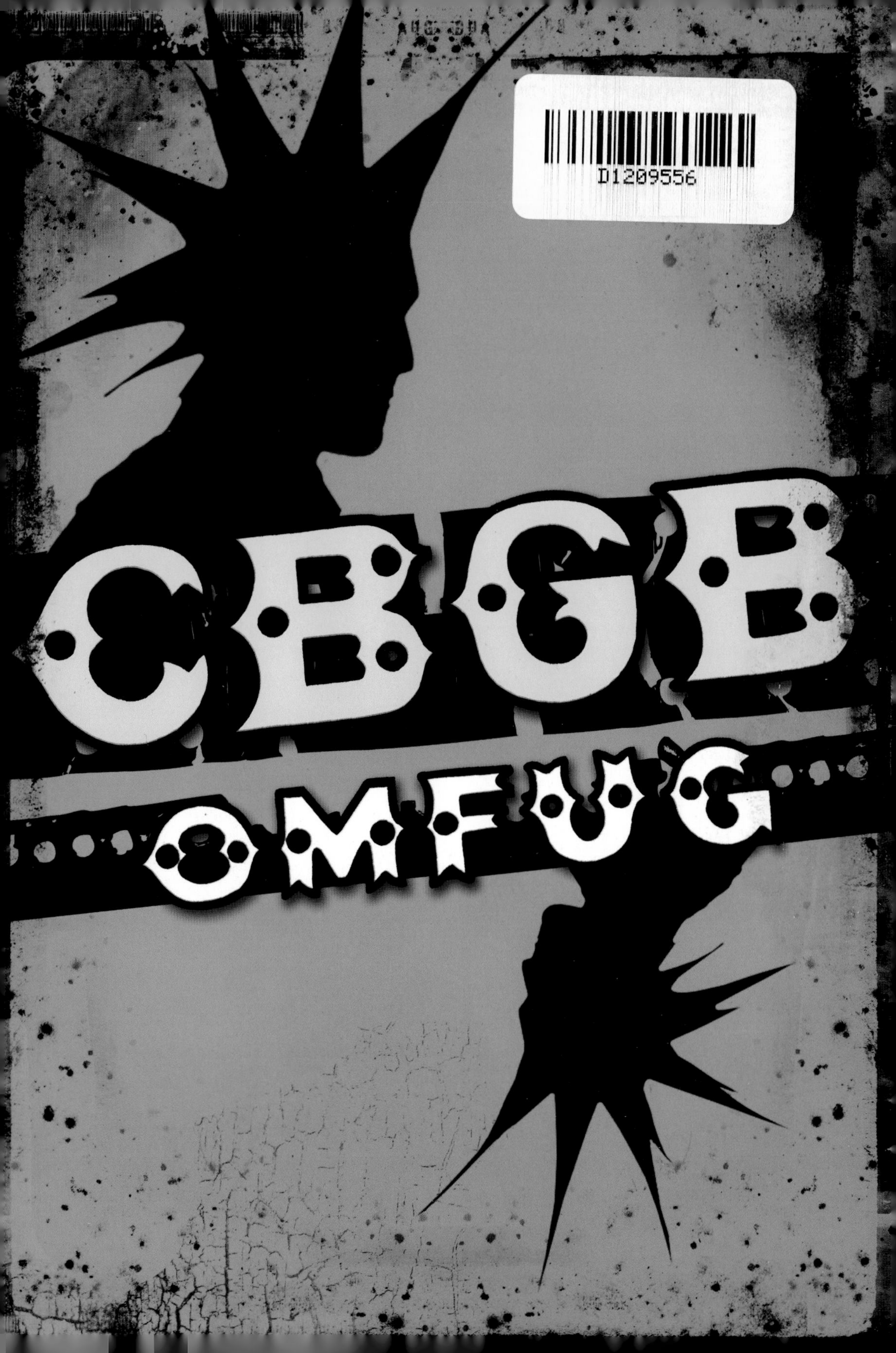
CBGB
OMFUG

OMFUG!
WRITTEN BY JESSE BLAZE SNIDER / ART BY CHUCK BB

A NYC PUNK CAROL
WRITTEN BY KIERON GILLEN / ART BY MARC ELLERBY

THE HELSINKI SYNDROME
WRITTEN BY SAM HUMPHRIES / ART BY ROB G

ROCK BLOCK
WRITTEN BY ANA MATRONIC / ART BY DAN DUNCAN

OOZY-SUZI-Q-TIP
WRITTEN AND ART BY MR. SHELDON

OF AND CONCERNING THE ANCIENT, MYSTICAL, AND HOLY ORIGINS OF THE MOST DOWN AND DIRTY 20TH CENTURY ROCK 'N' ROLL CLUB: CBGB
WRITTEN BY KIM KRIZAN / ART BY TOBY CYPRESS

ADVICE TO A YOUNG ARTIST
WRITTEN BY ROBERT STEVEN WILLIAMS AND LOUISE STALEY / ART BY GIORGIO PONTRELLI

COUNT 5 OR 6
WRITTEN BY KELLY SUE DECONNICK / ART BY CHUCK BB

NO FUTURE
WRITTEN BY R. ERIC LIEB / ART BY DAVID CROSLAND

SPECIAL THANKS TO EVERYONE AT CBGB HOLDINGS, LLC AND EXECUTIVE PRODUCER ROBERT STEVEN WILLIAMS

Ross Richie - Chief Executive Officer
Mark Waid - Chief Creative Officer
Matt Gagnon - Editor-in-Chief
Adam Fortier - VP-New Business
Wes Harris - VP-Publishing
Lance Kreiter - VP-Licensing & Merchandising
Chip Mosher - Marketing Director

Bryce Carlson - Managing Editor
Ian Brill - Editor
Dafna Pleban - Editor
Christopher Burns - Editor
Christopher Meyer - Editor
Shannon Watters - Assistant Editor

Neil Loughrie - Publishing Coordinator
Travis Beaty - Traffic Coordinator
Ivan Salazar - Marketing Assistant
Kate Hayden - Executive Assistant
Brian Latimer - Graphic Designer
Erika Terriquez - Graphic Designer

A catalog record for this book is available from OCLC and on our website www.boom-studios.com on the Librarians page.

First Edition: November 2010

10 9 8 7 6 5 4 3 2 1

Printed in U.S.A.

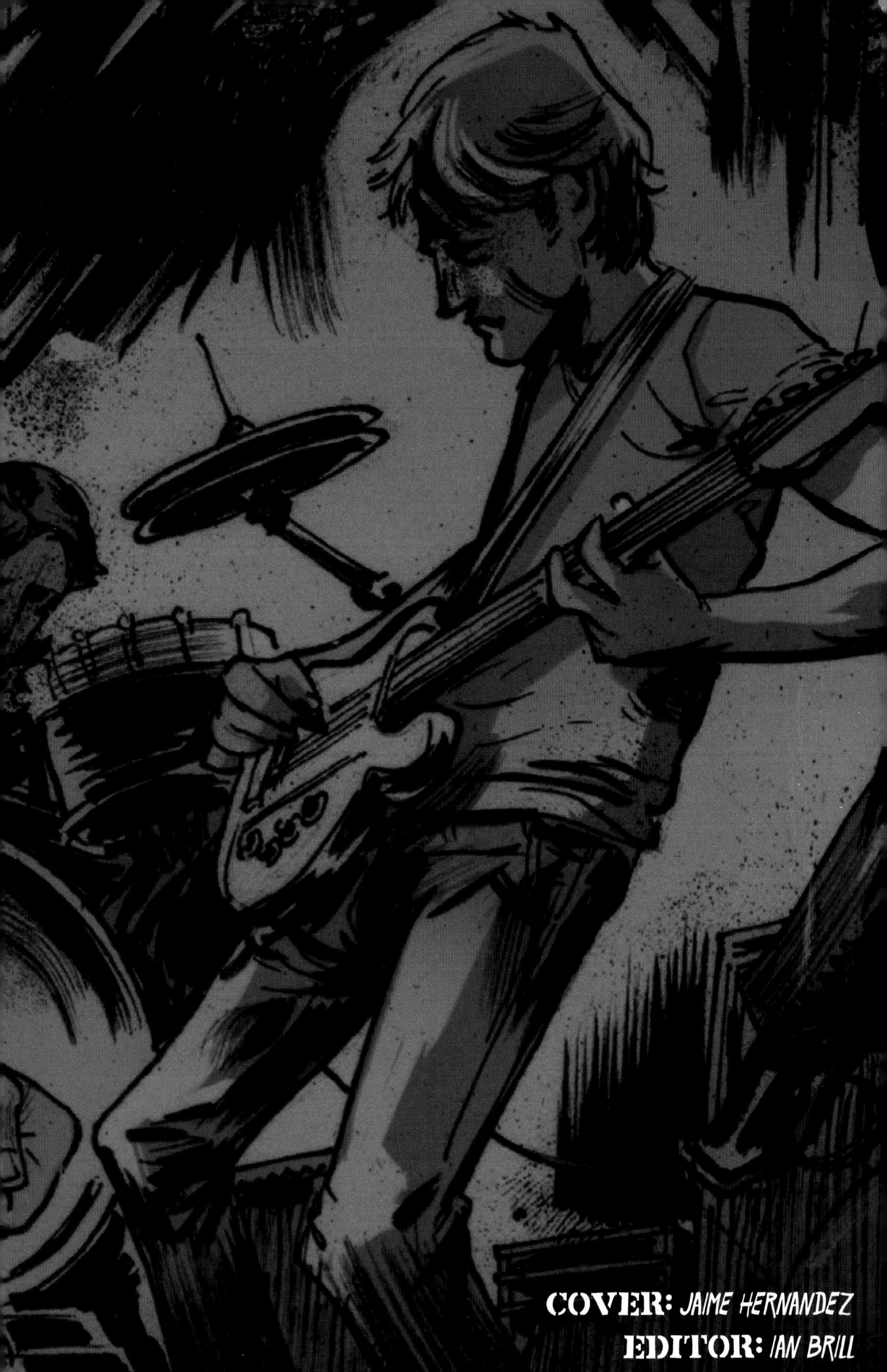

COVER: JAIME HERNANDEZ

EDITOR: IAN BRILL

DESIGNER: BRIAN LATIMER

FOR THE LATEST ON CBGB VISIT CBGB.COM OR BECOME A FACEBOOK FAN @ CBGB OMFUG

INTRODUCTION

IT'S ONLY FITTING THAT THE CARTOON WORLD OF CBGB SHOULD FIND ITSELF WITHIN THE PAGES OF A COMIC BOOK.

WHERE ELSE COULD AN ORDINARY MISFIT ENTER THE PHONE BOOTH THAT STOOD AT THE ENTRANCE OF THE CLUB AND EMERGE A SUPERHERO, GUITAR IN HAND, COMPLETE WITH DISTINCTIVE COSTUME AND LARGER—THAN—LIFE POWERS?

WHERE ELSE MIGHT THE CAST OF CHARACTERS LINING THE BAR ON ANY RANDOM NIGHT, THE VOLUPTUOUS FEMMES AND BLACK—ON—BLACK GARBED VILLAINS AND DISBELIEVING BYSTANDERS, BREATHE IN THE AIR OF PERPETUAL SURREALITY THAT SEEMED A PART OF THE OMFUG EXPERIENCE, ALL JOINED TOGETHER IN ELASTIC CARICATURES OF PEN AND INK AND CROSSHATCHED LINES OF SHADOW AND SHADE?

AND WHERE ELSE MIGHT THE TALES OF YOU—ARE—THERE BE TOLD THAN IN THE UNLIKELY PSYCHODRAMA AND HOMAGE THAT CHARACTERIZE THESE FABLES OF WHAT LIFE WAS LIKE IN THAT STAR—CROSSED LOCAL LOCALE THAN IN THE TWO DIMENSIONS OF GRAPHIC ART THAT SQUARE THEMSELVES INTO THE TRAVEL OF TIME?

I HAVE ALWAYS READ THE COMICS, FROM THE FIRST NEWSPAPER STRIPS THAT CAUGHT MY IMAGINATION — DICK TRACY, ALLEY OOP, POGO — TO THE CLASSIC COMICS THAT INTRODUCED ME TO LITERATURE BEFORE I COULD EVEN READ, TO COMIX THAT COUNTERED MY CULTURE — MR. NATURAL, THE FURRY FREAK BROTHERS, TRASHMAN — TO THE MANGA OF LONE WOLF AND CUB, AND MAI, THE PSYCHIC GIRL. THOUGH IT HAS BEEN SAID EVERMORE, NO OTHER MEDIUM INFUSES THE EN—VISUAL WITH ITS OWN ON—SCREEN DIALOGUE AS DO THE NARRATIVE PANELS OF ILLUSTRATIVE ART, ALLOWING FLIGHTS OF FANCY AND DERRING—DO IN WHICH THE SUSPENSION OF REALITY COMBINES WITH HYPERTEXT TO CREATE A WORLD OF ITS OWN.

AS DID CBGB, FROM THE FIRST MOMENT I ENTERED ITS BACKWATER CONFINES TO WITNESS A GROUP CALLED TELEVISION, WITH THEIR OWN SKEWED TRANSFERENCE OF MEDIA AND MESSAGE, AND STAYED AROUND FOR THE NEXT THIRTY THREE YEARS. A THIRD OF A CENTURY, AND YET, READING THESE HOMILIES OF WHERE—AND—WHEN, IT SEEMS AS IF A MYTHOS WHERE MORTALS MEET THE GODS MIGHT HAVE HAPPENED ANYTIME, ANY NIGHT, WHEN YOU WALKED THROUGH THAT BATTERED DOOR INTO THE PAGES OF WHAT IS PRESENTED HERE: COMICS BY GRAPHIC BOWERYITES. AT THE INTERSECTION OF BLEECKER.

LENNY KAYE

Lenny Kaye is the long-time guitarist with Patti Smith and a musician, producer, and writer who has worked with such diverse artists as Suzanne Vega, Jim Carroll, Allen Ginsberg, and Waylon Jennings. His compilation of sixties' garage-rock, "Nuggets: Original Artyfacts from the First Psychedelic Era," defined a genre.

OMFUG! FIRST PRESENTED IN SXSW FLYER ANNOUNCING THE CBGB GRAPHIC NOVEL

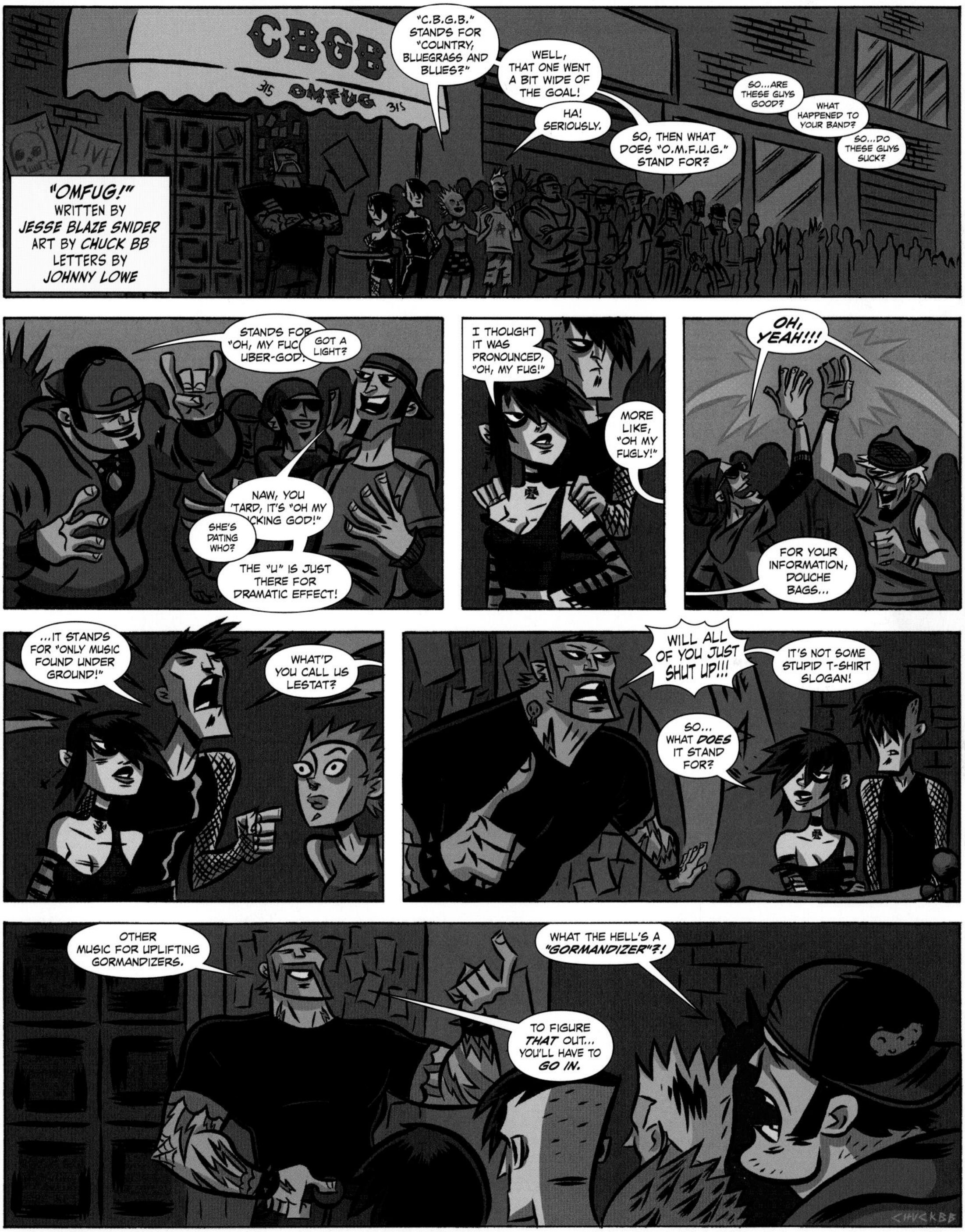
CBGB
OMFUG
315
"OMFUG!"
WRITTEN BY JESSE BLAZE SNIDER
ART BY CHUCK BB
LETTERS BY JOHNNY LOWE
"C.B.G.B." STANDS FOR "COUNTRY, BLUEGRASS AND BLUES?"
WELL, THAT ONE WENT A BIT WIDE OF THE GOAL!
HA! SERIOUSLY.
SO, THEN WHAT DOES "O.M.F.U.G." STAND FOR?
SO...ARE THESE GUYS GOOD?
WHAT HAPPENED TO YOUR BAND?
SO...DO THESE GUYS SUCK?
STANDS FOR "OH, MY FUC
GOT A LIGHT?
UBER-GOD."
NAW, YOU 'TARD, IT'S "OH MY
CKING GOD!"
SHE'S DATING WHO?
THE "U" IS JUST THERE FOR DRAMATIC EFFECT!
I THOUGHT IT WAS PRONOUNCED, "OH, MY FUG!"
MORE LIKE, "OH MY FUGLY!"
OH, YEAH!!!
FOR YOUR INFORMATION, DOUCHE BAGS...
...IT STANDS FOR "ONLY MUSIC FOUND UNDER GROUND!"
WHAT'D YOU CALL US LESTAT?
WILL ALL OF YOU JUST SHUT UP!!!
IT'S NOT SOME STUPID T-SHIRT SLOGAN!
SO... WHAT DOES IT STAND FOR?
OTHER MUSIC FOR UPLIFTING GORMANDIZERS.
WHAT THE HELL'S A "GORMANDIZER"?!
TO FIGURE THAT OUT... YOU'LL HAVE TO GO IN.
CHUCKBB

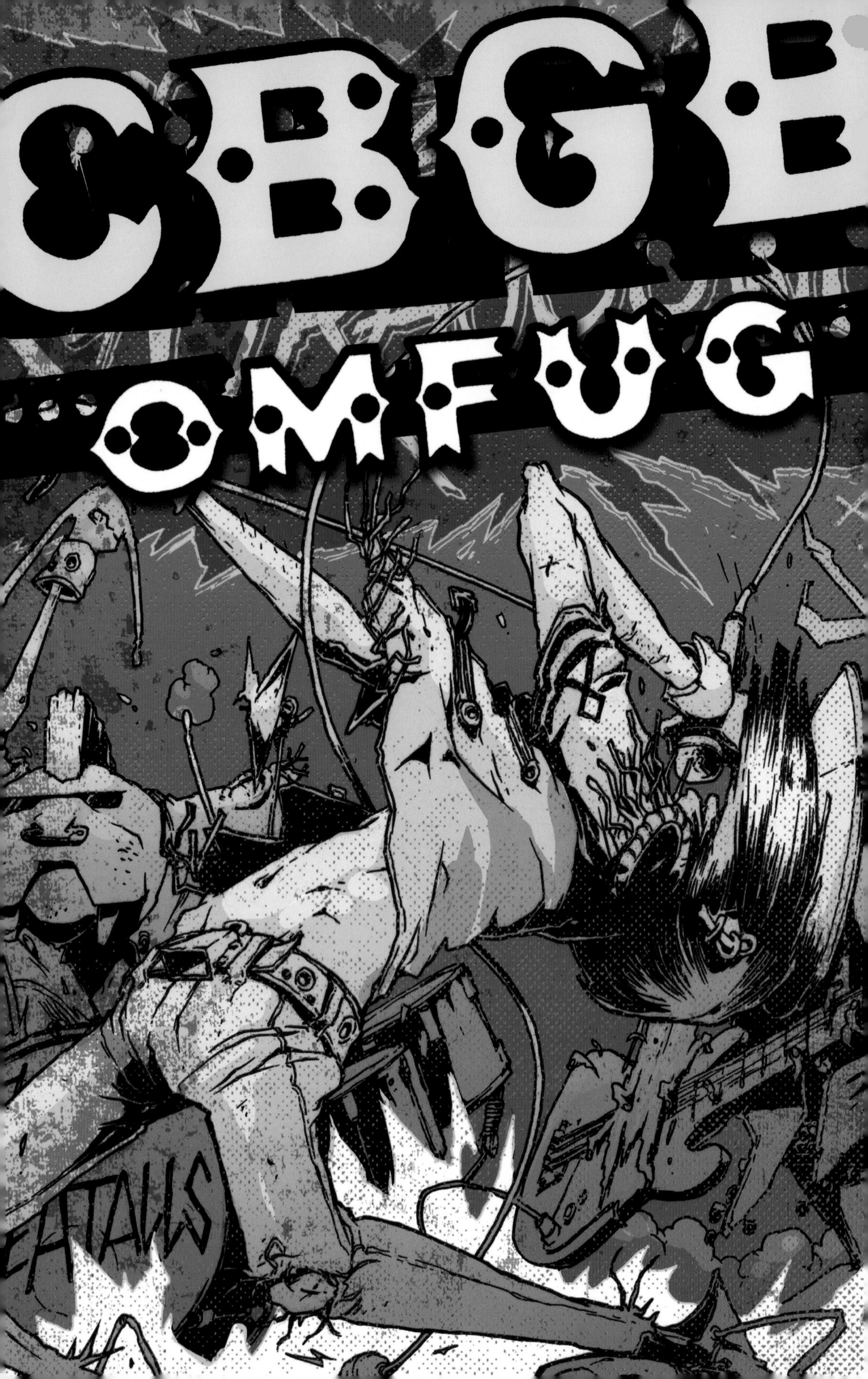
CBGB
OMFUG

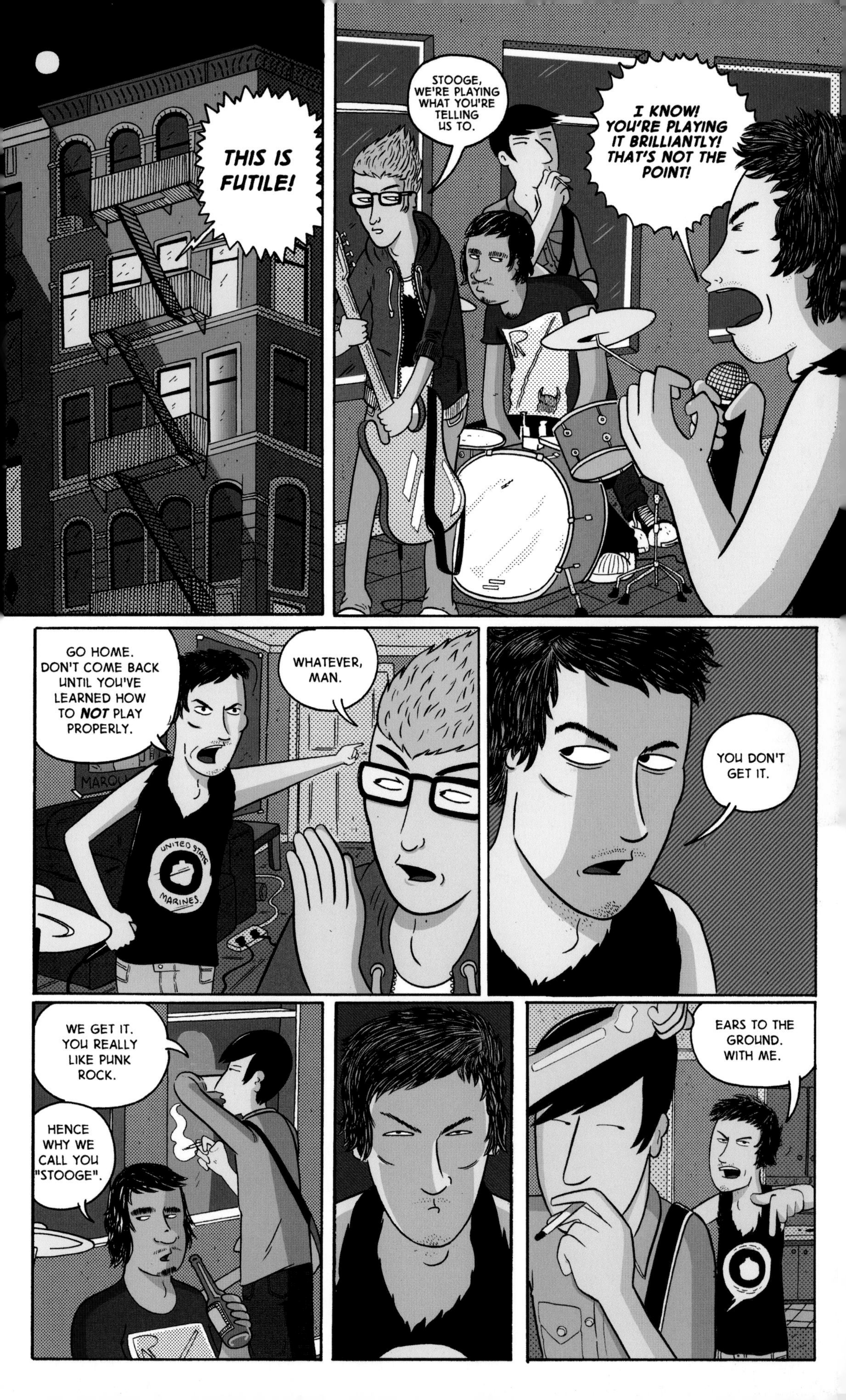
THIS IS FUTILE!
STOOGE, WE'RE PLAYING WHAT YOU'RE TELLING US TO.
I KNOW! YOU'RE PLAYING IT BRILLIANTLY! THAT'S NOT THE POINT!
GO HOME. DON'T COME BACK UNTIL YOU'VE LEARNED HOW TO NOT PLAY PROPERLY.
WHATEVER, MAN.
YOU DON'T GET IT.
WE GET IT. YOU REALLY LIKE PUNK ROCK.
HENCE WHY WE CALL YOU "STOOGE".
EARS TO THE GROUND. WITH ME.

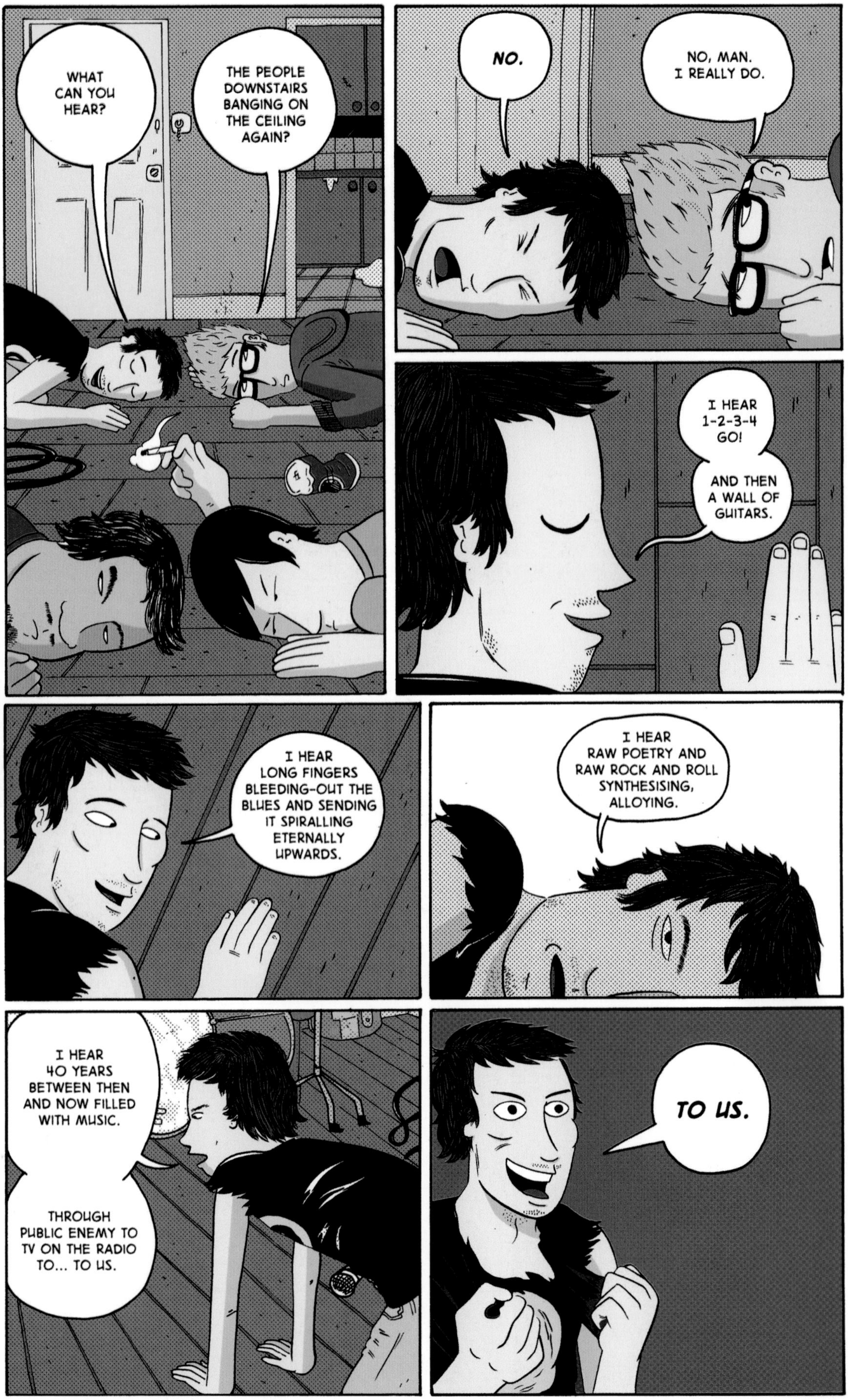
WHAT CAN YOU HEAR?
THE PEOPLE DOWNSTAIRS BANGING ON THE CEILING AGAIN?
NO.
NO, MAN. I REALLY DO.
I HEAR 1-2-3-4 GO!
AND THEN A WALL OF GUITARS.
I HEAR LONG FINGERS BLEEDING-OUT THE BLUES AND SENDING IT SPIRALLING ETERNALLY UPWARDS.
I HEAR RAW POETRY AND RAW ROCK AND ROLL SYNTHESISING, ALLOYING.
I HEAR 40 YEARS BETWEEN THEN AND NOW FILLED WITH MUSIC.
THROUGH PUBLIC ENEMY TO TV ON THE RADIO TO... TO US.
TO US.

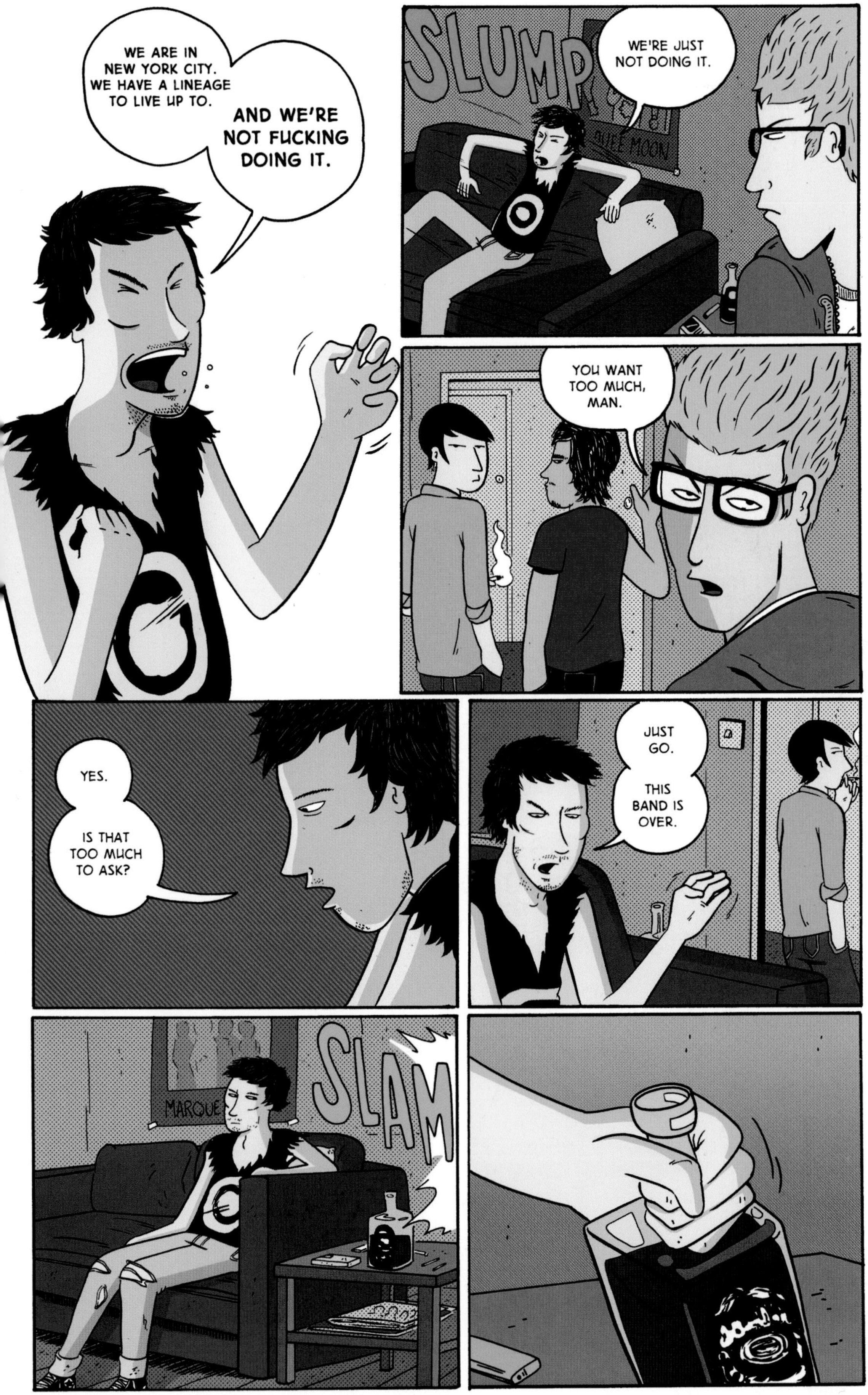
WE ARE IN NEW YORK CITY. WE HAVE A LINEAGE TO LIVE UP TO.
AND WE'RE NOT FUCKING DOING IT.
SLUMP
WE'RE JUST NOT DOING IT.
YOU WANT TOO MUCH, MAN.
YES.
IS THAT TOO MUCH TO ASK?
JUST GO.
THIS BAND IS OVER.
MARQUEE
SLAM

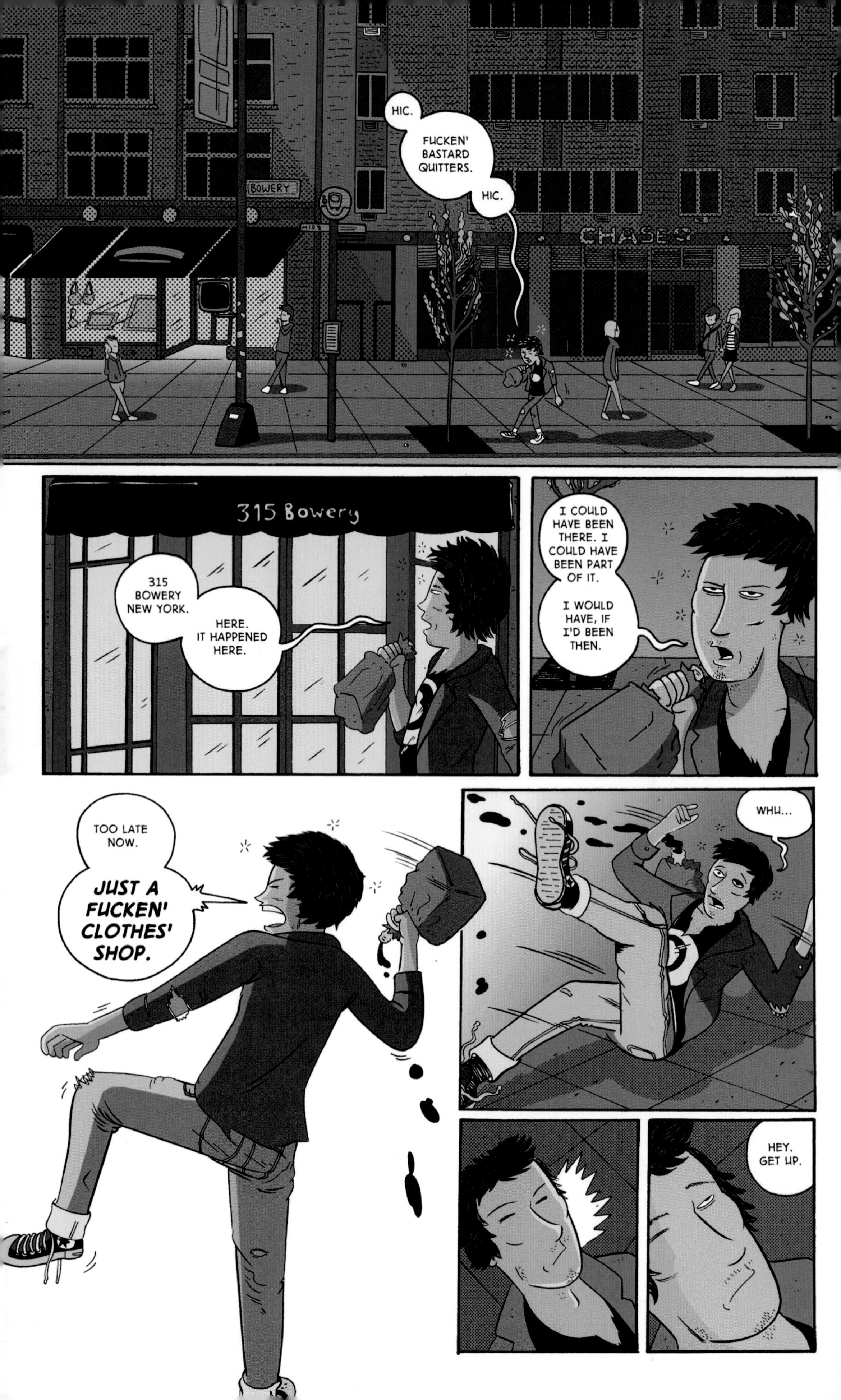

BOWERY
CHASES
HIC.
FUCKEN' BASTARD QUITTERS.
HIC.
315 Bowery
315 BOWERY NEW YORK.
HERE. IT HAPPENED HERE.
I COULD HAVE BEEN THERE. I COULD HAVE BEEN PART OF IT.
I WOULD HAVE, IF I'D BEEN THEN.
TOO LATE NOW.
JUST A FUCKEN' CLOTHES' SHOP.
WHU...
HEY. GET UP.

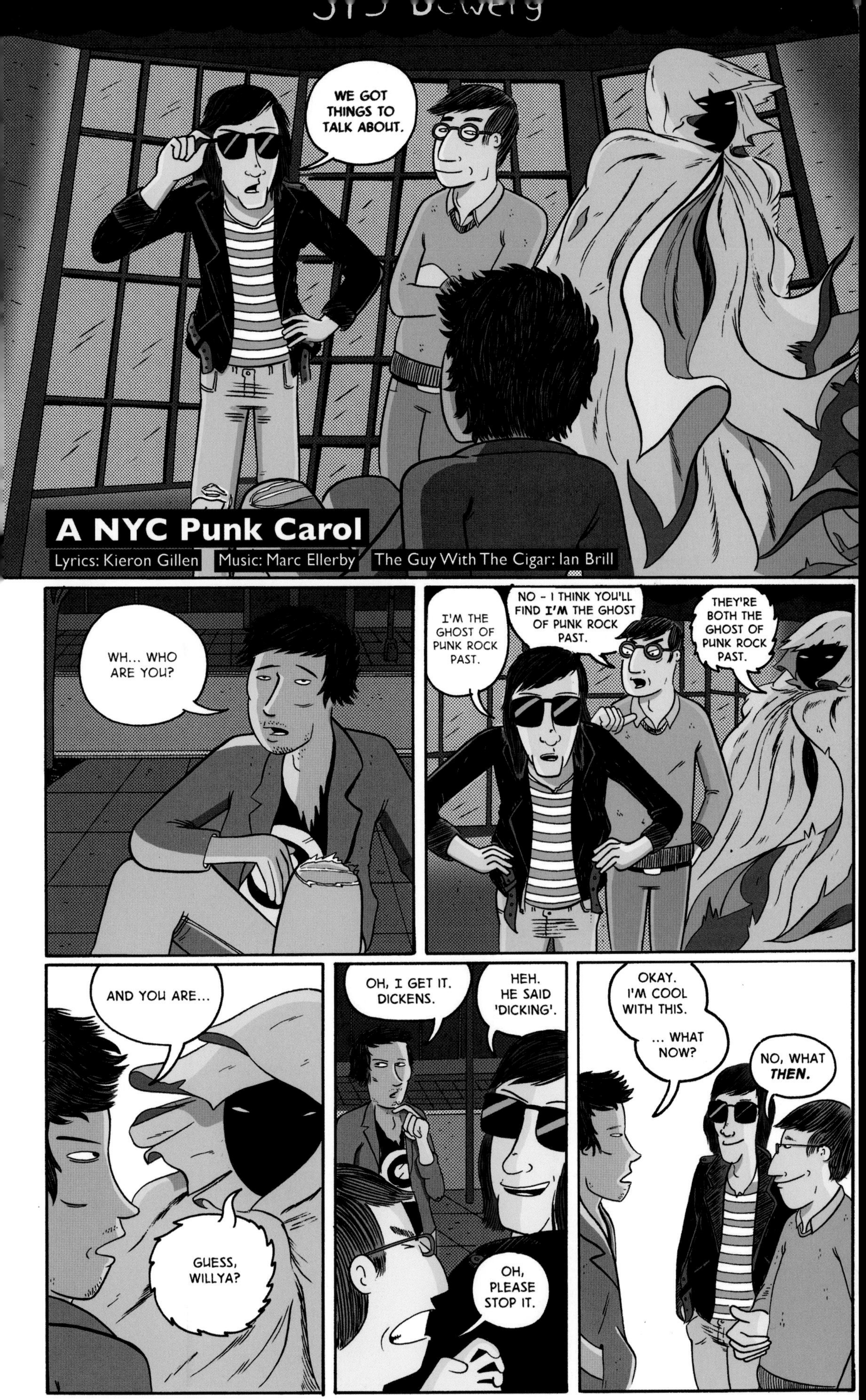

WE GOT THINGS TO TALK ABOUT.
A NYC Punk Carol
Lyrics: Kieron Gillen
Music: Marc Ellerby
The Guy With The Cigar: Ian Brill
WH... WHO ARE YOU?
I'M THE GHOST OF PUNK ROCK PAST.
NO - I THINK YOU'LL FIND I'M THE GHOST OF PUNK ROCK PAST.
THEY'RE BOTH THE GHOST OF PUNK ROCK PAST.
AND YOU ARE...
GUESS, WILLYA?
OH, I GET IT. DICKENS.
HEH. HE SAID 'DICKING'.
OH, PLEASE STOP IT.
OKAY. I'M COOL WITH THIS.
... WHAT NOW?
NO, WHAT THEN.

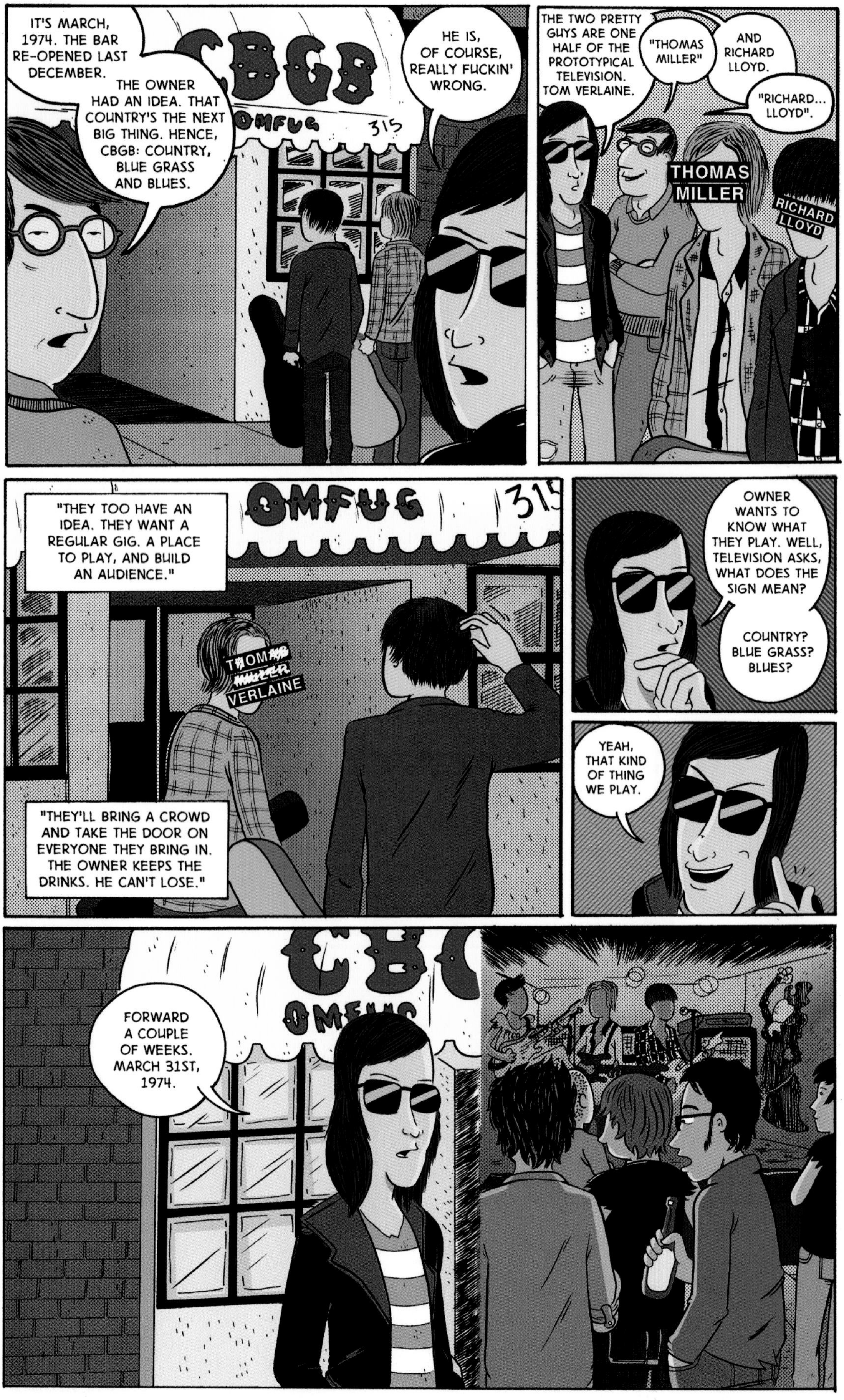
CBGB
OMFUG
315
IT'S MARCH, 1974. THE BAR RE-OPENED LAST DECEMBER.
THE OWNER HAD AN IDEA. THAT COUNTRY'S THE NEXT BIG THING. HENCE, CBGB: COUNTRY, BLUE GRASS AND BLUES.
HE IS, OF COURSE, REALLY FUCKIN' WRONG.
THE TWO PRETTY GUYS ARE ONE HALF OF THE PROTOTYPICAL TELEVISION. TOM VERLAINE.
"THOMAS MILLER"
AND RICHARD LLOYD.
"RICHARD... LLOYD".
THOMAS MILLER
RICHARD LLOYD
OMFUG
315
"THEY TOO HAVE AN IDEA. THEY WANT A REGULAR GIG. A PLACE TO PLAY, AND BUILD AN AUDIENCE."
THOM
VERLAINE
"THEY'LL BRING A CROWD AND TAKE THE DOOR ON EVERYONE THEY BRING IN. THE OWNER KEEPS THE DRINKS. HE CAN'T LOSE."
OWNER WANTS TO KNOW WHAT THEY PLAY. WELL, TELEVISION ASKS, WHAT DOES THE SIGN MEAN?
COUNTRY? BLUE GRASS? BLUES?
YEAH, THAT KIND OF THING WE PLAY.
FORWARD A COUPLE OF WEEKS. MARCH 31ST, 1974.

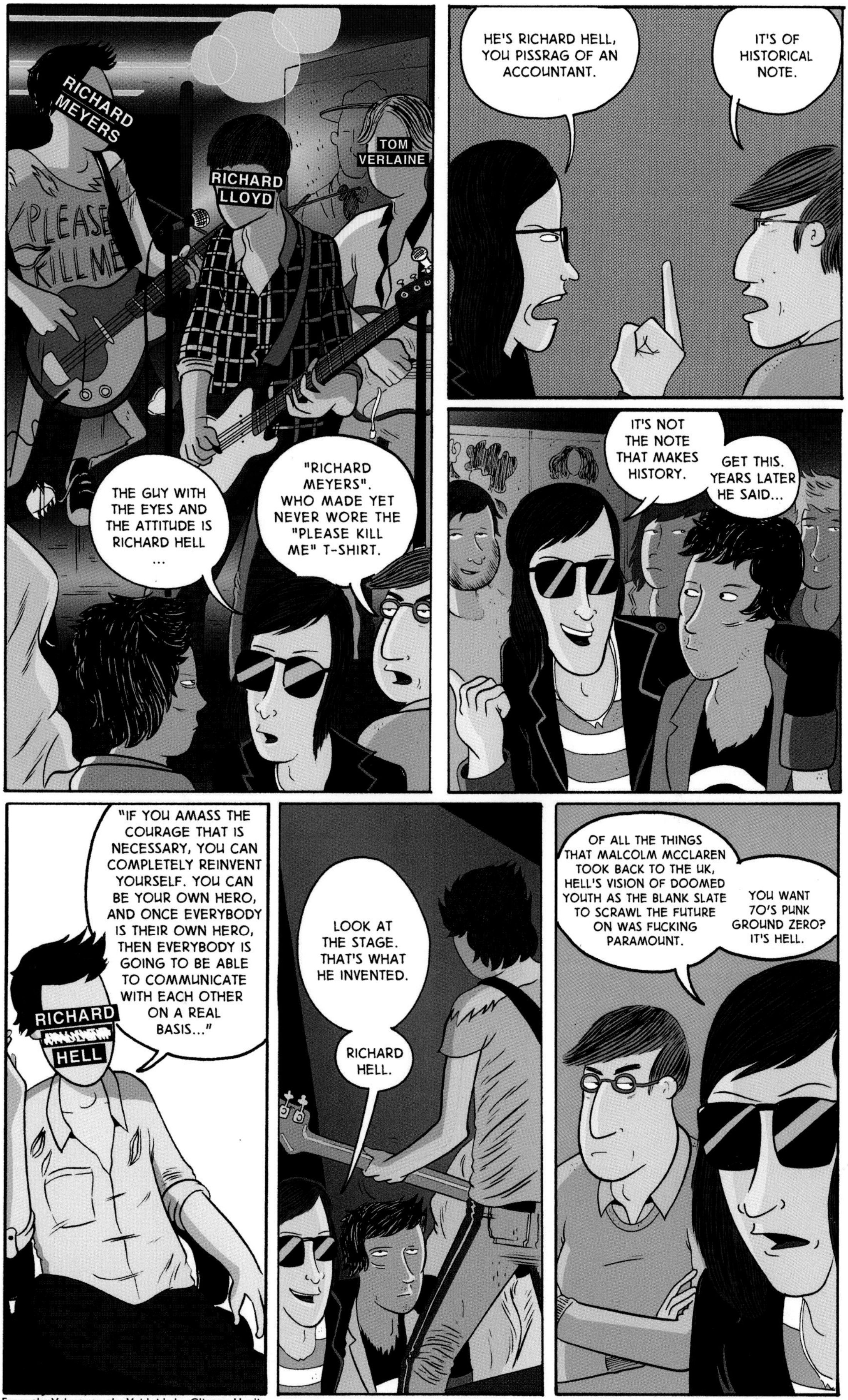
RICHARD MEYERS
RICHARD LLOYD
TOM VERLAINE
PLEASE KILL ME
THE GUY WITH THE EYES AND THE ATTITUDE IS RICHARD HELL ...
"RICHARD MEYERS". WHO MADE YET NEVER WORE THE "PLEASE KILL ME" T-SHIRT.
HE'S RICHARD HELL, YOU PISSRAG OF AN ACCOUNTANT.
IT'S OF HISTORICAL NOTE.
IT'S NOT THE NOTE THAT MAKES HISTORY.
GET THIS. YEARS LATER HE SAID...
"IF YOU AMASS THE COURAGE THAT IS NECESSARY, YOU CAN COMPLETELY REINVENT YOURSELF. YOU CAN BE YOUR OWN HERO, AND ONCE EVERYBODY IS THEIR OWN HERO, THEN EVERYBODY IS GOING TO BE ABLE TO COMMUNICATE WITH EACH OTHER ON A REAL BASIS..."
RICHARD
HELL
LOOK AT THE STAGE. THAT'S WHAT HE INVENTED.
RICHARD HELL.
OF ALL THE THINGS THAT MALCOLM MCCLAREN TOOK BACK TO THE UK, HELL'S VISION OF DOOMED YOUTH AS THE BLANK SLATE TO SCRAWL THE FUTURE ON WAS FUCKING PARAMOUNT.
YOU WANT 70'S PUNK GROUND ZERO? IT'S HELL.
From the Velvets to the Voidoids by Clinton Heylin

ANYWAY - THEY PLAY THEIR FIRST GIG ON THE 31ST.

IT WAS FUCKING EXPLOSIVE. IT WAS HISTORIC.

IT WAS 20-30 PEOPLE, TOPS. FOR WEEKS.

DIDN'T MATTER. STEP ASIDE FROM THE MYTH.

LET'S LOOK AT THE COLDEST OF FACTS.

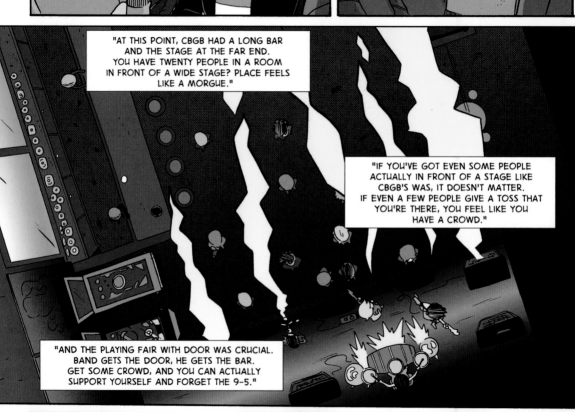

"AT THIS POINT, CBGB HAD A LONG BAR AND THE STAGE AT THE FAR END. YOU HAVE TWENTY PEOPLE IN A ROOM IN FRONT OF A WIDE STAGE? PLACE FEELS LIKE A MORGUE."

"IF YOU'VE GOT EVEN SOME PEOPLE ACTUALLY IN FRONT OF A STAGE LIKE CBGB'S WAS, IT DOESN'T MATTER. IF EVEN A FEW PEOPLE GIVE A TOSS THAT YOU'RE THERE, YOU FEEL LIKE YOU HAVE A CROWD."

"AND THE PLAYING FAIR WITH DOOR WAS CRUCIAL. BAND GETS THE DOOR, HE GETS THE BAR. GET SOME CROWD, AND YOU CAN ACTUALLY SUPPORT YOURSELF AND FORGET THE 9-5."

ESPECIALLY IN AN AFFORDABLE SHITHOLE LIKE THE BOWERY WAS THEN. WHICH IS ALSO KEY, BUT ANOTHER STORY.

THAT'S WHAT CBGB WAS. IT WAS A PLACE TO BE. IT WAS A NUCLEUS WHICH A SCENE COULD CONGREGATE.

FUCK. I WISH I COULD FIND A PLACE TO GIVE US THE DOOR NOW. IS THERE ANY CHANCE OF...

ABSOLUTELY NONE.

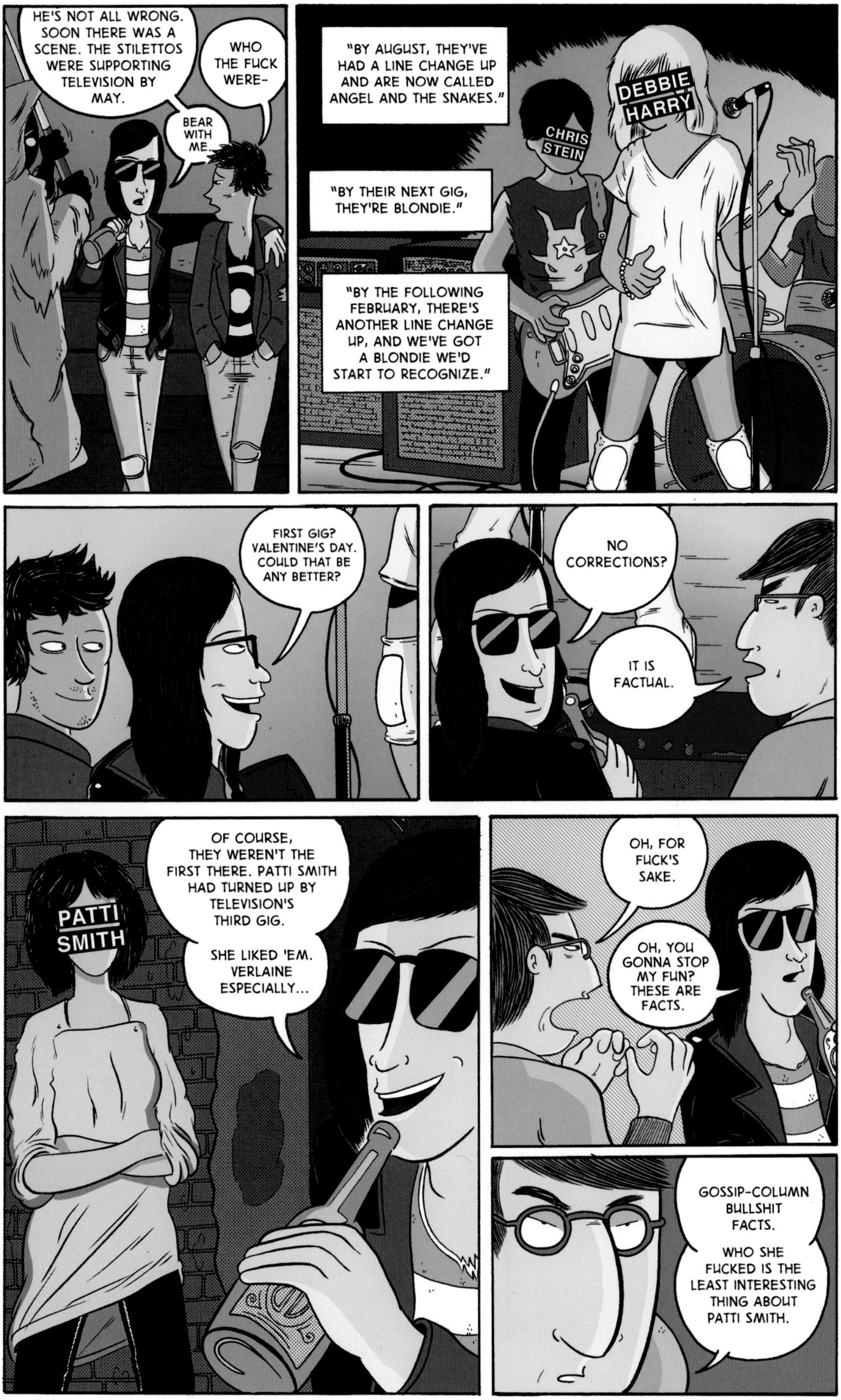

HE'S NOT ALL WRONG. SOON THERE WAS A SCENE. THE STILETTOS WERE SUPPORTING TELEVISION BY MAY.
WHO THE FUCK WERE-
BEAR WITH ME.
"BY AUGUST, THEY'VE HAD A LINE CHANGE UP AND ARE NOW CALLED ANGEL AND THE SNAKES."
"BY THEIR NEXT GIG, THEY'RE BLONDIE."
"BY THE FOLLOWING FEBRUARY, THERE'S ANOTHER LINE CHANGE UP, AND WE'VE GOT A BLONDIE WE'D START TO RECOGNIZE."
DEBBIE HARRY
CHRIS STEIN
FIRST GIG? VALENTINE'S DAY. COULD THAT BE ANY BETTER?
NO CORRECTIONS?
IT IS FACTUAL.
PATTI SMITH
OF COURSE, THEY WEREN'T THE FIRST THERE. PATTI SMITH HAD TURNED UP BY TELEVISION'S THIRD GIG.
SHE LIKED 'EM. VERLAINE ESPECIALLY...
OH, FOR FUCK'S SAKE.
OH, YOU GONNA STOP MY FUN? THESE ARE FACTS.
GOSSIP-COLUMN BULLSHIT FACTS.
WHO SHE FUCKED IS THE LEAST INTERESTING THING ABOUT PATTI SMITH.

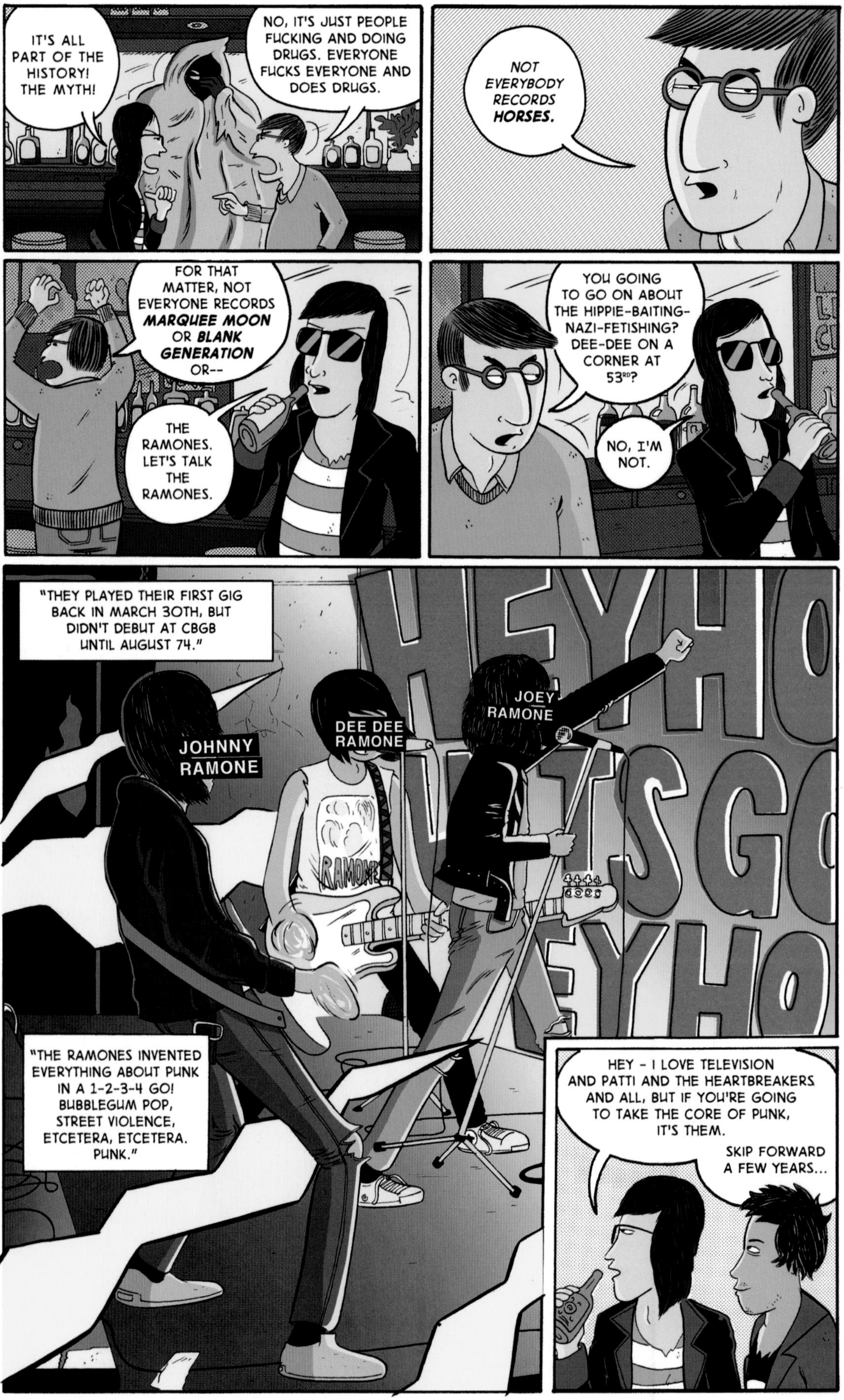
IT'S ALL PART OF THE HISTORY! THE MYTH!
NO, IT'S JUST PEOPLE FUCKING AND DOING DRUGS. EVERYONE FUCKS EVERYONE AND DOES DRUGS.
NOT EVERYBODY RECORDS HORSES.
FOR THAT MATTER, NOT EVERYONE RECORDS MARQUEE MOON OR BLANK GENERATION OR--
THE RAMONES. LET'S TALK THE RAMONES.
YOU GOING TO GO ON ABOUT THE HIPPIE-BAITING-NAZI-FETISHING? DEE-DEE ON A CORNER AT 53RD?
NO, I'M NOT.
"THEY PLAYED THEIR FIRST GIG BACK IN MARCH 30TH, BUT DIDN'T DEBUT AT CBGB UNTIL AUGUST 74."
HEY HO LETS GO HEY HO
JOEY RAMONE
DEE DEE RAMONE
JOHNNY RAMONE
RAMONES
"THE RAMONES INVENTED EVERYTHING ABOUT PUNK IN A 1-2-3-4 GO! BUBBLEGUM POP, STREET VIOLENCE, ETCETERA, ETCETERA. PUNK."
HEY - I LOVE TELEVISION AND PATTI AND THE HEARTBREAKERS AND ALL, BUT IF YOU'RE GOING TO TAKE THE CORE OF PUNK, IT'S THEM.
SKIP FORWARD A FEW YEARS...

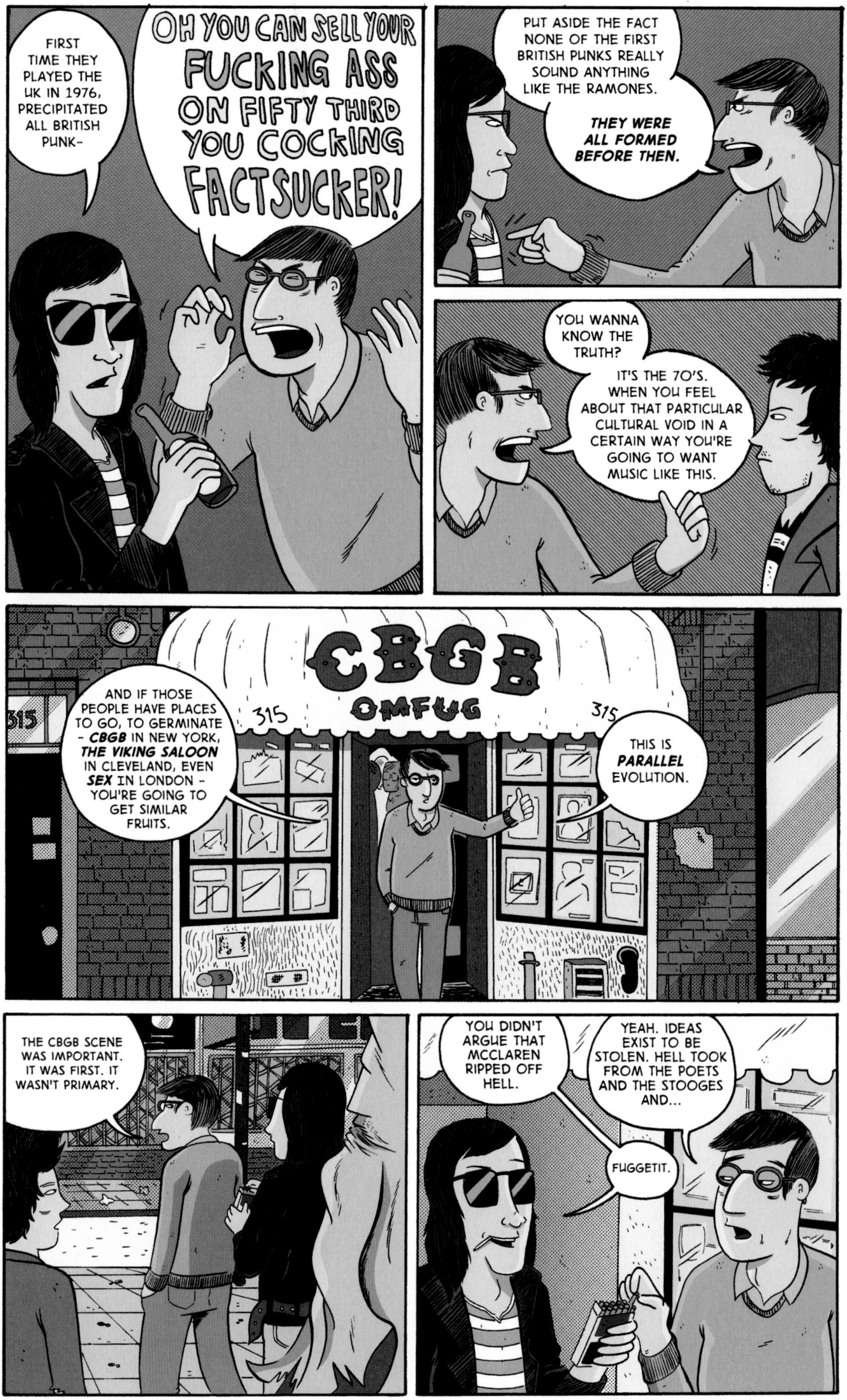

FIRST TIME THEY PLAYED THE UK IN 1976, PRECIPITATED ALL BRITISH PUNK-
OH YOU CAN SELL YOUR FUCKING ASS ON FIFTY THIRD YOU COCKING FACTSUCKER!
PUT ASIDE THE FACT NONE OF THE FIRST BRITISH PUNKS REALLY SOUND ANYTHING LIKE THE RAMONES.
THEY WERE ALL FORMED BEFORE THEN.
YOU WANNA KNOW THE TRUTH?
IT'S THE 70'S. WHEN YOU FEEL ABOUT THAT PARTICULAR CULTURAL VOID IN A CERTAIN WAY YOU'RE GOING TO WANT MUSIC LIKE THIS.
CBGB
OMFUG
315
315
315
AND IF THOSE PEOPLE HAVE PLACES TO GO, TO GERMINATE - CBGB IN NEW YORK, THE VIKING SALOON IN CLEVELAND, EVEN SEX IN LONDON - YOU'RE GOING TO GET SIMILAR FRUITS.
THIS IS PARALLEL EVOLUTION.
THE CBGB SCENE WAS IMPORTANT. IT WAS FIRST. IT WASN'T PRIMARY.
YOU DIDN'T ARGUE THAT MCCLAREN RIPPED OFF HELL.
YEAH. IDEAS EXIST TO BE STOLEN. HELL TOOK FROM THE POETS AND THE STOOGES AND...
FUGGETIT.

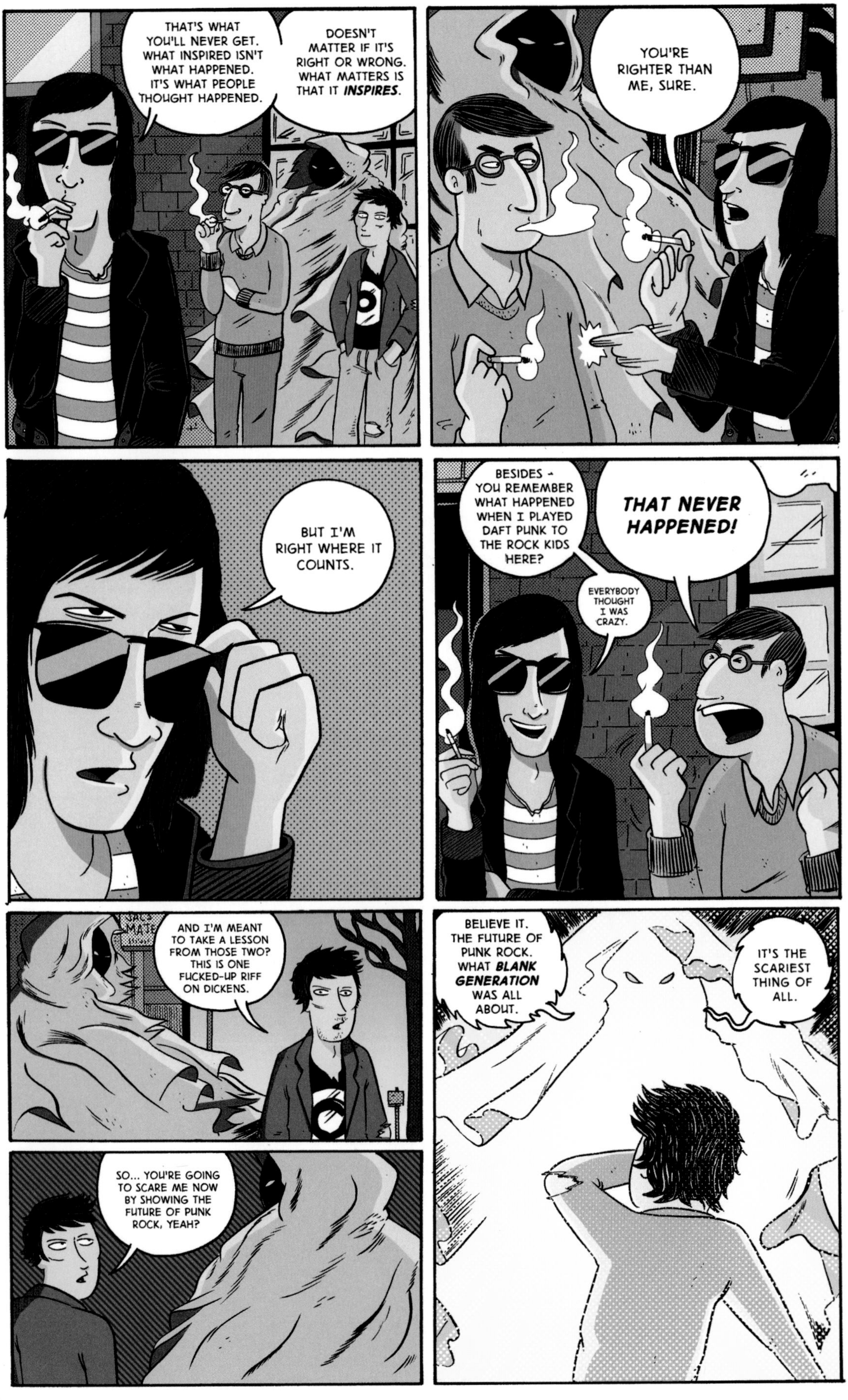
THAT'S WHAT YOU'LL NEVER GET. WHAT INSPIRED ISN'T WHAT HAPPENED. IT'S WHAT PEOPLE THOUGHT HAPPENED.
DOESN'T MATTER IF IT'S RIGHT OR WRONG. WHAT MATTERS IS THAT IT INSPIRES.
YOU'RE RIGHTER THAN ME, SURE.
BUT I'M RIGHT WHERE IT COUNTS.
BESIDES - YOU REMEMBER WHAT HAPPENED WHEN I PLAYED DAFT PUNK TO THE ROCK KIDS HERE?
EVERYBODY THOUGHT I WAS CRAZY.
THAT NEVER HAPPENED!
AND I'M MEANT TO TAKE A LESSON FROM THOSE TWO? THIS IS ONE FUCKED-UP RIFF ON DICKENS.
SO... YOU'RE GOING TO SCARE ME NOW BY SHOWING THE FUTURE OF PUNK ROCK, YEAH?
BELIEVE IT. THE FUTURE OF PUNK ROCK. WHAT BLANK GENERATION WAS ALL ABOUT.
IT'S THE SCARIEST THING OF ALL.

THE FUTURE OF PUNK ROCK

AS CONCEIVED AND EXECUTED BY _____.

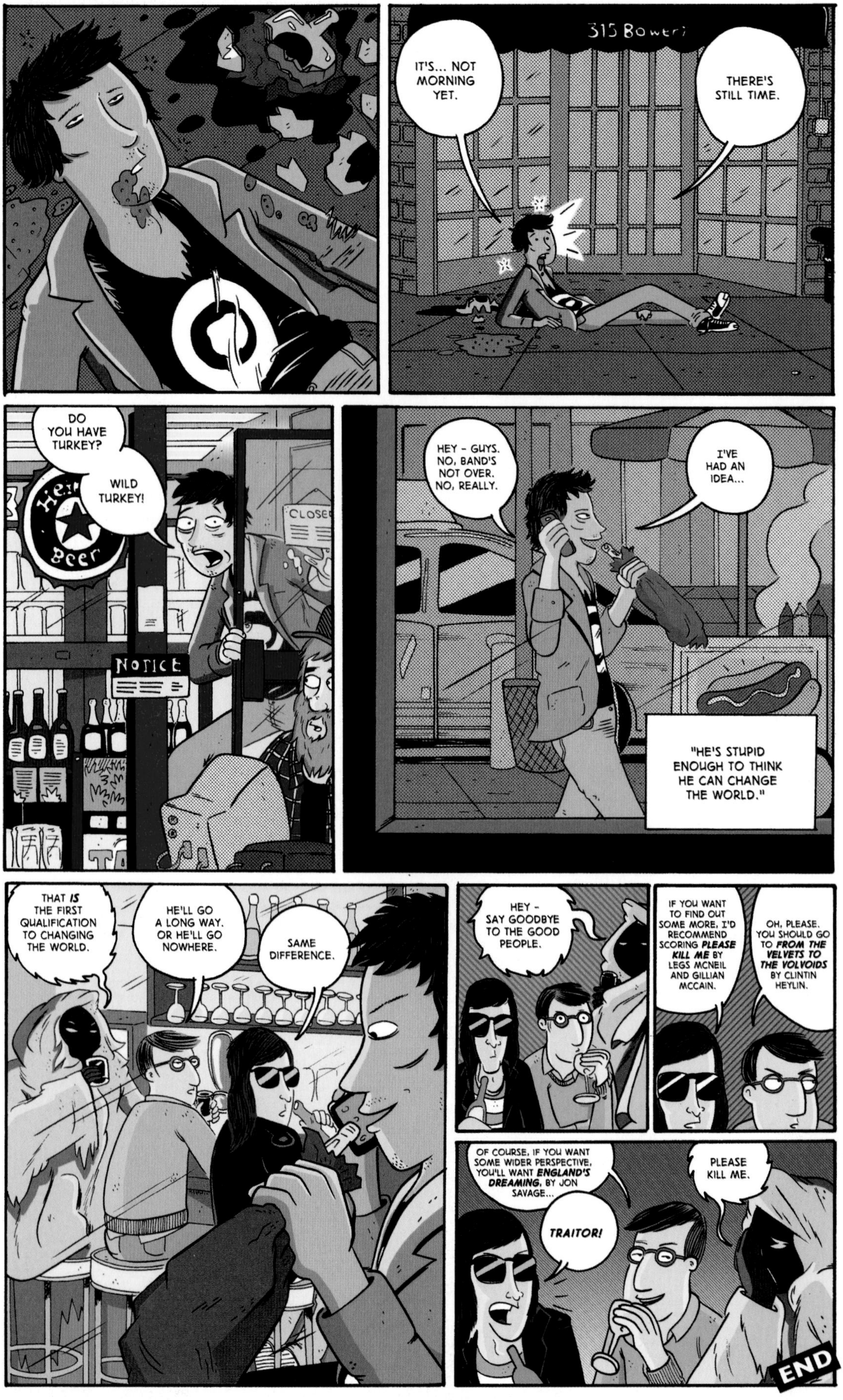
315 Bowery
IT'S... NOT MORNING YET.
THERE'S STILL TIME.
DO YOU HAVE TURKEY?
WILD TURKEY!
Heineken Beer
CLOSED
NOTICE
HEY - GUYS. NO, BAND'S NOT OVER. NO, REALLY.
I'VE HAD AN IDEA...
"HE'S STUPID ENOUGH TO THINK HE CAN CHANGE THE WORLD."
THAT *IS* THE FIRST QUALIFICATION TO CHANGING THE WORLD.
HE'LL GO A LONG WAY. OR HE'LL GO NOWHERE.
SAME DIFFERENCE.
HEY - SAY GOODBYE TO THE GOOD PEOPLE.
IF YOU WANT TO FIND OUT SOME MORE, I'D RECOMMEND SCORING ***PLEASE KILL ME*** BY LEGS MCNEIL AND GILLIAN MCCAIN.
OH, PLEASE. YOU SHOULD GO TO ***FROM THE VELVETS TO THE VOLVOIDS*** BY CLINTIN HEYLIN.
OF COURSE, IF YOU WANT SOME WIDER PERSPECTIVE, YOU'LL WANT ***ENGLAND'S DREAMING***, BY JON SAVAGE...
PLEASE KILL ME.
TRAITOR!
END

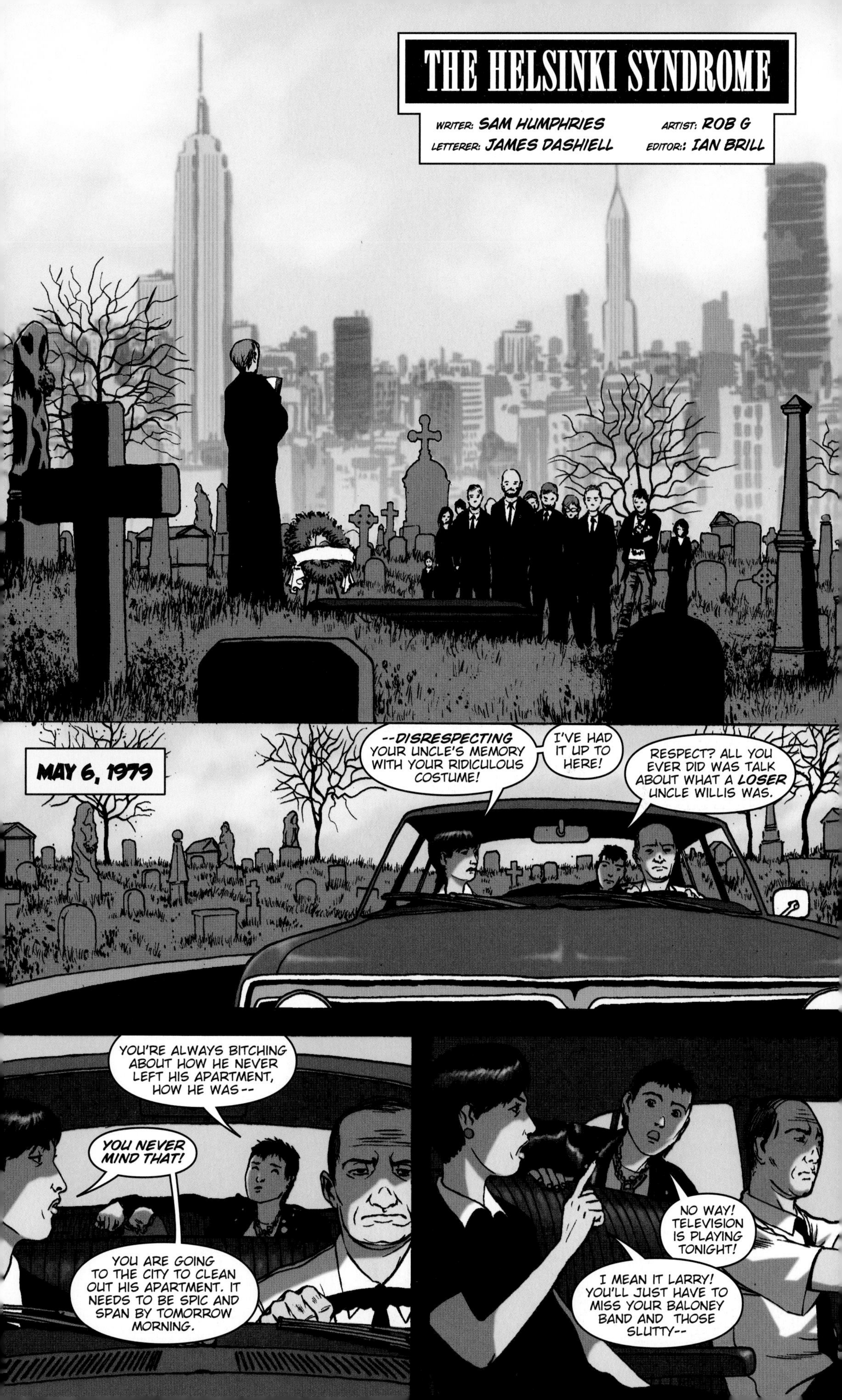
THE HELSINKI SYNDROME
WRITER: SAM HUMPHRIES
ARTIST: ROB G
LETTERER: JAMES DASHIELL
EDITOR:: IAN BRILL
MAY 6, 1979
--DISRESPECTING YOUR UNCLE'S MEMORY WITH YOUR RIDICULOUS COSTUME!
I'VE HAD IT UP TO HERE!
RESPECT? ALL YOU EVER DID WAS TALK ABOUT WHAT A LOSER UNCLE WILLIS WAS.
YOU'RE ALWAYS BITCHING ABOUT HOW HE NEVER LEFT HIS APARTMENT, HOW HE WAS--
YOU NEVER MIND THAT!
YOU ARE GOING TO THE CITY TO CLEAN OUT HIS APARTMENT. IT NEEDS TO BE SPIC AND SPAN BY TOMORROW MORNING.
NO WAY! TELEVISION IS PLAYING TONIGHT!
I MEAN IT LARRY! YOU'LL JUST HAVE TO MISS YOUR BALONEY BAND AND THOSE SLUTTY--

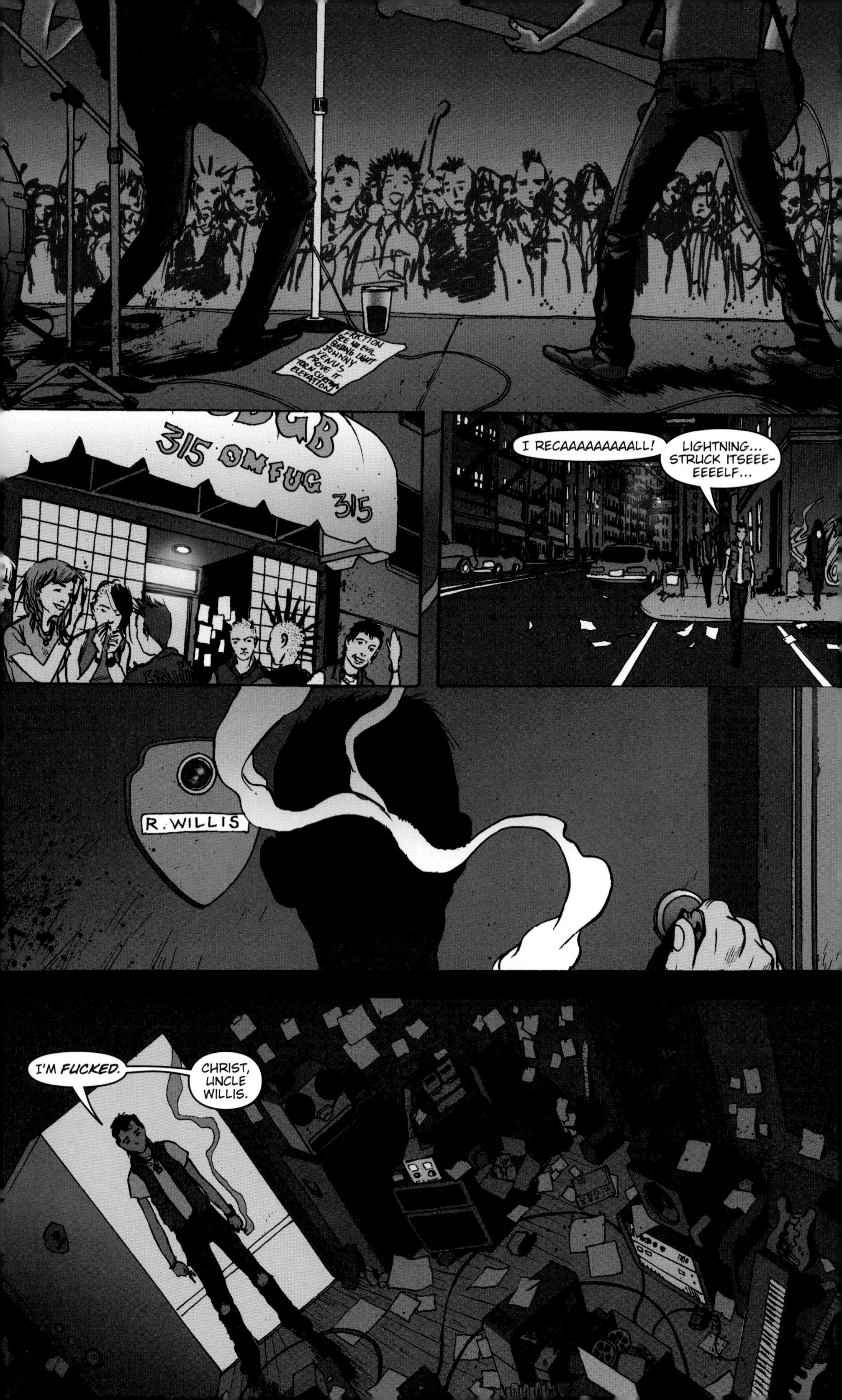
FRICTION
SEE NO EVIL
BLINDING LIGHT
JOHNNY
VENUS
PROVE IT
TORN CURTAIN
ELEVATION
315 OMFUG 315
I RECAAAAAAAAAALL!
LIGHTNING... STRUCK ITSEEE-EEEELF...
R. WILLIS
I'M *FUCKED.*
CHRIST, UNCLE WILLIS.

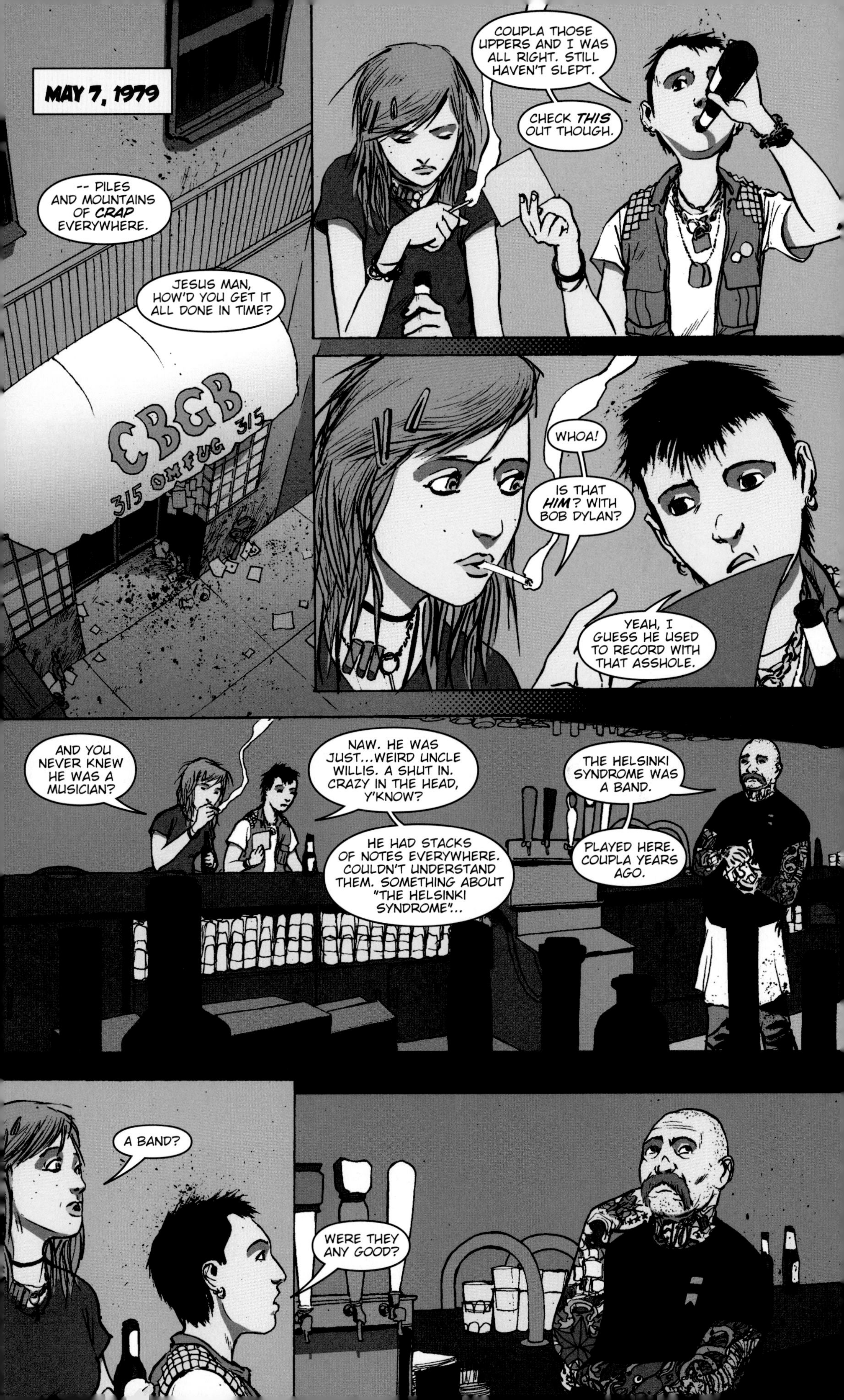
MAY 7, 1979
-- PILES AND MOUNTAINS OF CRAP EVERYWHERE.
JESUS MAN, HOW'D YOU GET IT ALL DONE IN TIME?
CBGB 315 OMFUG 315
COUPLA THOSE UPPERS AND I WAS ALL RIGHT. STILL HAVEN'T SLEPT.
CHECK THIS OUT THOUGH.
WHOA!
IS THAT HIM? WITH BOB DYLAN?
YEAH, I GUESS HE USED TO RECORD WITH THAT ASSHOLE.
AND YOU NEVER KNEW HE WAS A MUSICIAN?
NAW. HE WAS JUST...WEIRD UNCLE WILLIS. A SHUT IN. CRAZY IN THE HEAD, Y'KNOW?
HE HAD STACKS OF NOTES EVERYWHERE. COULDN'T UNDERSTAND THEM. SOMETHING ABOUT "THE HELSINKI SYNDROME"...
THE HELSINKI SYNDROME WAS A BAND.
PLAYED HERE. COUPLA YEARS AGO.
A BAND?
WERE THEY ANY GOOD?

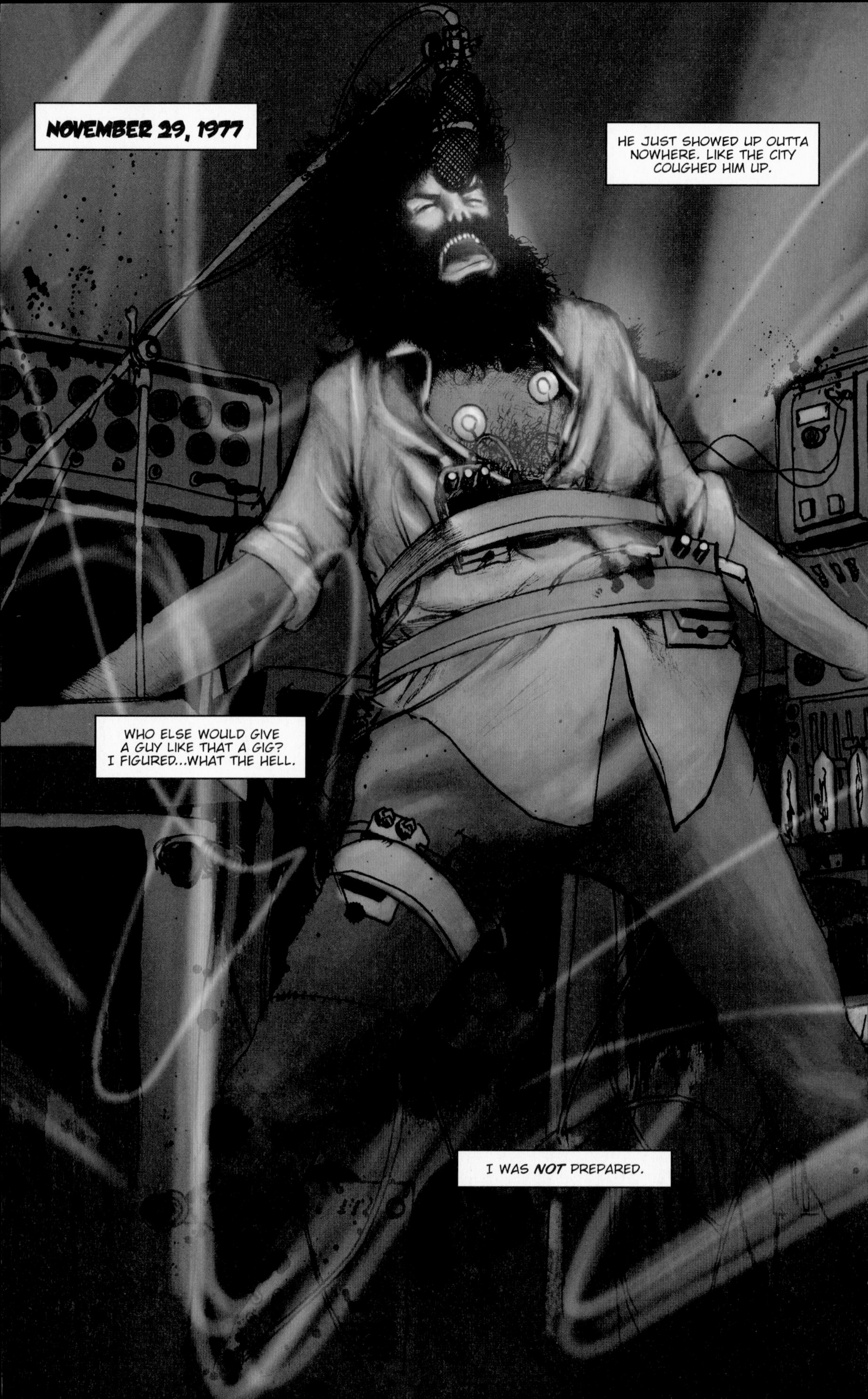
NOVEMBER 29, 1977
HE JUST SHOWED UP OUTTA NOWHERE. LIKE THE CITY COUGHED HIM UP.
WHO ELSE WOULD GIVE A GUY LIKE THAT A GIG? I FIGURED...WHAT THE HELL.
I WAS *NOT* PREPARED.

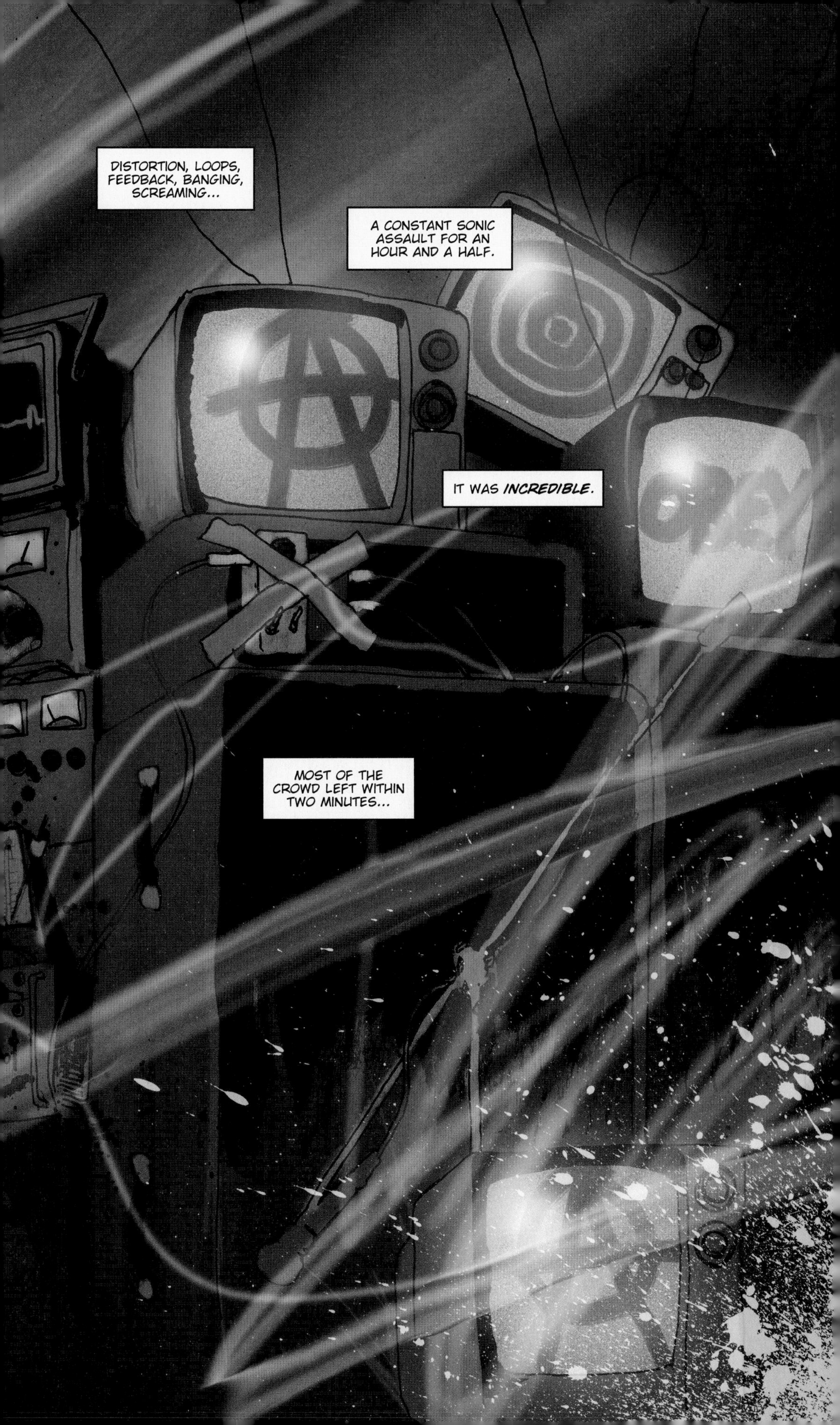
DISTORTION, LOOPS, FEEDBACK, BANGING, SCREAMING...
A CONSTANT SONIC ASSAULT FOR AN HOUR AND A HALF.
IT WAS *INCREDIBLE*.
MOST OF THE CROWD LEFT WITHIN TWO MINUTES...

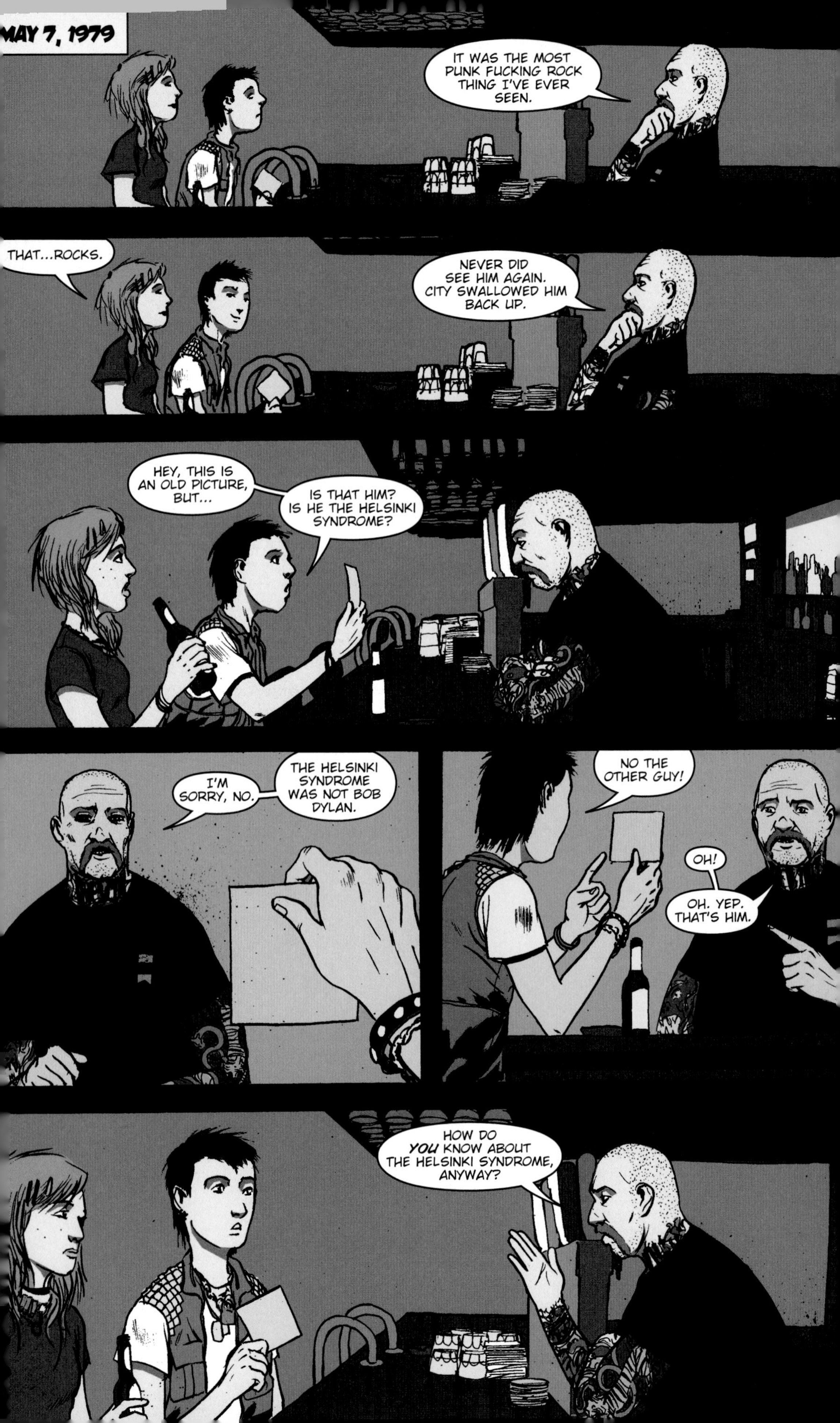
MAY 7, 1979
IT WAS THE MOST PUNK FUCKING ROCK THING I'VE EVER SEEN.
THAT...ROCKS.
NEVER DID SEE HIM AGAIN. CITY SWALLOWED HIM BACK UP.
HEY, THIS IS AN OLD PICTURE, BUT...
IS THAT HIM? IS HE THE HELSINKI SYNDROME?
I'M SORRY, NO.
THE HELSINKI SYNDROME WAS NOT BOB DYLAN.
NO THE OTHER GUY!
OH!
OH. YEP. THAT'S HIM.
HOW DO *YOU* KNOW ABOUT THE HELSINKI SYNDROME, ANYWAY?

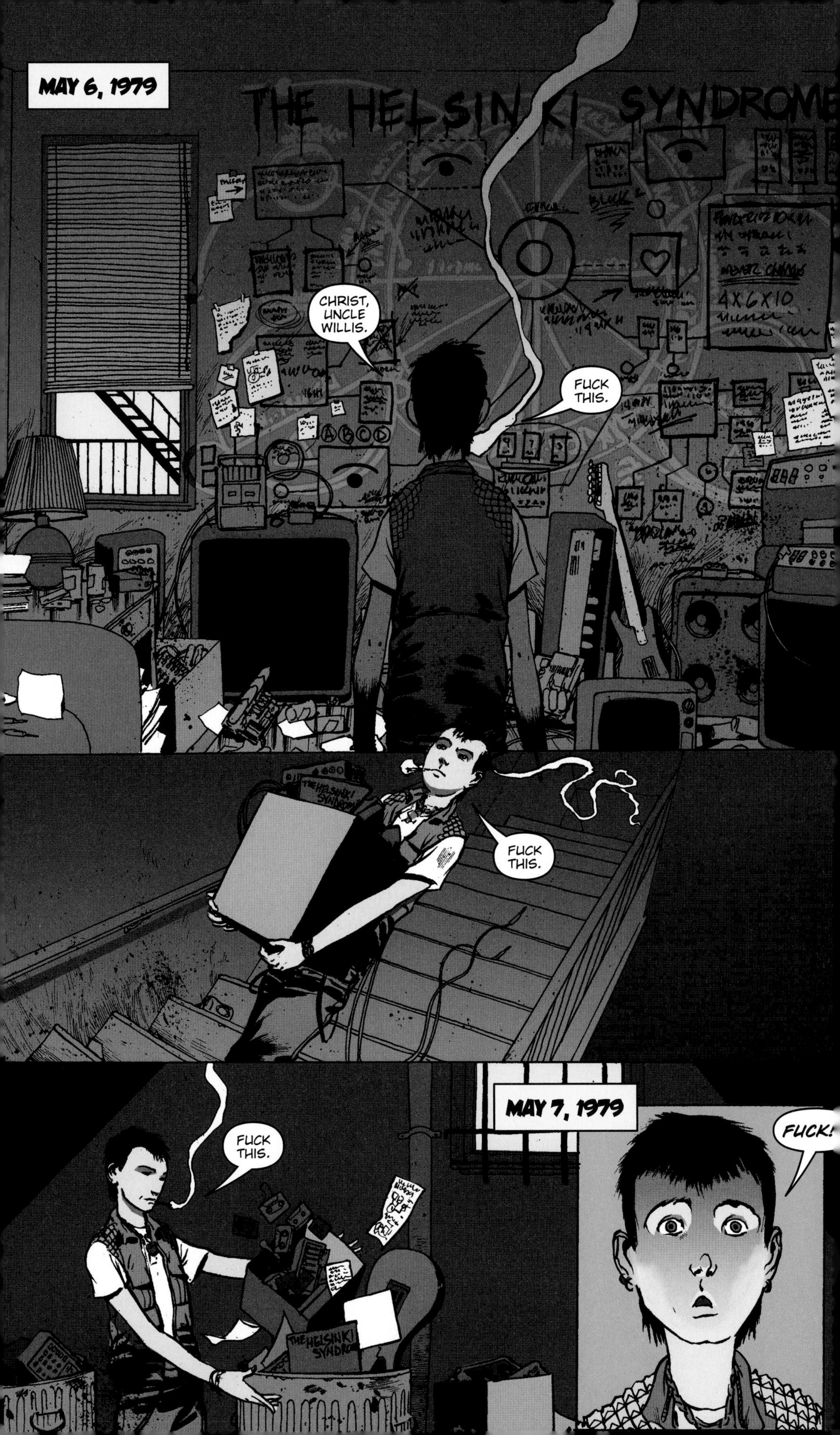
MAY 6, 1979
CHRIST, UNCLE WILLIS.
FUCK THIS.
FUCK THIS.
FUCK THIS.
MAY 7, 1979
FUCK!

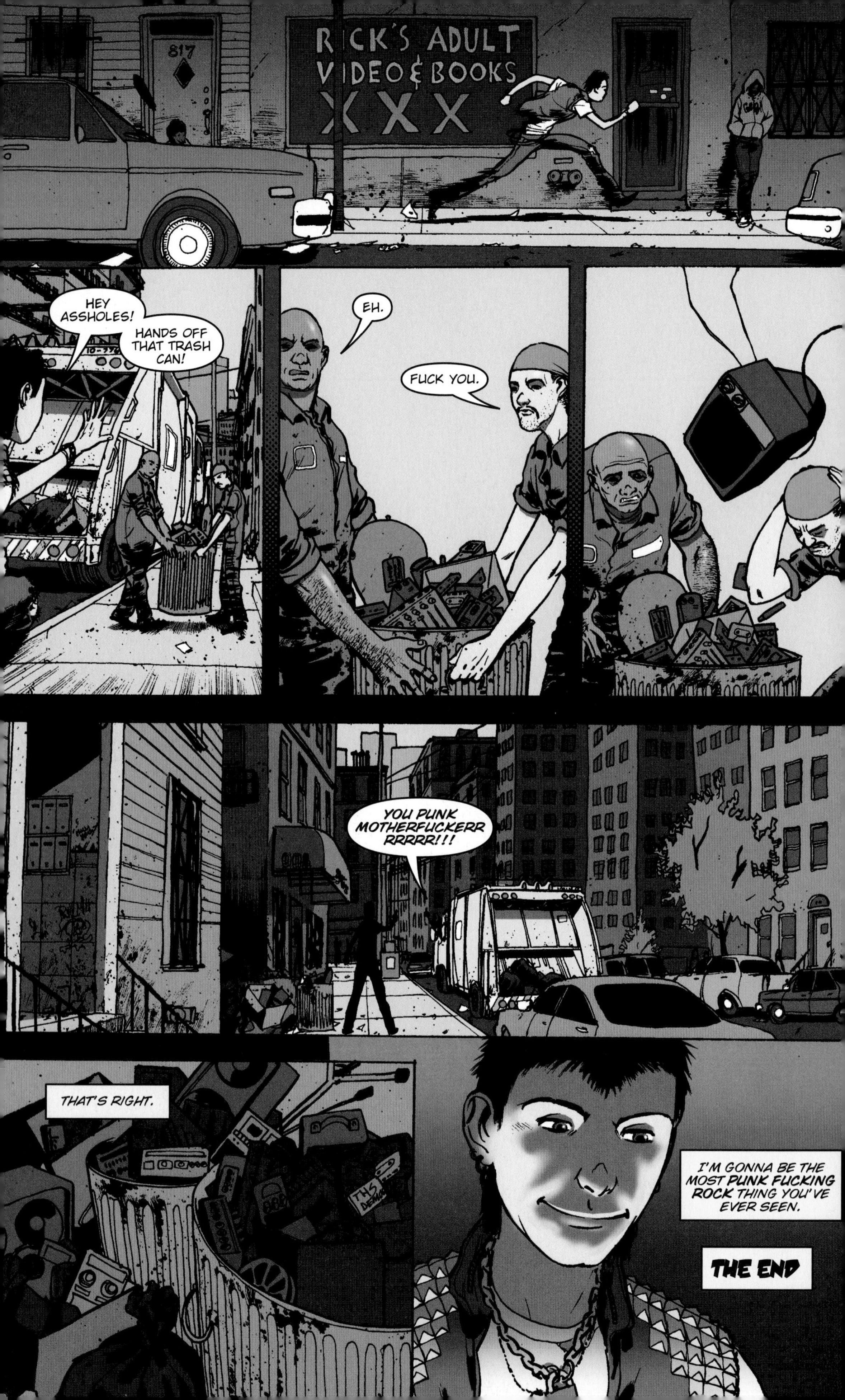
RICK'S ADULT VIDEO & BOOKS XXX
817
HEY ASSHOLES!
HANDS OFF THAT TRASH CAN!
EH.
FUCK YOU.
YOU PUNK MOTHERFUCKERR RRRRR!!!
THAT'S RIGHT.
I'M GONNA BE THE MOST PUNK FUCKING ROCK THING YOU'VE EVER SEEN.
THE END

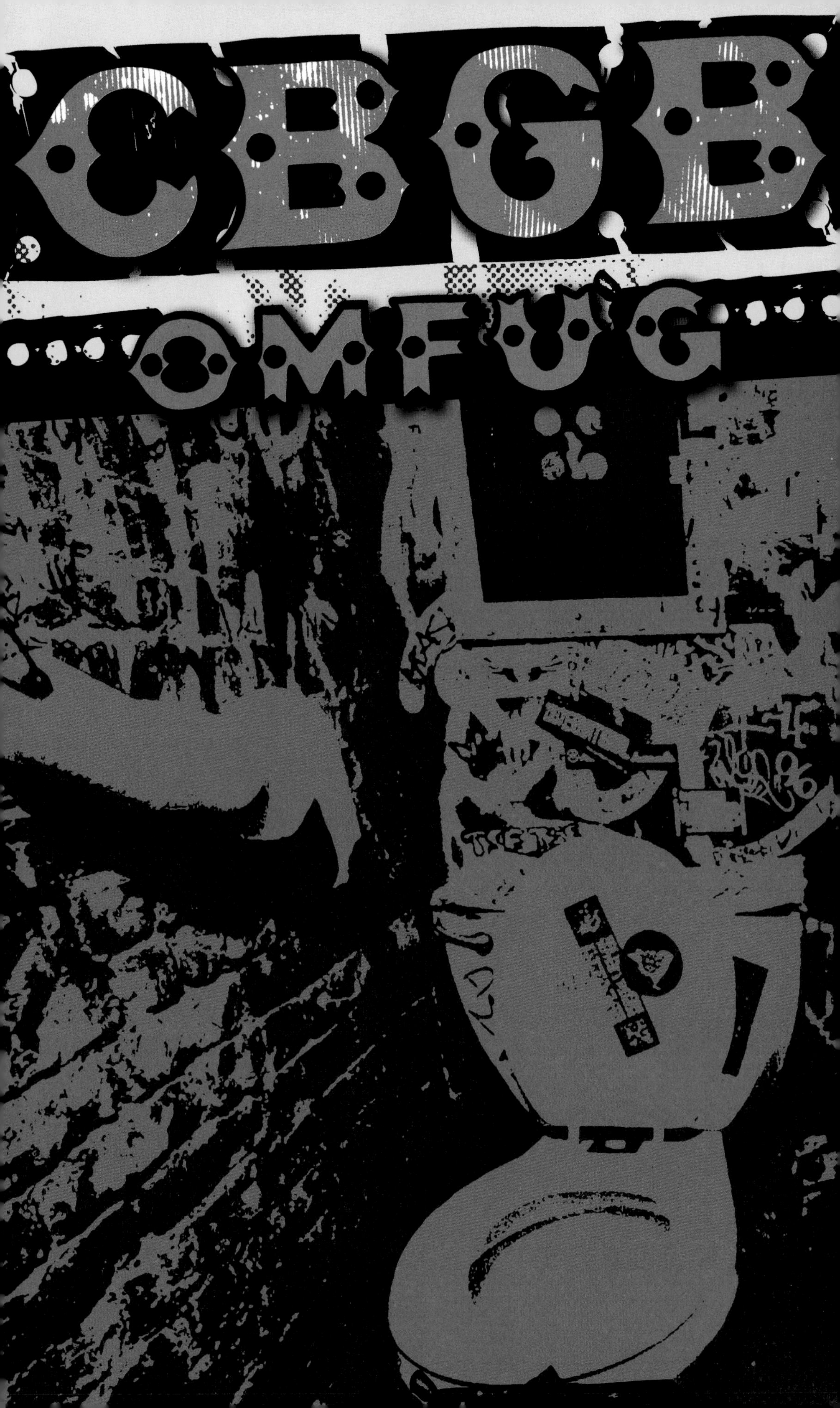
CBGB
OMFUG

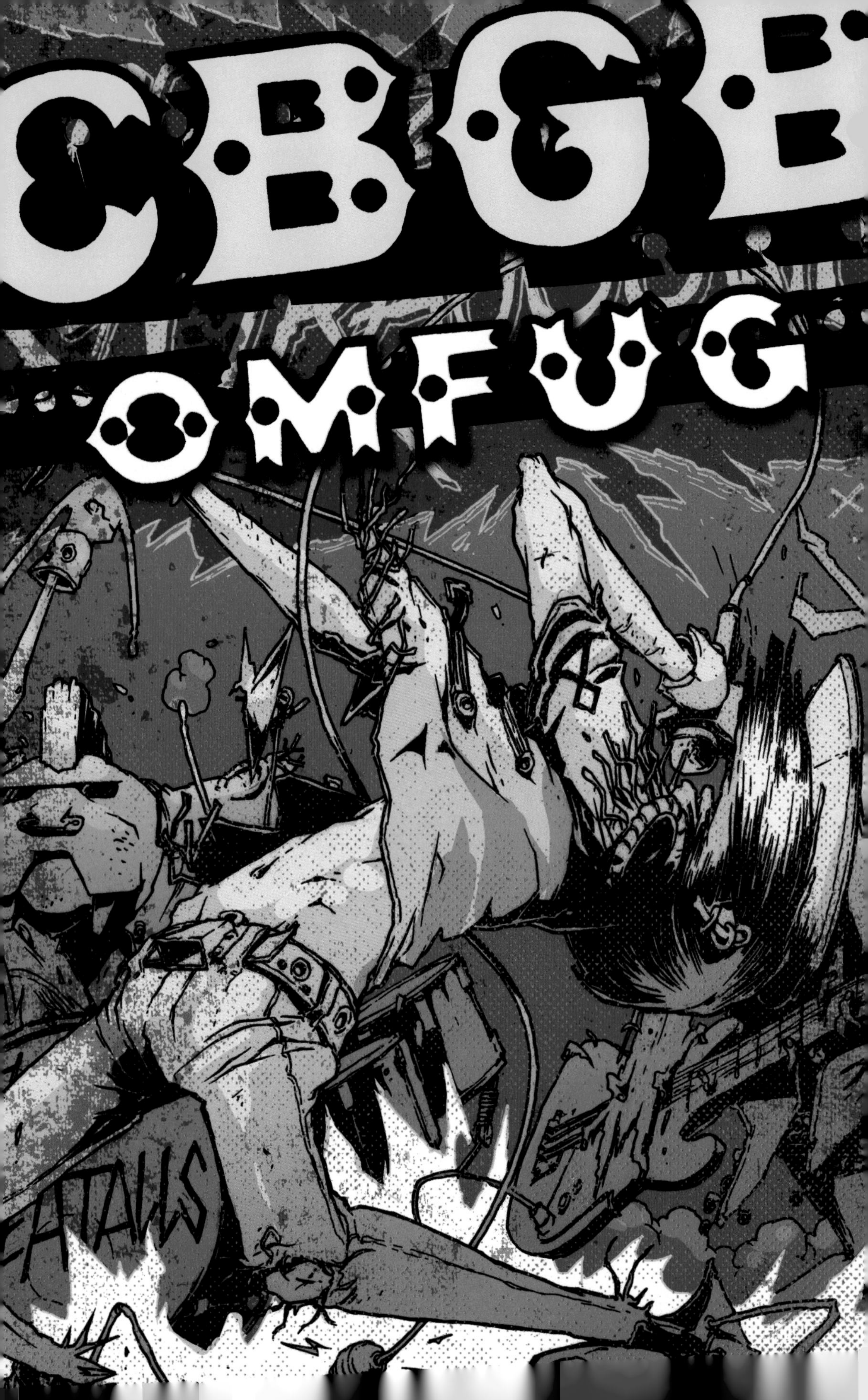
CBGB
OMFUG

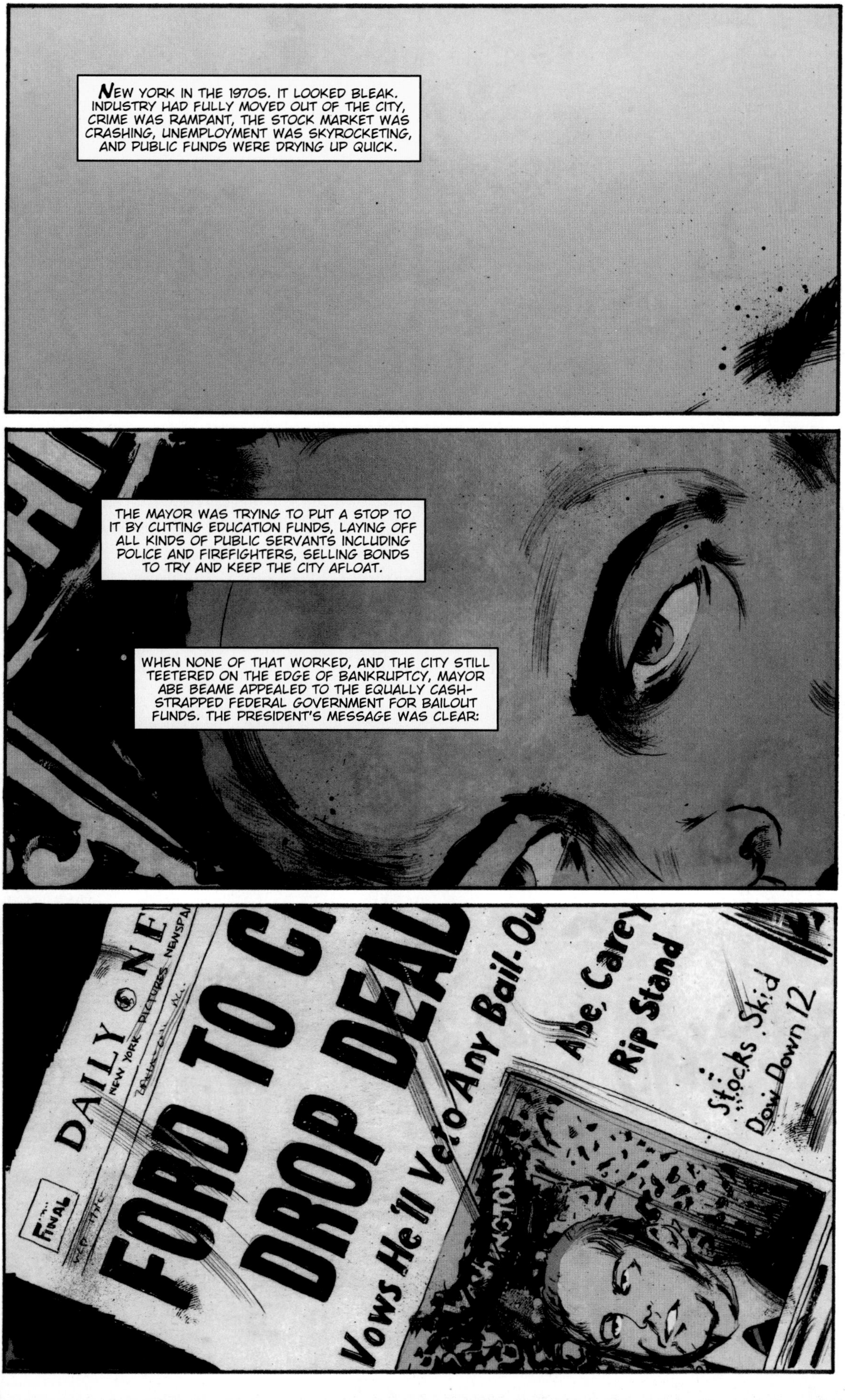
NEW YORK IN THE 1970S. IT LOOKED BLEAK. INDUSTRY HAD FULLY MOVED OUT OF THE CITY, CRIME WAS RAMPANT, THE STOCK MARKET WAS CRASHING, UNEMPLOYMENT WAS SKYROCKETING, AND PUBLIC FUNDS WERE DRYING UP QUICK.
THE MAYOR WAS TRYING TO PUT A STOP TO IT BY CUTTING EDUCATION FUNDS, LAYING OFF ALL KINDS OF PUBLIC SERVANTS INCLUDING POLICE AND FIREFIGHTERS, SELLING BONDS TO TRY AND KEEP THE CITY AFLOAT.
WHEN NONE OF THAT WORKED, AND THE CITY STILL TEETERED ON THE EDGE OF BANKRUPTCY, MAYOR ABE BEAME APPEALED TO THE EQUALLY CASH-STRAPPED FEDERAL GOVERNMENT FOR BAILOUT FUNDS. THE PRESIDENT'S MESSAGE WAS CLEAR:
DAILY NE
NEW YORK PICTURES NEWSPA
FINAL
FORD TO CI
DROP DEAD
Vows He'll Veto Any Bail-Ou
Abe, Carey Rip Stand
Stocks Skid Dow Down 12

ROCK BLOCK

WRITER: ANA MATRONIC ARTIST: DAN DUNCAN
COLORIST: RENATO FACCINI LETTERER: JAMES DASHIELL EDITOR: IAN BRILL

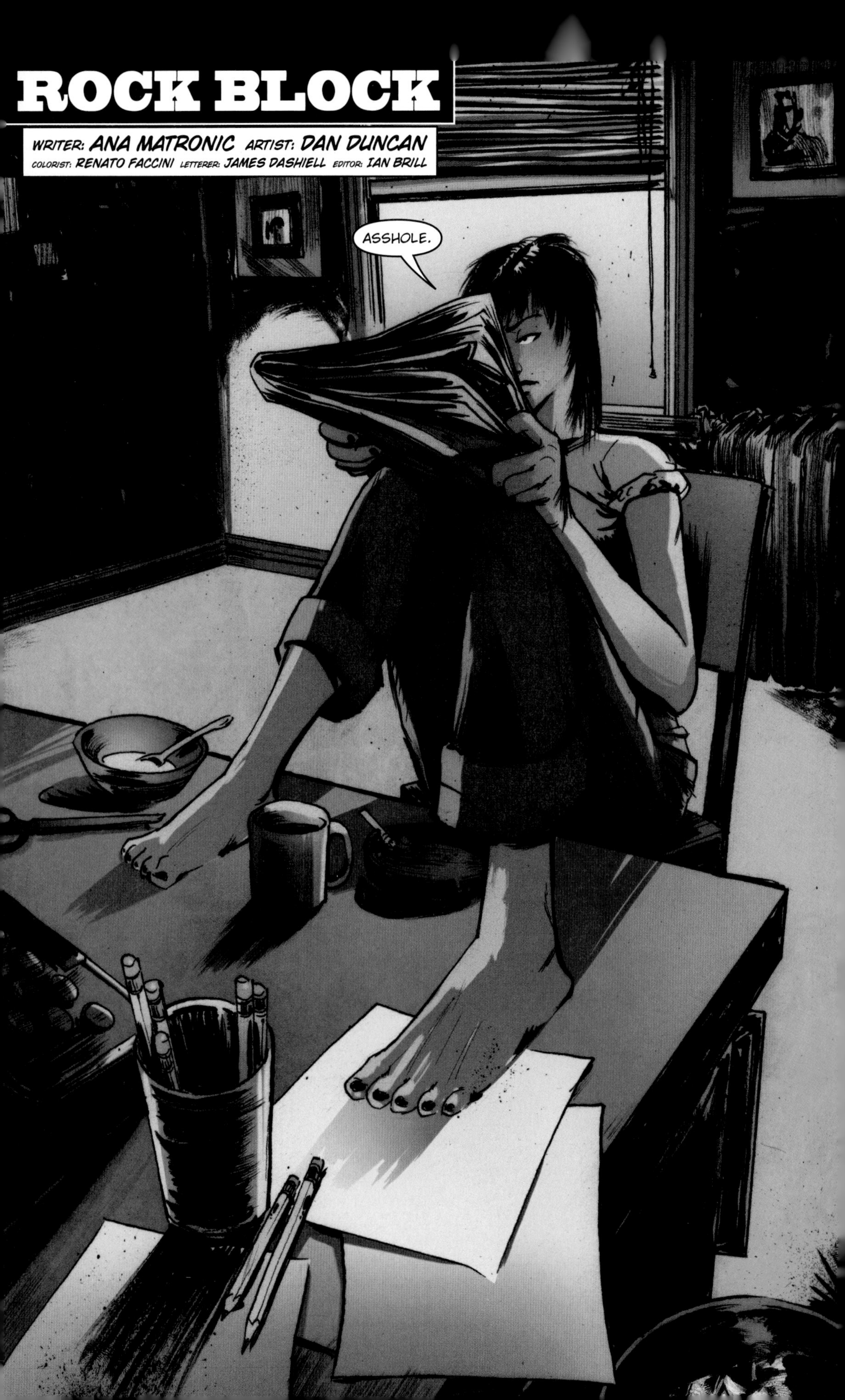
ASSHOLE.

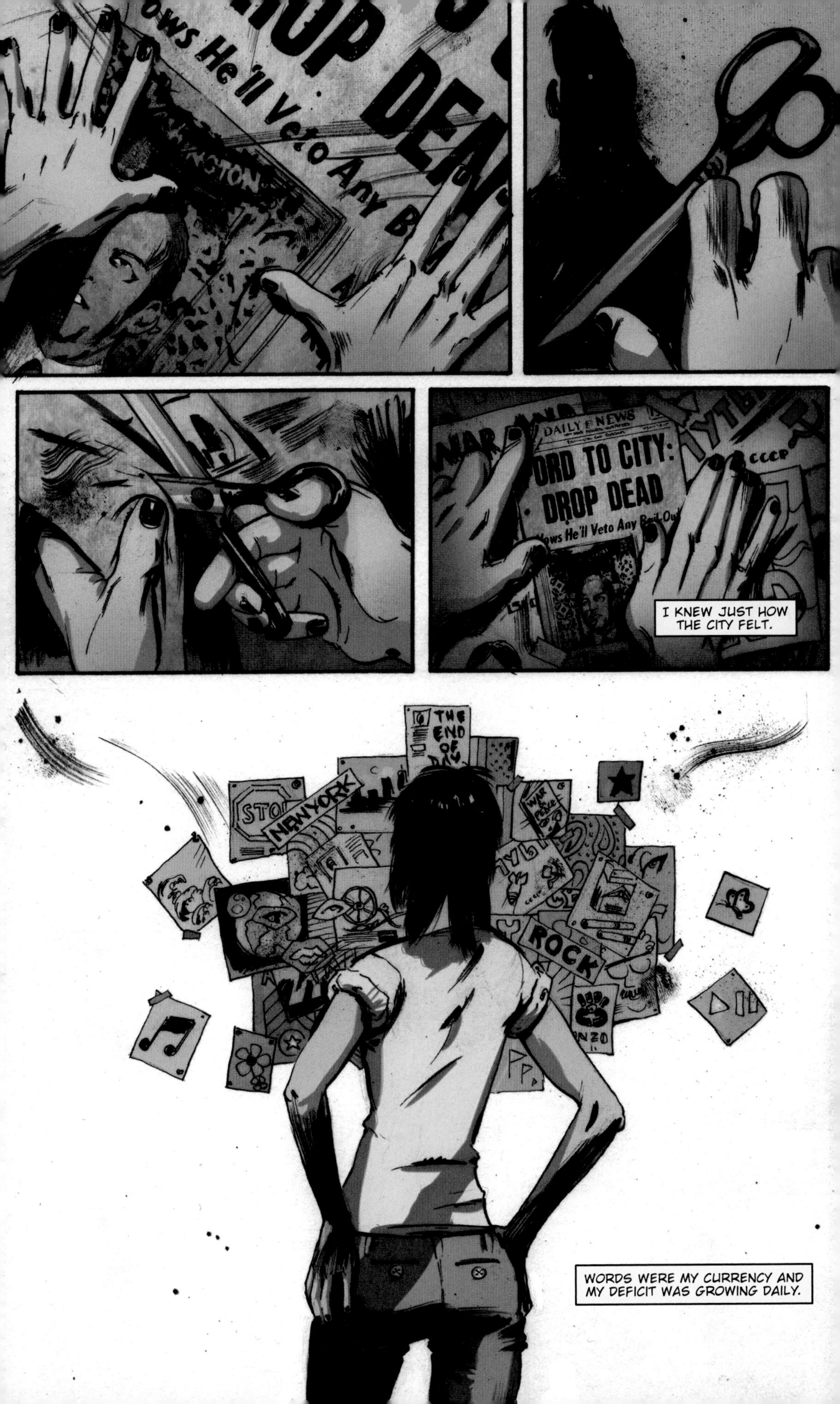

ORD TO CITY:
DROP DEAD
I KNEW JUST HOW THE CITY FELT.
THE END OF
NEW YORK
ROCK
WORDS WERE MY CURRENCY AND MY DEFICIT WAS GROWING DAILY.

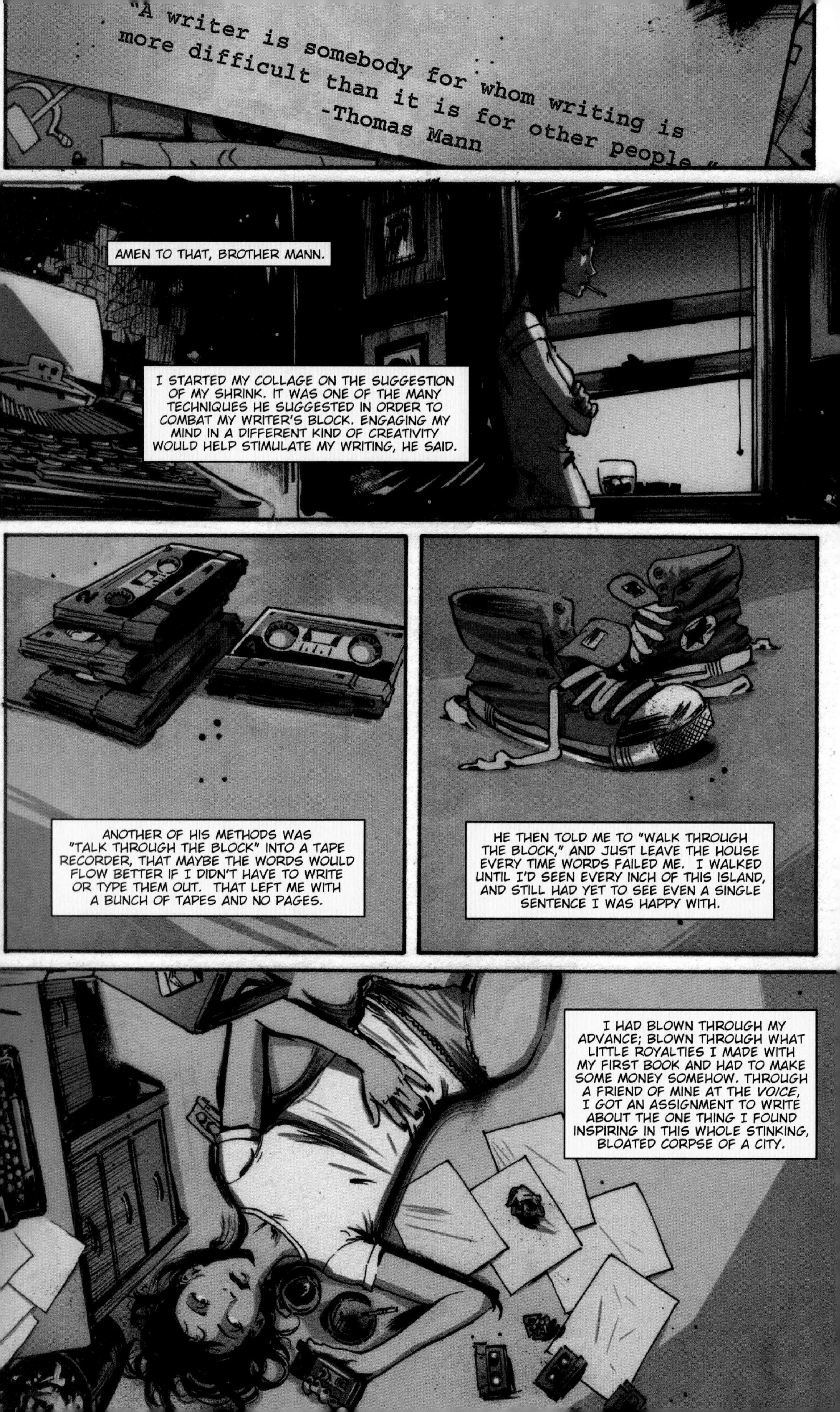
"A writer is somebody for whom writing is more difficult than it is for other people."
-Thomas Mann
AMEN TO THAT, BROTHER MANN.
I STARTED MY COLLAGE ON THE SUGGESTION OF MY SHRINK. IT WAS ONE OF THE MANY TECHNIQUES HE SUGGESTED IN ORDER TO COMBAT MY WRITER'S BLOCK. ENGAGING MY MIND IN A DIFFERENT KIND OF CREATIVITY WOULD HELP STIMULATE MY WRITING, HE SAID.
ANOTHER OF HIS METHODS WAS "TALK THROUGH THE BLOCK" INTO A TAPE RECORDER, THAT MAYBE THE WORDS WOULD FLOW BETTER IF I DIDN'T HAVE TO WRITE OR TYPE THEM OUT. THAT LEFT ME WITH A BUNCH OF TAPES AND NO PAGES.
HE THEN TOLD ME TO "WALK THROUGH THE BLOCK," AND JUST LEAVE THE HOUSE EVERY TIME WORDS FAILED ME. I WALKED UNTIL I'D SEEN EVERY INCH OF THIS ISLAND, AND STILL HAD YET TO SEE EVEN A SINGLE SENTENCE I WAS HAPPY WITH.
I HAD BLOWN THROUGH MY ADVANCE; BLOWN THROUGH WHAT LITTLE ROYALTIES I MADE WITH MY FIRST BOOK AND HAD TO MAKE SOME MONEY SOMEHOW. THROUGH A FRIEND OF MINE AT THE *VOICE*, I GOT AN ASSIGNMENT TO WRITE ABOUT THE ONE THING I FOUND INSPIRING IN THIS WHOLE STINKING, BLOATED CORPSE OF A CITY.

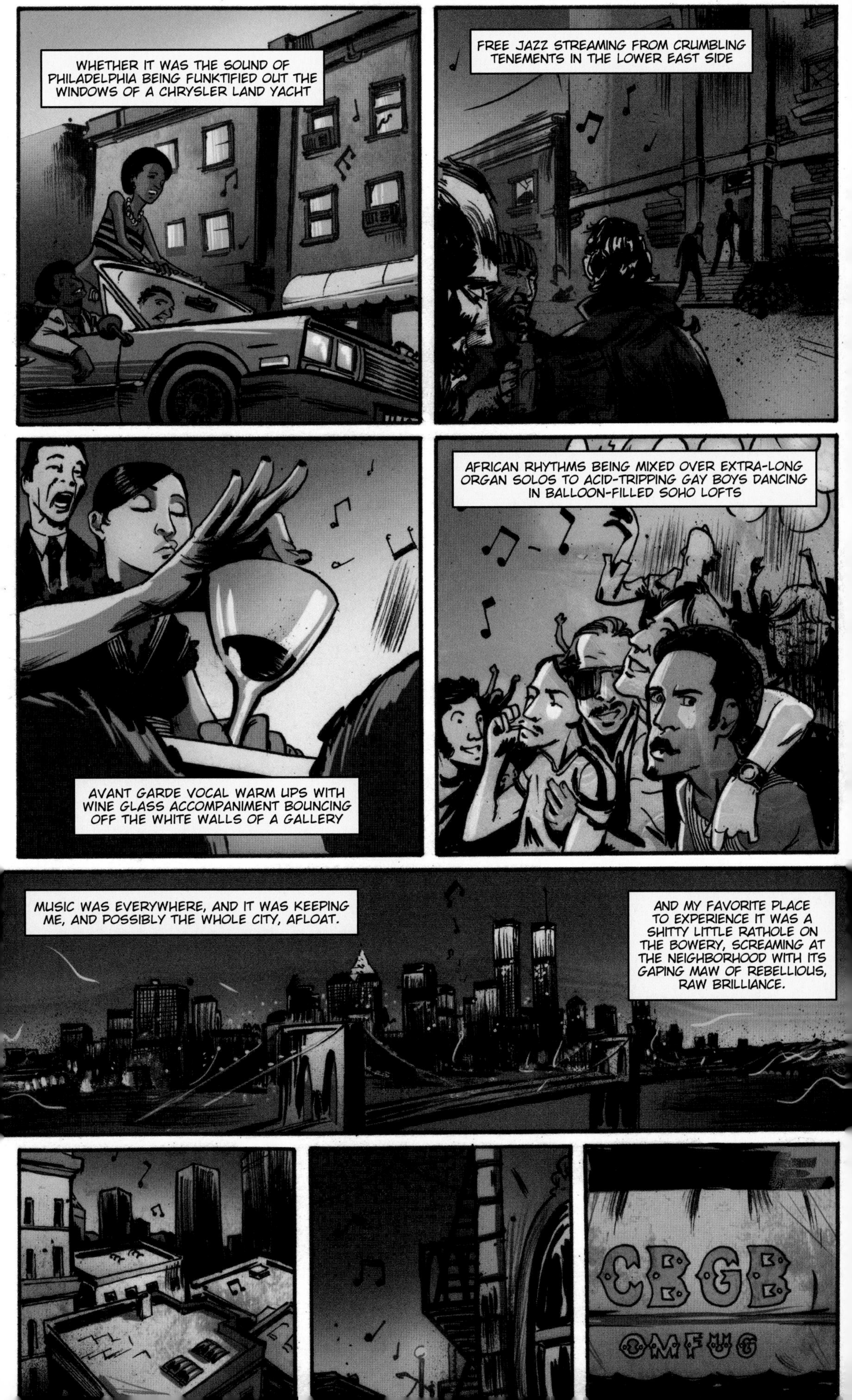
WHETHER IT WAS THE SOUND OF PHILADELPHIA BEING FUNKTIFIED OUT THE WINDOWS OF A CHRYSLER LAND YACHT
FREE JAZZ STREAMING FROM CRUMBLING TENEMENTS IN THE LOWER EAST SIDE
AVANT GARDE VOCAL WARM UPS WITH WINE GLASS ACCOMPANIMENT BOUNCING OFF THE WHITE WALLS OF A GALLERY
AFRICAN RHYTHMS BEING MIXED OVER EXTRA-LONG ORGAN SOLOS TO ACID-TRIPPING GAY BOYS DANCING IN BALLOON-FILLED SOHO LOFTS
MUSIC WAS EVERYWHERE, AND IT WAS KEEPING ME, AND POSSIBLY THE WHOLE CITY, AFLOAT.
AND MY FAVORITE PLACE TO EXPERIENCE IT WAS A SHITTY LITTLE RATHOLE ON THE BOWERY, SCREAMING AT THE NEIGHBORHOOD WITH ITS GAPING MAW OF REBELLIOUS, RAW BRILLIANCE.
CBGB
OMFUG

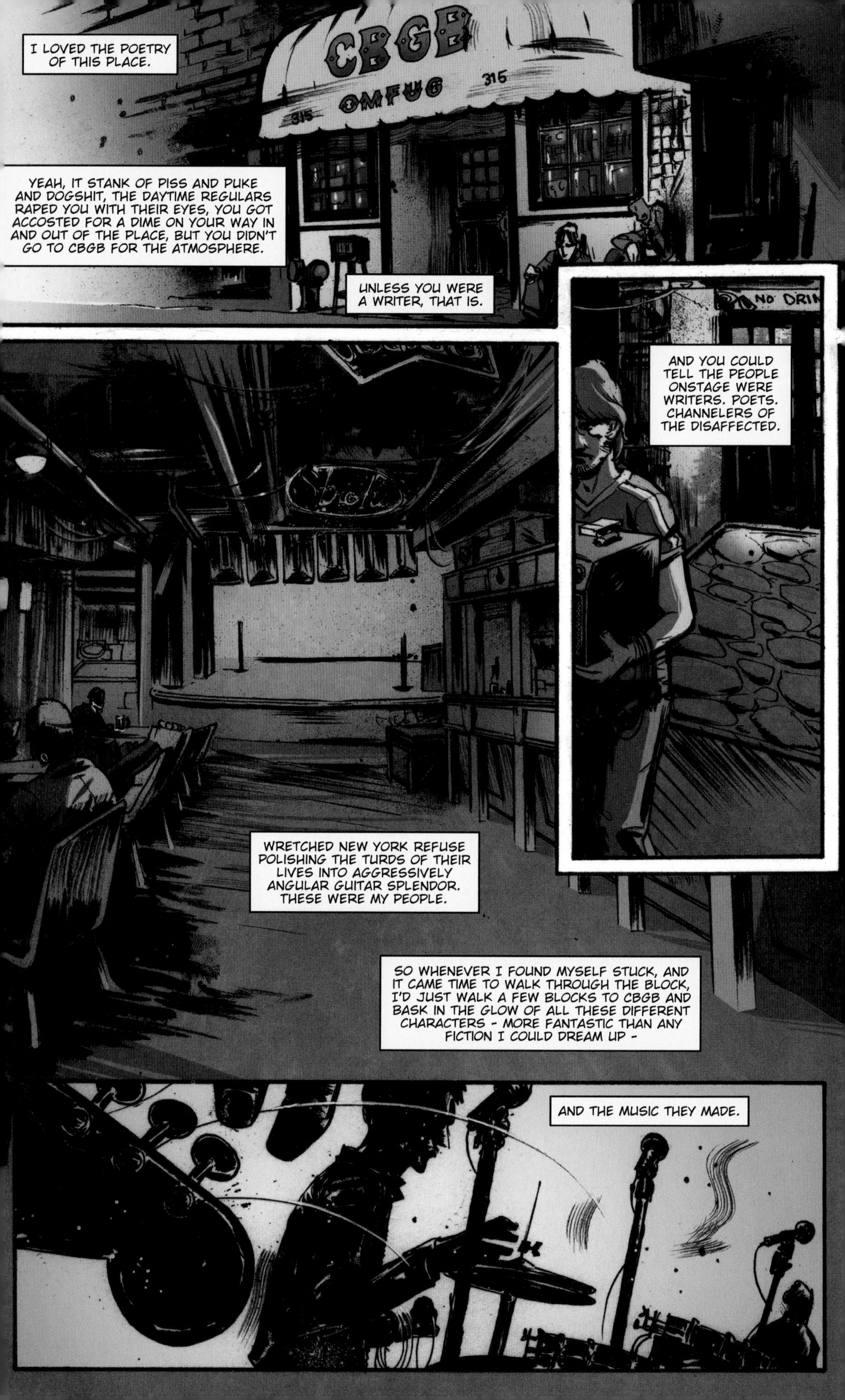
I LOVED THE POETRY OF THIS PLACE.
CBGB
OMFUG
315
YEAH, IT STANK OF PISS AND PUKE AND DOGSHIT, THE DAYTIME REGULARS RAPED YOU WITH THEIR EYES, YOU GOT ACCOSTED FOR A DIME ON YOUR WAY IN AND OUT OF THE PLACE, BUT YOU DIDN'T GO TO CBGB FOR THE ATMOSPHERE.
UNLESS YOU WERE A WRITER, THAT IS.
AND YOU COULD TELL THE PEOPLE ONSTAGE WERE WRITERS. POETS. CHANNELERS OF THE DISAFFECTED.
WRETCHED NEW YORK REFUSE POLISHING THE TURDS OF THEIR LIVES INTO AGGRESSIVELY ANGULAR GUITAR SPLENDOR. THESE WERE MY PEOPLE.
SO WHENEVER I FOUND MYSELF STUCK, AND IT CAME TIME TO WALK THROUGH THE BLOCK, I'D JUST WALK A FEW BLOCKS TO CBGB AND BASK IN THE GLOW OF ALL THESE DIFFERENT CHARACTERS - MORE FANTASTIC THAN ANY FICTION I COULD DREAM UP -
AND THE MUSIC THEY MADE.

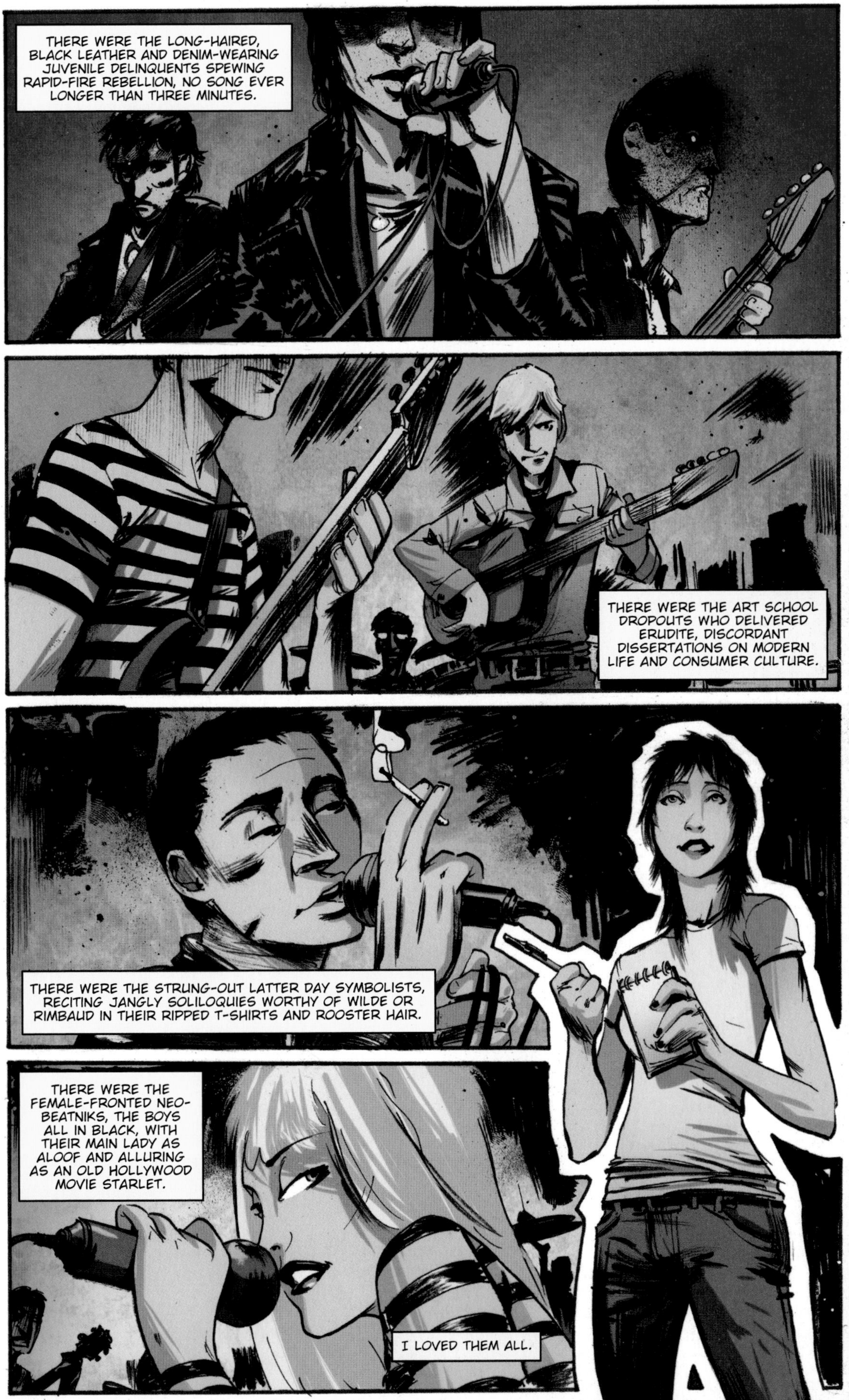
THERE WERE THE LONG-HAIRED, BLACK LEATHER AND DENIM-WEARING JUVENILE DELINQUENTS SPEWING RAPID-FIRE REBELLION, NO SONG EVER LONGER THAN THREE MINUTES.
THERE WERE THE ART SCHOOL DROPOUTS WHO DELIVERED ERUDITE, DISCORDANT DISSERTATIONS ON MODERN LIFE AND CONSUMER CULTURE.
THERE WERE THE STRUNG-OUT LATTER DAY SYMBOLISTS, RECITING JANGLY SOLILOQUIES WORTHY OF WILDE OR RIMBAUD IN THEIR RIPPED T-SHIRTS AND ROOSTER HAIR.
THERE WERE THE FEMALE-FRONTED NEO-BEATNIKS, THE BOYS ALL IN BLACK, WITH THEIR MAIN LADY AS ALOOF AND ALLURING AS AN OLD HOLLYWOOD MOVIE STARLET.
I LOVED THEM ALL.

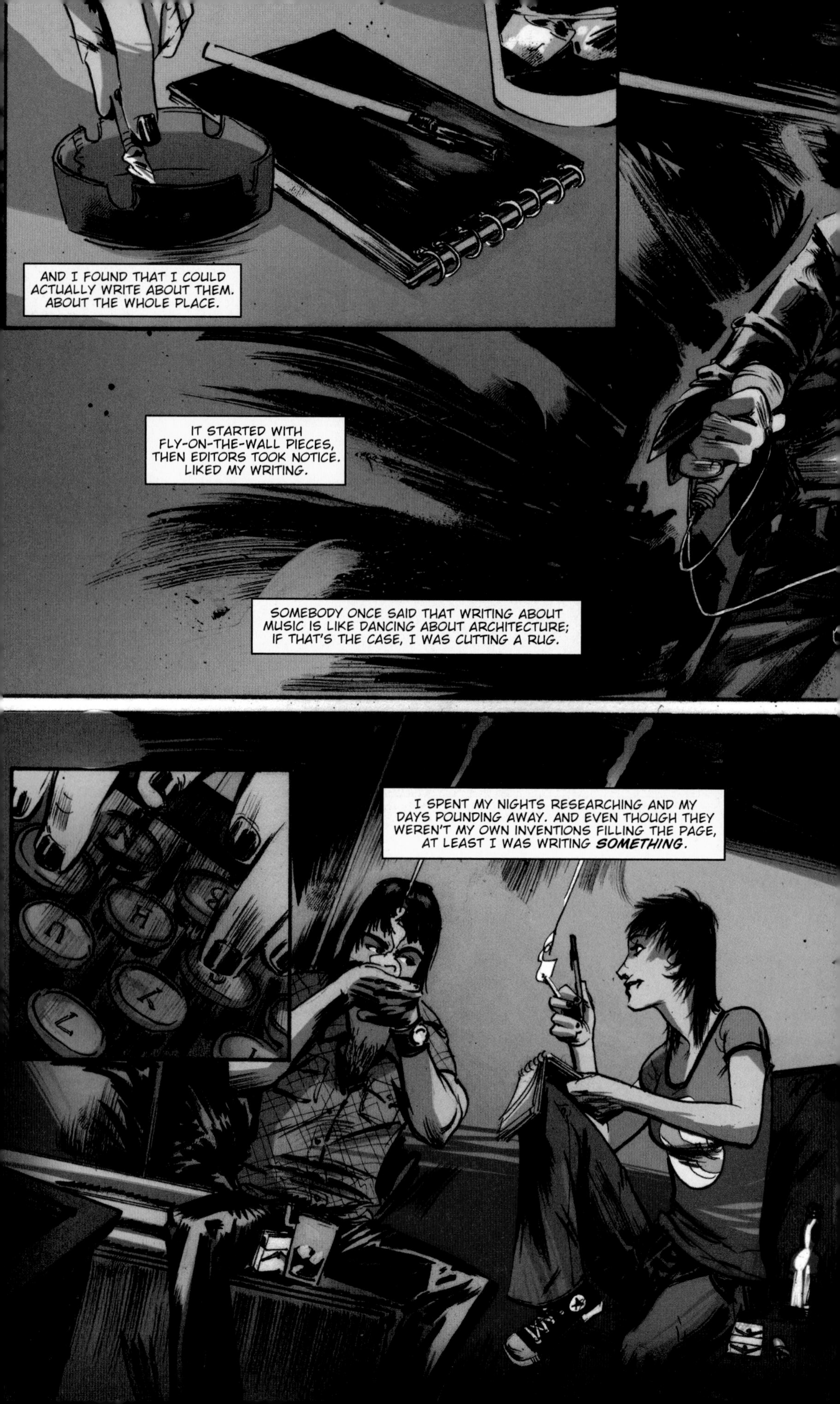

AND I FOUND THAT I COULD ACTUALLY WRITE ABOUT THEM. ABOUT THE WHOLE PLACE.
IT STARTED WITH FLY-ON-THE-WALL PIECES, THEN EDITORS TOOK NOTICE. LIKED MY WRITING.
SOMEBODY ONCE SAID THAT WRITING ABOUT MUSIC IS LIKE DANCING ABOUT ARCHITECTURE; IF THAT'S THE CASE, I WAS CUTTING A RUG.
I SPENT MY NIGHTS RESEARCHING AND MY DAYS POUNDING AWAY. AND EVEN THOUGH THEY WEREN'T MY OWN INVENTIONS FILLING THE PAGE, AT LEAST I WAS WRITING *SOMETHING*.

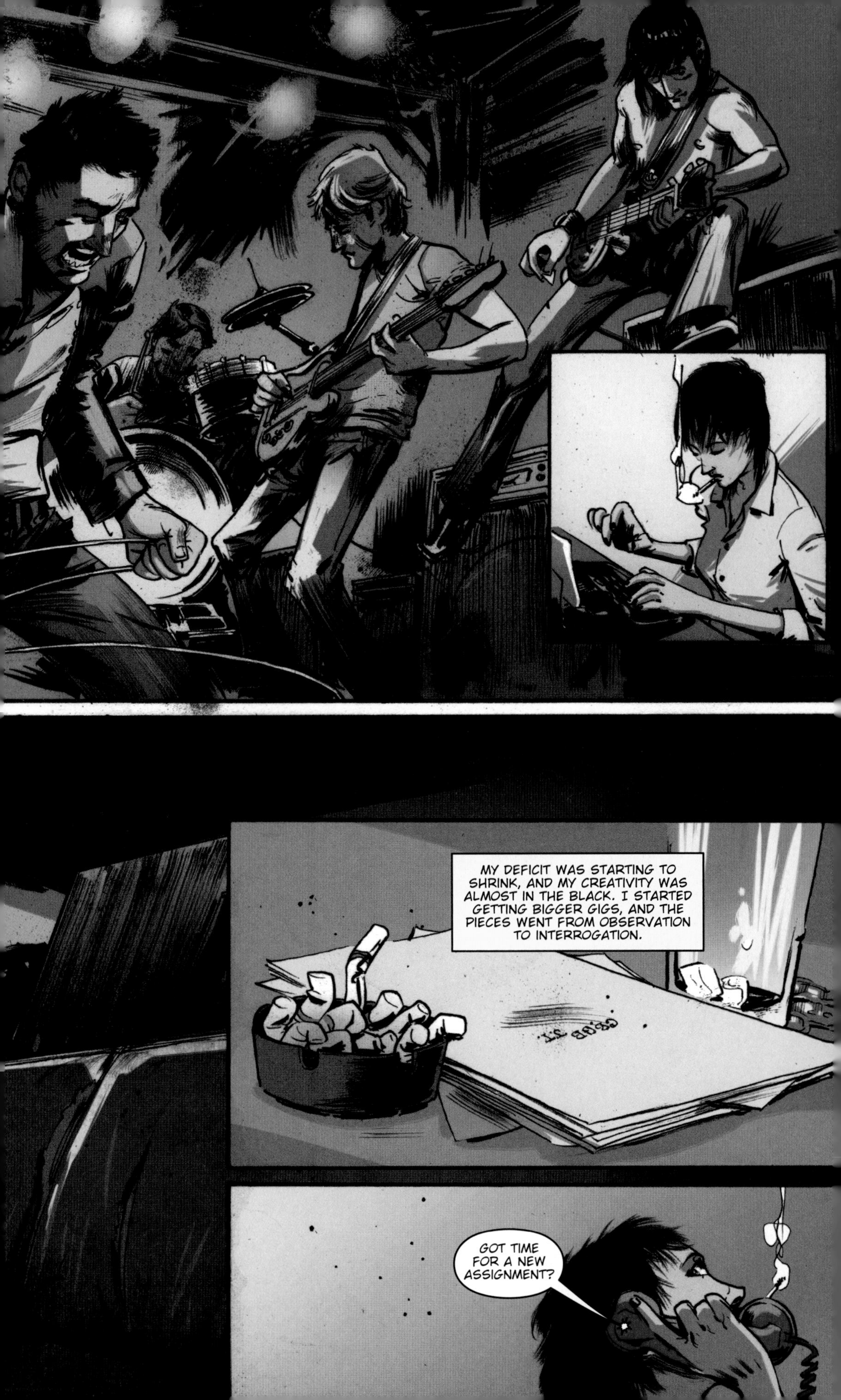
MY DEFICIT WAS STARTING TO SHRINK, AND MY CREATIVITY WAS ALMOST IN THE BLACK. I STARTED GETTING BIGGER GIGS, AND THE PIECES WENT FROM OBSERVATION TO INTERROGATION.
GOT TIME FOR A NEW ASSIGNMENT?

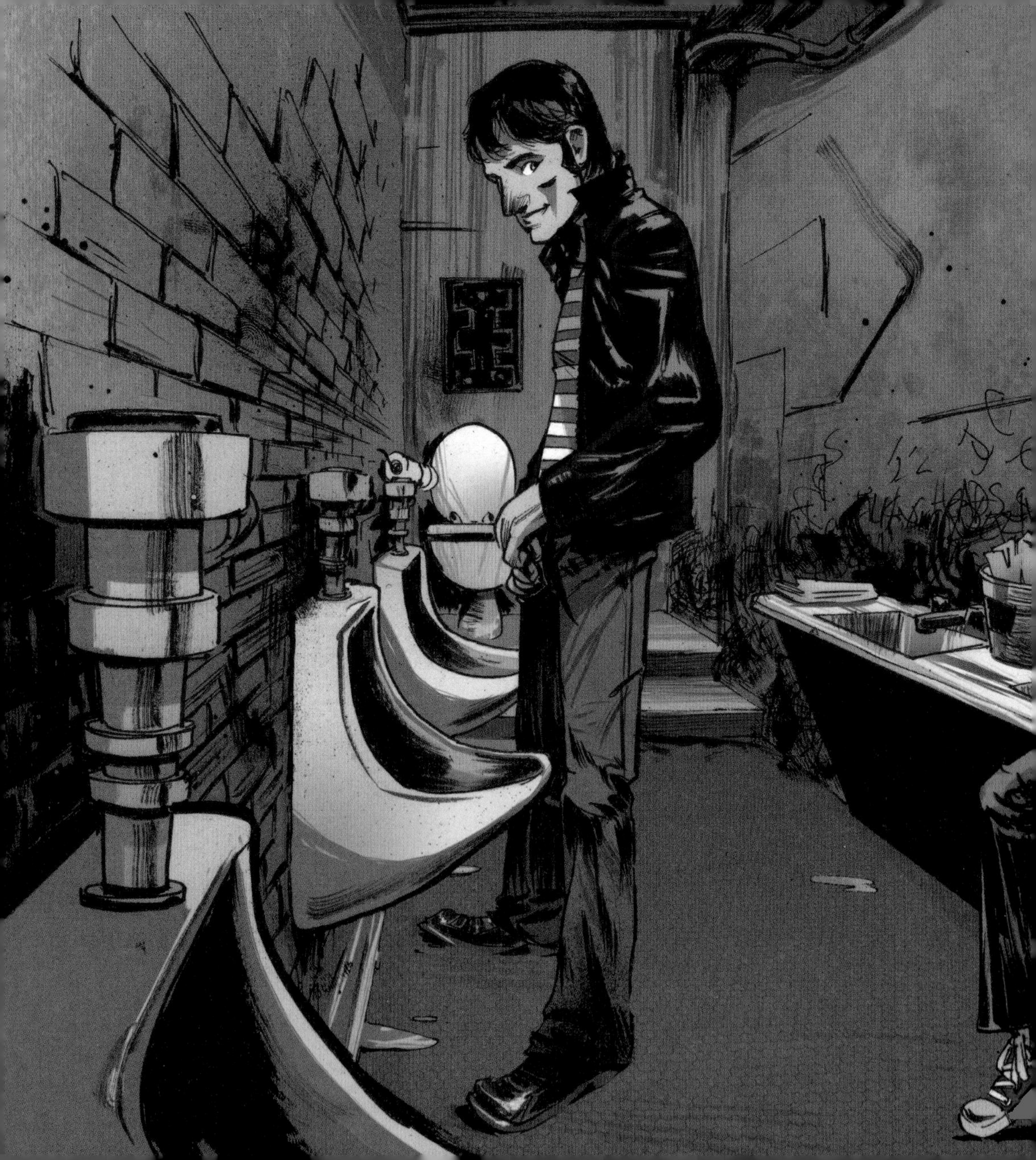

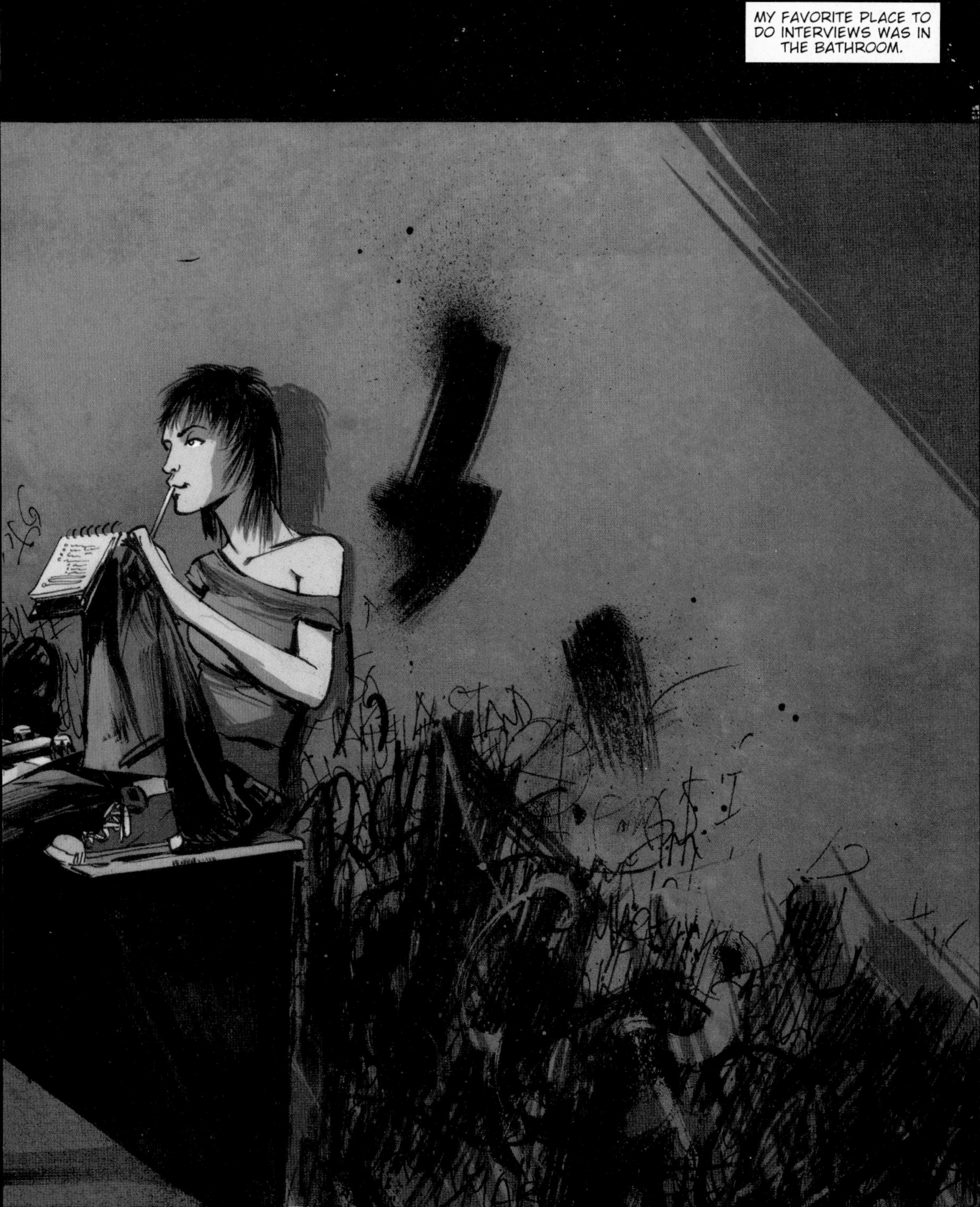
MY FAVORITE PLACE TO DO INTERVIEWS WAS IN THE BATHROOM.

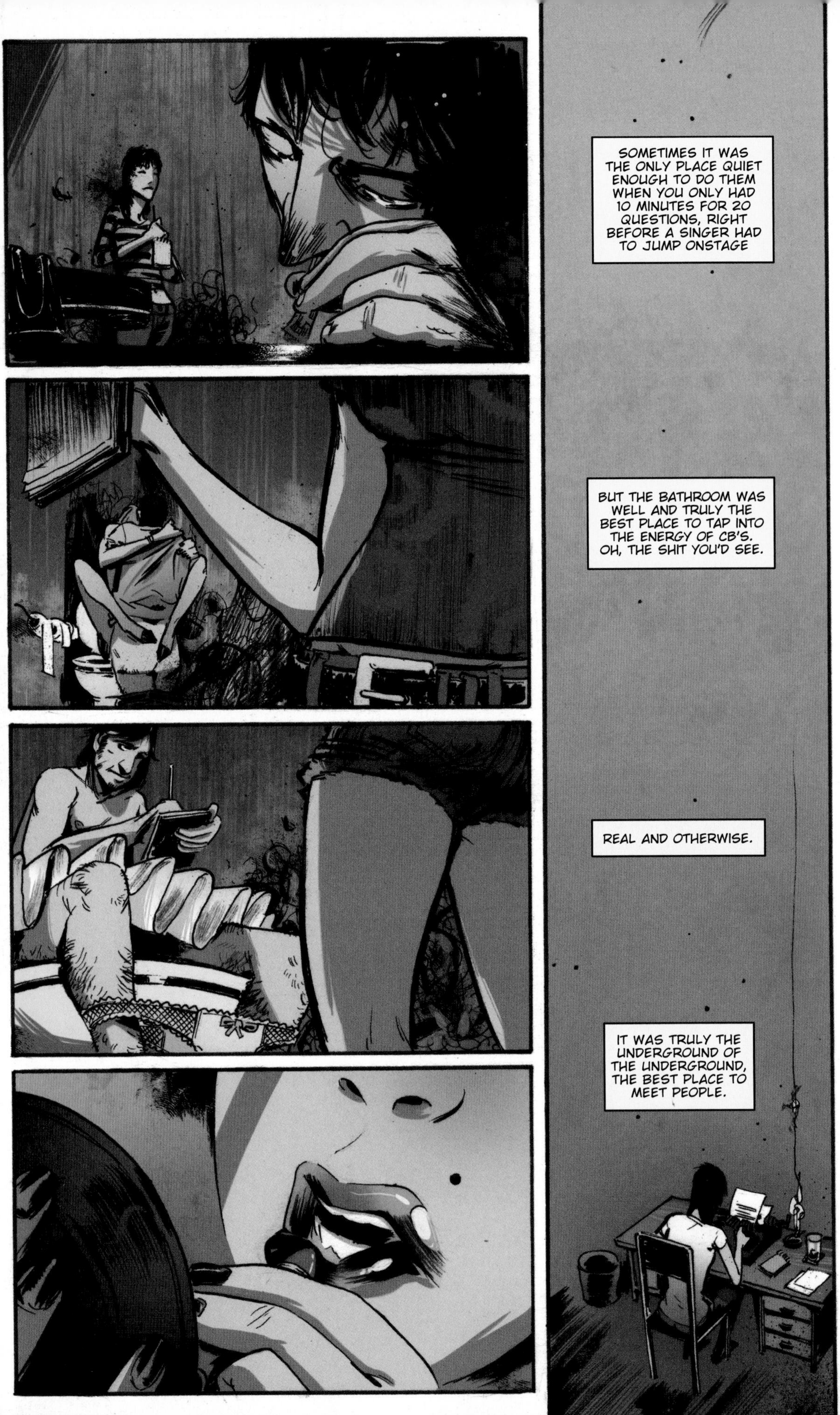
SOMETIMES IT WAS THE ONLY PLACE QUIET ENOUGH TO DO THEM WHEN YOU ONLY HAD 10 MINUTES FOR 20 QUESTIONS, RIGHT BEFORE A SINGER HAD TO JUMP ONSTAGE
BUT THE BATHROOM WAS WELL AND TRULY THE BEST PLACE TO TAP INTO THE ENERGY OF CB'S. OH, THE SHIT YOU'D SEE.
REAL AND OTHERWISE.
IT WAS TRULY THE UNDERGROUND OF THE UNDERGROUND, THE BEST PLACE TO MEET PEOPLE.

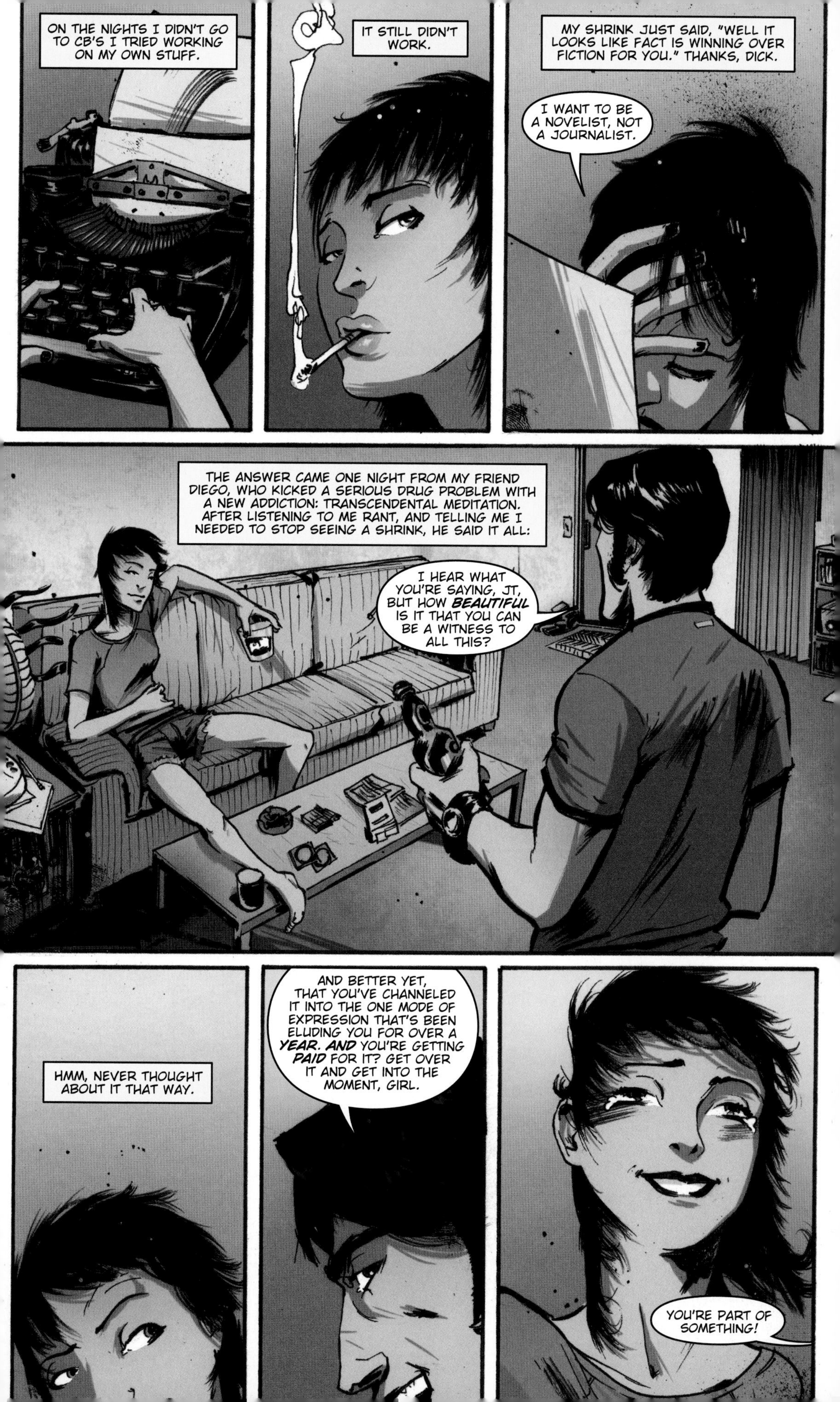

ON THE NIGHTS I DIDN'T GO TO CB'S I TRIED WORKING ON MY OWN STUFF.
IT STILL DIDN'T WORK.
MY SHRINK JUST SAID, "WELL IT LOOKS LIKE FACT IS WINNING OVER FICTION FOR YOU." THANKS, DICK.
I WANT TO BE A NOVELIST, NOT A JOURNALIST.
THE ANSWER CAME ONE NIGHT FROM MY FRIEND DIEGO, WHO KICKED A SERIOUS DRUG PROBLEM WITH A NEW ADDICTION: TRANSCENDENTAL MEDITATION. AFTER LISTENING TO ME RANT, AND TELLING ME I NEEDED TO STOP SEEING A SHRINK, HE SAID IT ALL:
I HEAR WHAT YOU'RE SAYING, JT, BUT HOW ***BEAUTIFUL*** IS IT THAT YOU CAN BE A WITNESS TO ALL THIS?
HMM, NEVER THOUGHT ABOUT IT THAT WAY.
AND BETTER YET, THAT YOU'VE CHANNELED IT INTO THE ONE MODE OF EXPRESSION THAT'S BEEN ELUDING YOU FOR OVER A ***YEAR. AND*** YOU'RE GETTING ***PAID*** FOR IT? GET OVER IT AND GET INTO THE MOMENT, GIRL.
YOU'RE PART OF SOMETHING!

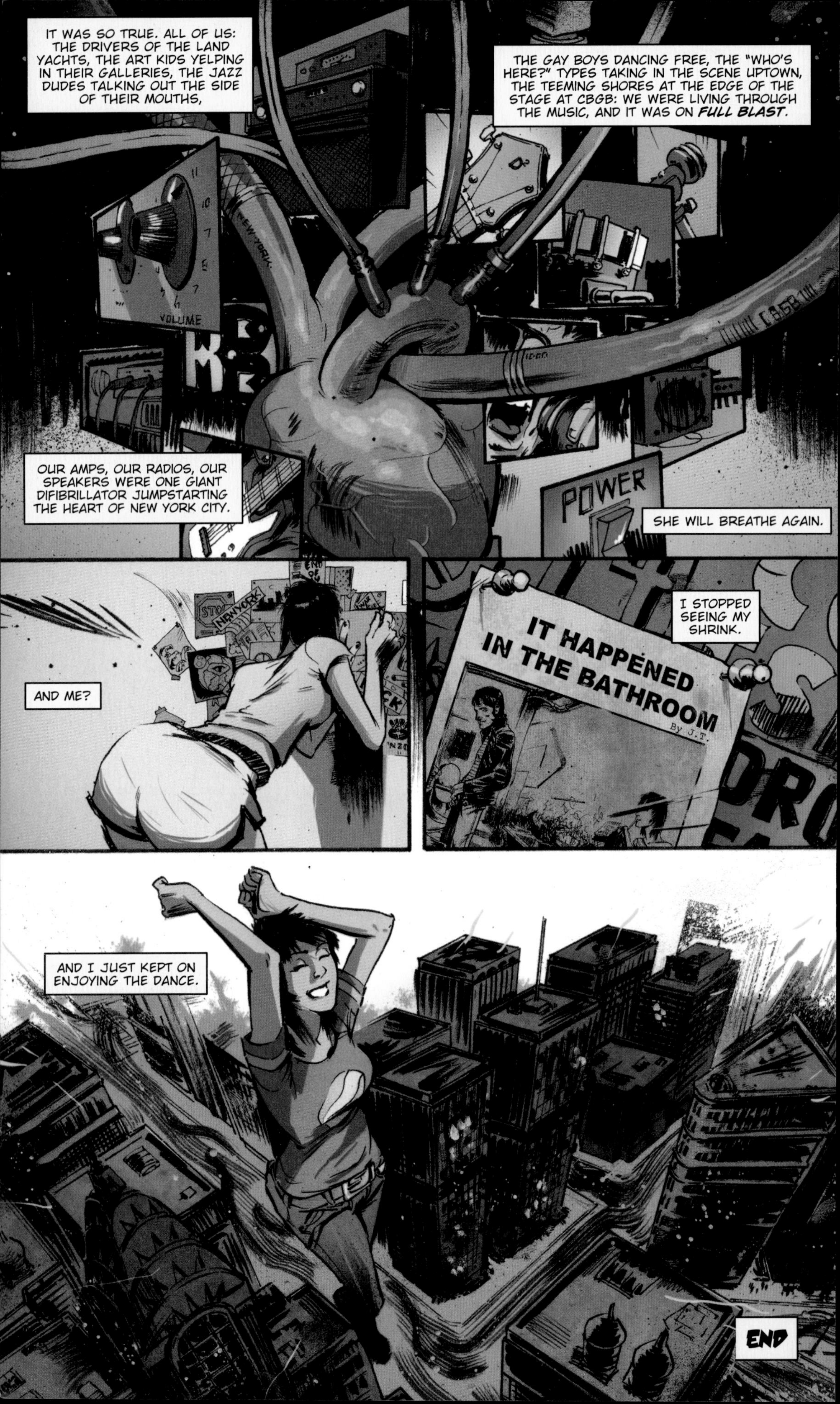
IT WAS SO TRUE. ALL OF US: THE DRIVERS OF THE LAND YACHTS, THE ART KIDS YELPING IN THEIR GALLERIES, THE JAZZ DUDES TALKING OUT THE SIDE OF THEIR MOUTHS,
THE GAY BOYS DANCING FREE, THE "WHO'S HERE?" TYPES TAKING IN THE SCENE UPTOWN, THE TEEMING SHORES AT THE EDGE OF THE STAGE AT CBGB: WE WERE LIVING THROUGH THE MUSIC, AND IT WAS ON FULL BLAST.
VOLUME
NEW YORK
POWER
OUR AMPS, OUR RADIOS, OUR SPEAKERS WERE ONE GIANT DIFIBRILLATOR JUMPSTARTING THE HEART OF NEW YORK CITY.
SHE WILL BREATHE AGAIN.
AND ME?
I STOPPED SEEING MY SHRINK.
IT HAPPENED IN THE BATHROOM
By J.T.
AND I JUST KEPT ON ENJOYING THE DANCE.
END

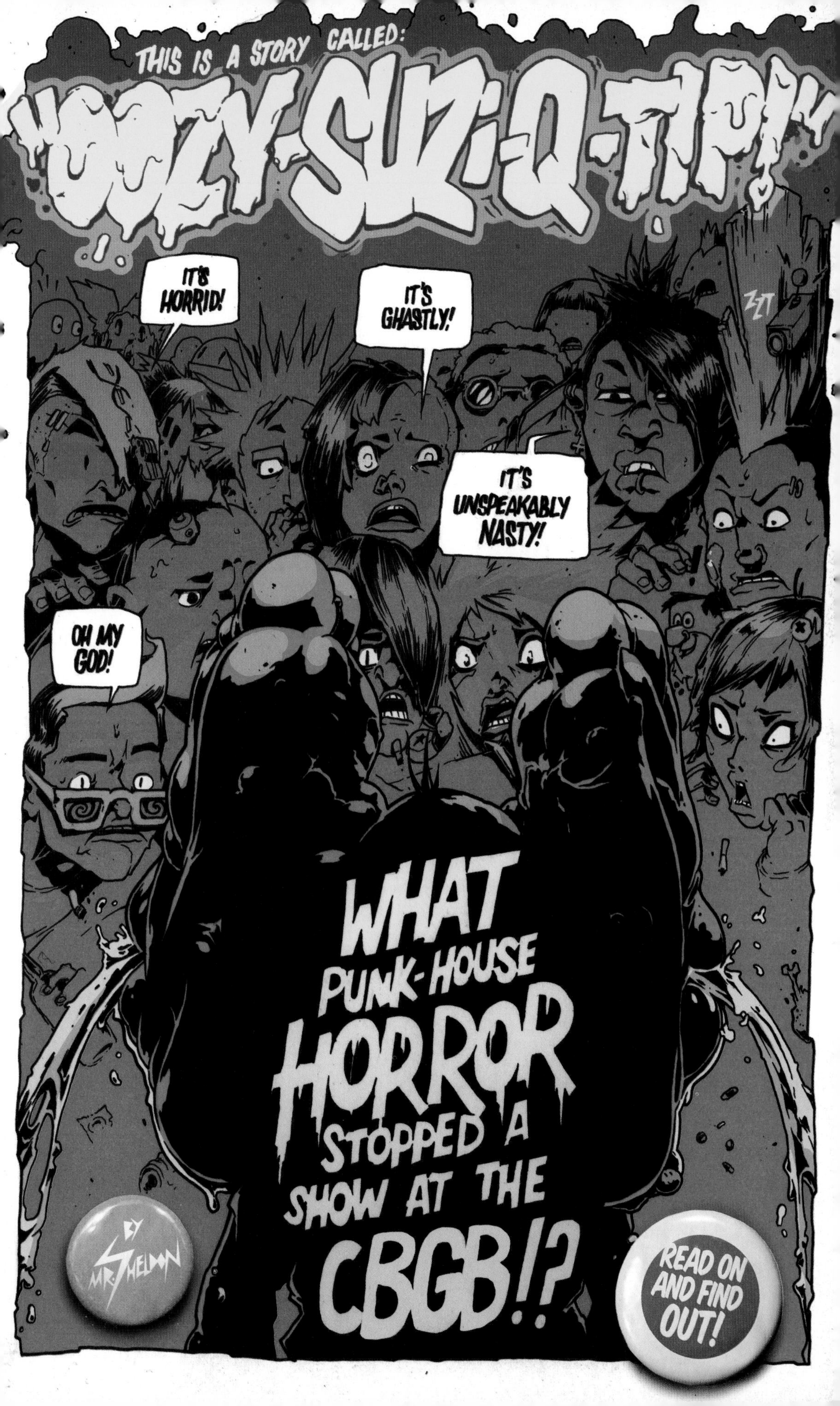
THIS IS A STORY CALLED:
"OOZY-SUZI-Q-TIP!"
IT'S HORRID!
IT'S GHASTLY!
IT'S UNSPEAKABLY NASTY!
OH MY GOD!
ZZT
WHAT PUNK-HOUSE HORROR STOPPED A SHOW AT THE CBGB!?
BY MR. SHELDON
READ ON AND FIND OUT!

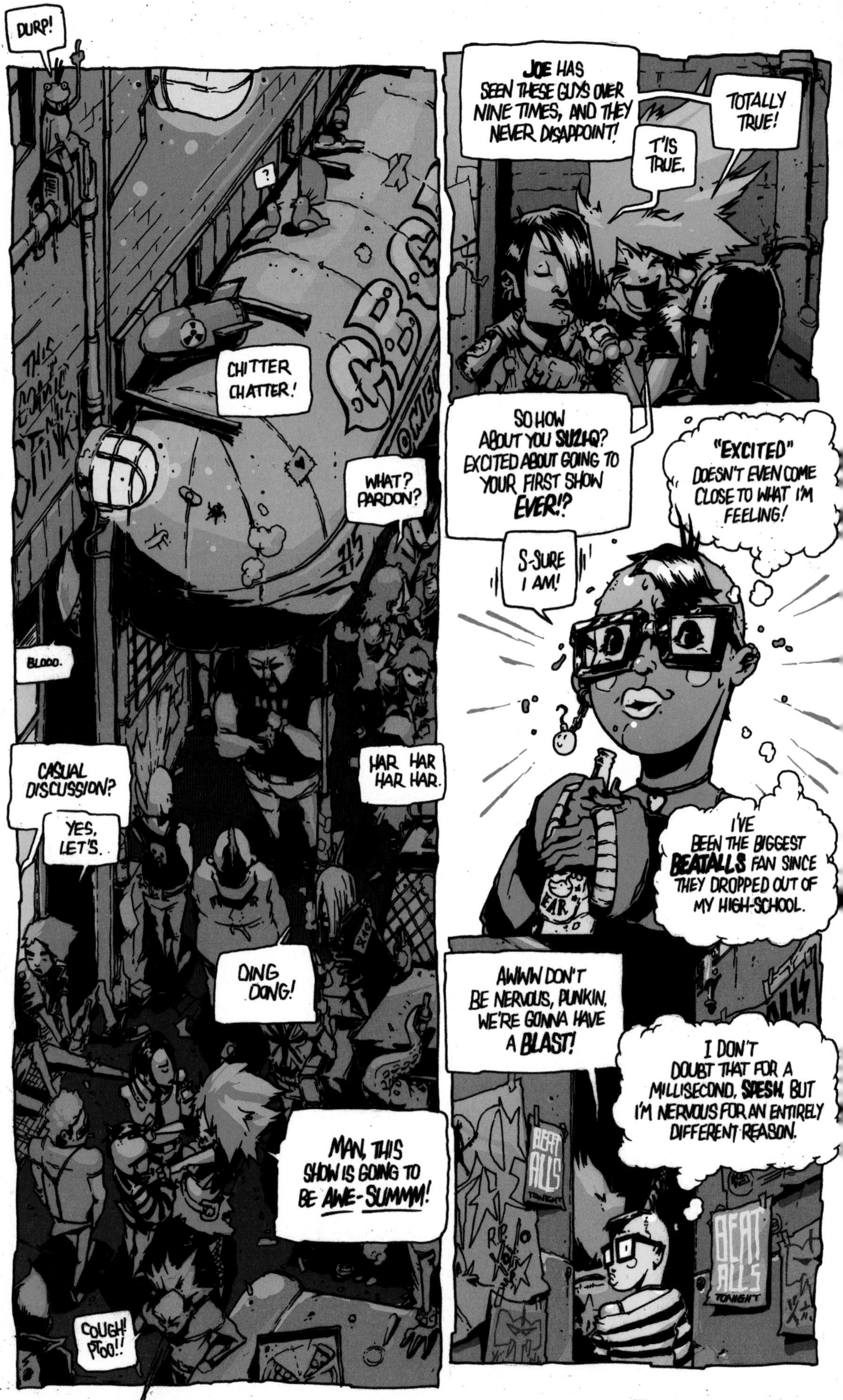
DURP!
?
CHITTER CHATTER!
THIS COMIC STINKS
WHAT? PARDON?
BLOOO.
CASUAL DISCUSSION?
YES, LET'S.
HAR HAR HAR HAR.
DING DONG!
MAN, THIS SHOW IS GOING TO BE AWE-SUMMM!
COUGH! PTOO!!
JOE HAS SEEN THESE GUYS OVER NINE TIMES, AND THEY NEVER DISAPPOINT!
T'IS TRUE.
TOTALLY TRUE!
SO HOW ABOUT YOU SUZI-Q? EXCITED ABOUT GOING TO YOUR FIRST SHOW EVER!?
S-SURE I AM!
"EXCITED" DOESN'T EVEN COME CLOSE TO WHAT I'M FEELING!
I'VE BEEN THE BIGGEST BEATALLS FAN SINCE THEY DROPPED OUT OF MY HIGH-SCHOOL.
AWWW DON'T BE NERVOUS, PUNKIN, WE'RE GONNA HAVE A BLAST!
I DON'T DOUBT THAT FOR A MILLISECOND, SPESH, BUT I'M NERVOUS FOR AN ENTIRELY DIFFERENT REASON.
BEAT ALLS TONIGHT
BEAT ALLS TONIGHT

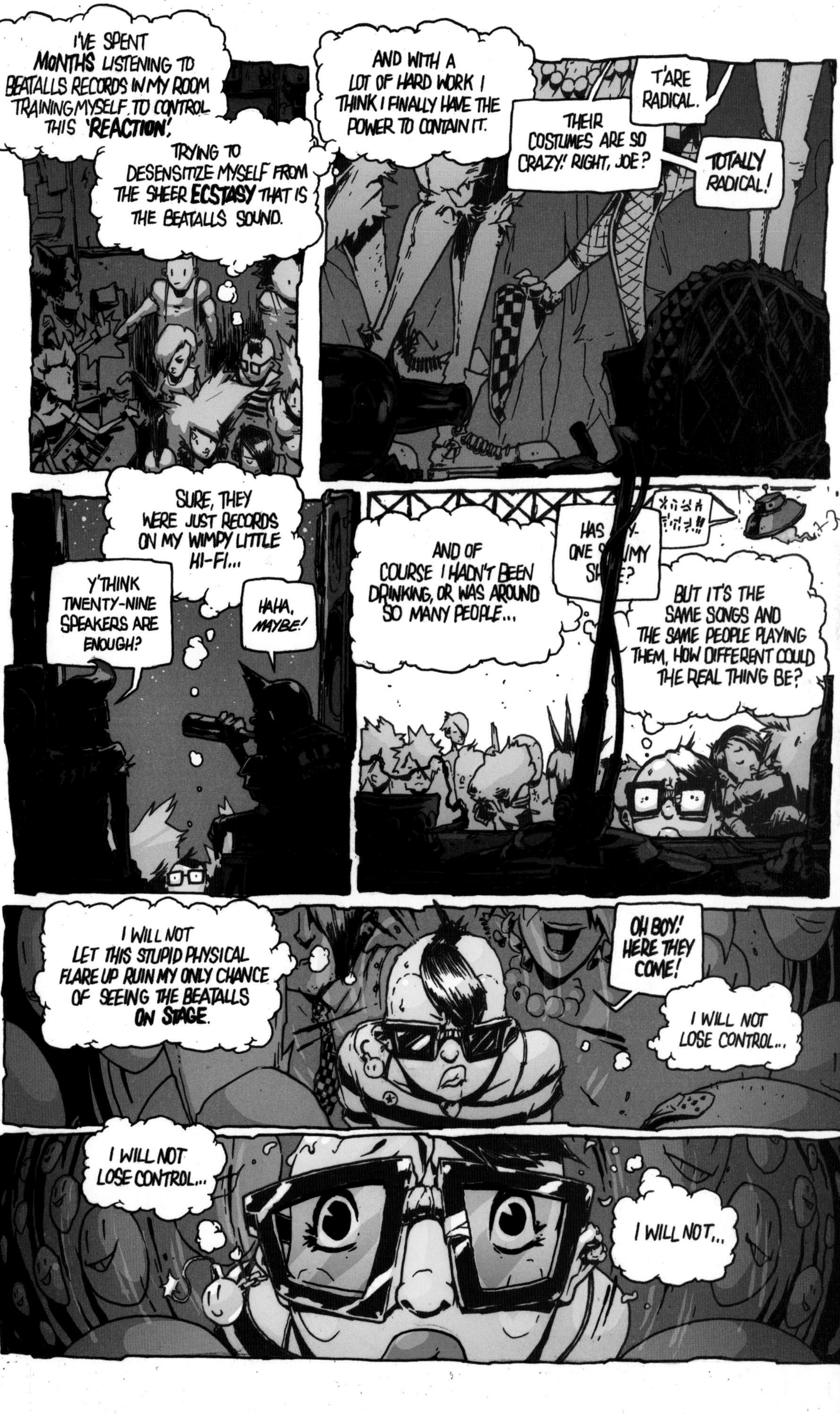

I'VE SPENT MONTHS LISTENING TO BEATALLS RECORDS IN MY ROOM TRAINING MYSELF TO CONTROL THIS 'REACTION'.
TRYING TO DESENSITIZE MYSELF FROM THE SHEER ECSTASY THAT IS THE BEATALLS SOUND.
AND WITH A LOT OF HARD WORK I THINK I FINALLY HAVE THE POWER TO CONTAIN IT.
THEIR COSTUMES ARE SO CRAZY! RIGHT, JOE?
T'ARE RADICAL.
TOTALLY RADICAL!
SURE, THEY WERE JUST RECORDS ON MY WIMPY LITTLE HI-FI...
Y'THINK TWENTY-NINE SPEAKERS ARE ENOUGH?
HAHA, MAYBE!
AND OF COURSE I HADN'T BEEN DRINKING, OR WAS AROUND SO MANY PEOPLE...
BUT IT'S THE SAME SONGS AND THE SAME PEOPLE PLAYING THEM, HOW DIFFERENT COULD THE REAL THING BE?
I WILL NOT LET THIS STUPID PHYSICAL FLARE UP RUIN MY ONLY CHANCE OF SEEING THE BEATALLS ON STAGE.
OH BOY! HERE THEY COME!
I WILL NOT LOSE CONTROL...
I WILL NOT LOSE CONTROL...
I WILL NOT...

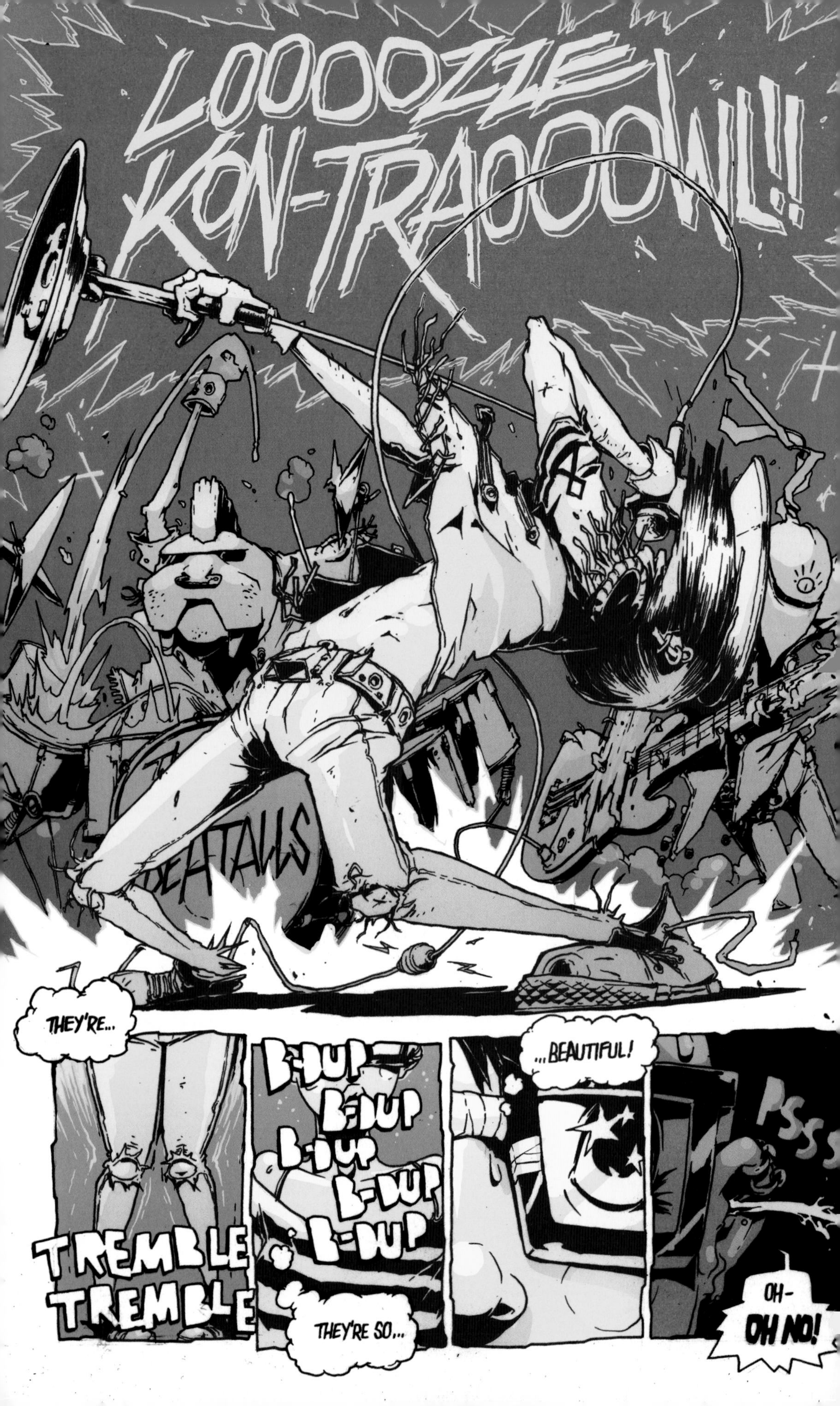
LOOOOZZE KON-TRAOOOWL!!
DEATTAILS
THEY'RE...
TREMBLE
TREMBLE
B-DUP
B-DUP
B-DUP
B-DUP
B-DUP
THEY'RE SO...
...BEAUTIFUL!
PSSS
OH-
OH NO!

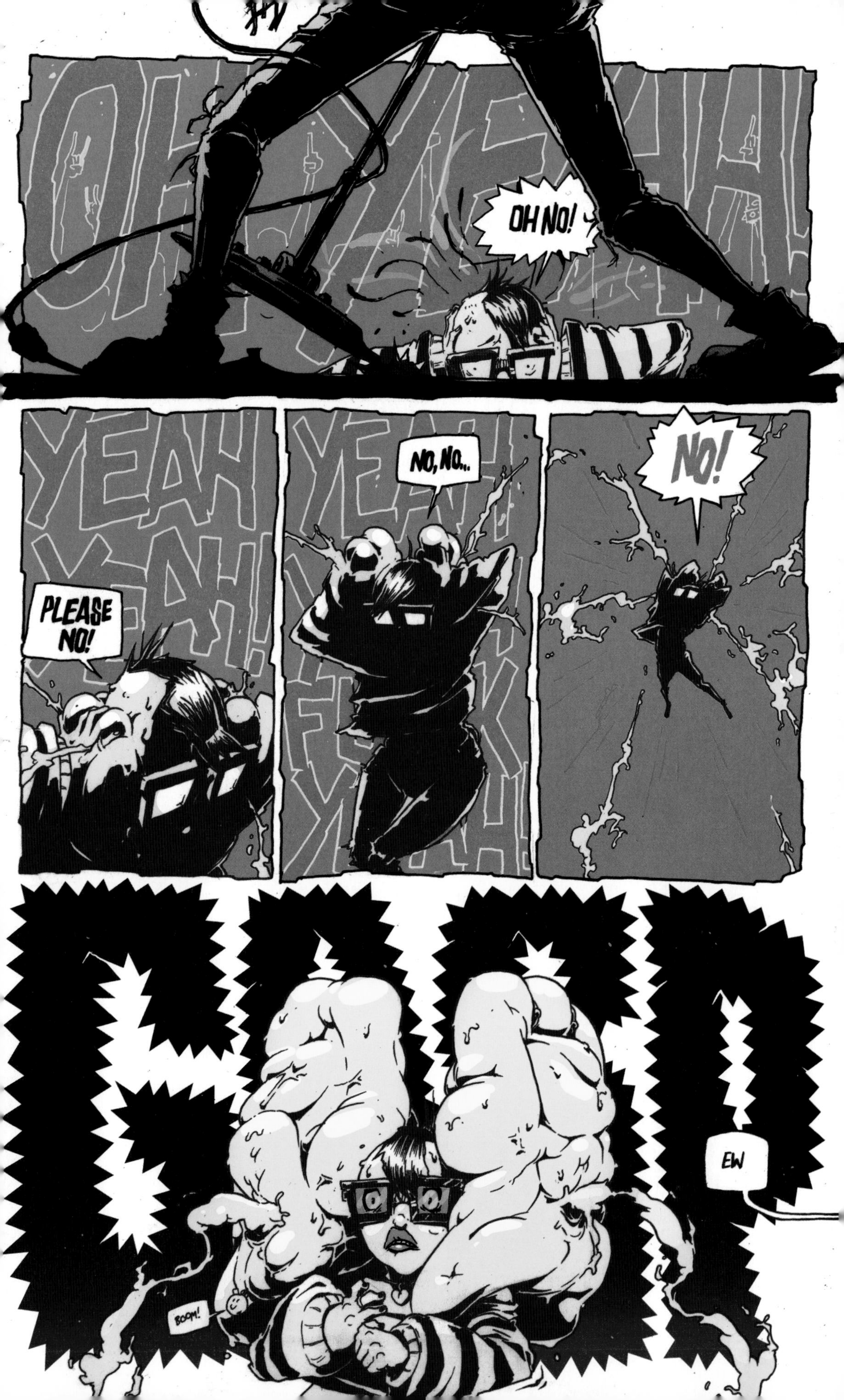
OH NO!
YEAH
PLEASE NO!
NO, NO...
NO!
EW
BOOM!

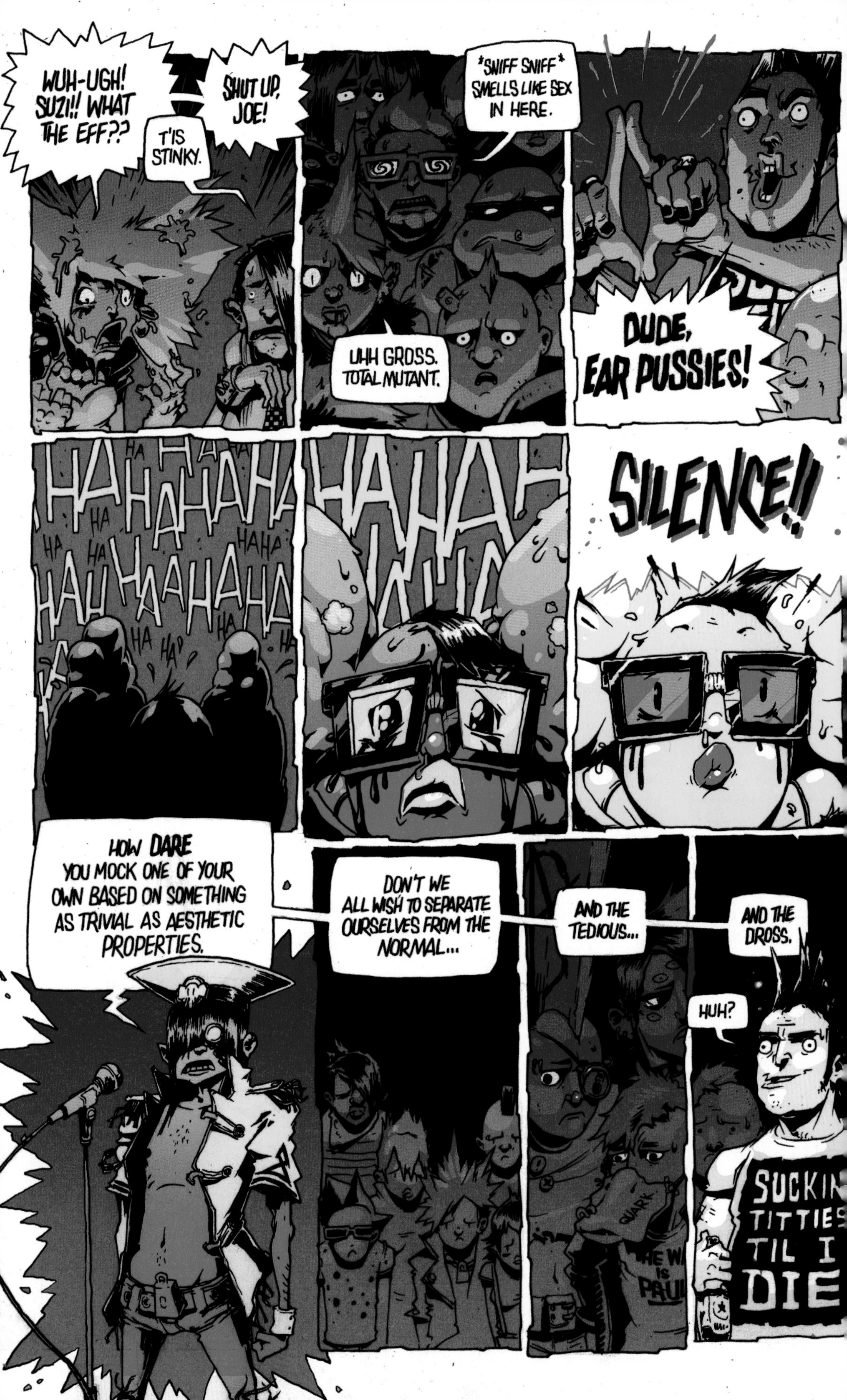
WUH-UGH! SUZI!! WHAT THE EFF??
T'IS STINKY.
SHUT UP, JOE!
SNIFF SNIFF SMELLS LIKE SEX IN HERE.
UHH GROSS. TOTAL MUTANT.
DUDE, EAR PUSSIES!
HAHAHAHAHA HAHAHAHAHA
HAHAHA
SILENCE!!
HOW DARE YOU MOCK ONE OF YOUR OWN BASED ON SOMETHING AS TRIVIAL AS AESTHETIC PROPERTIES.
DON'T WE ALL WISH TO SEPARATE OURSELVES FROM THE NORMAL...
AND THE TEDIOUS...
AND THE DROSS.
HUH?
SUCKIN TITTIES TIL I DIE

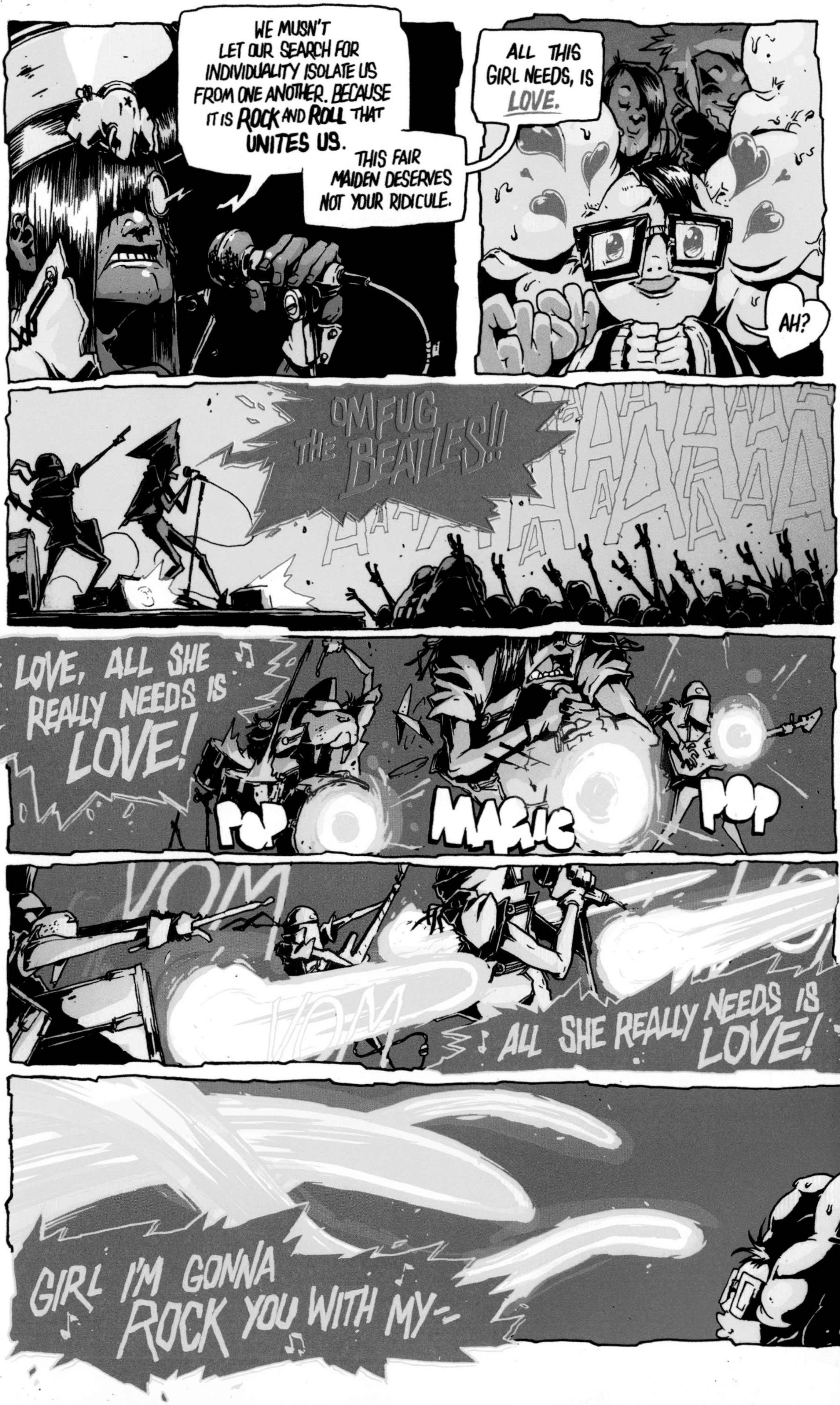
WE MUSN'T LET OUR SEARCH FOR INDIVIDUALITY ISOLATE US FROM ONE ANOTHER. BECAUSE IT IS ROCK AND ROLL THAT UNITES US.
THIS FAIR MAIDEN DESERVES NOT YOUR RIDICULE.
ALL THIS GIRL NEEDS, IS LOVE.
AH?
OMFUG THE BEATLES!!
AAAAAAAAAH
LOVE, ALL SHE REALLY NEEDS IS LOVE!
POP
MAGIC
POP
VOM
VOM
ALL SHE REALLY NEEDS IS LOVE!
GIRL I'M GONNA ROCK YOU WITH MY-

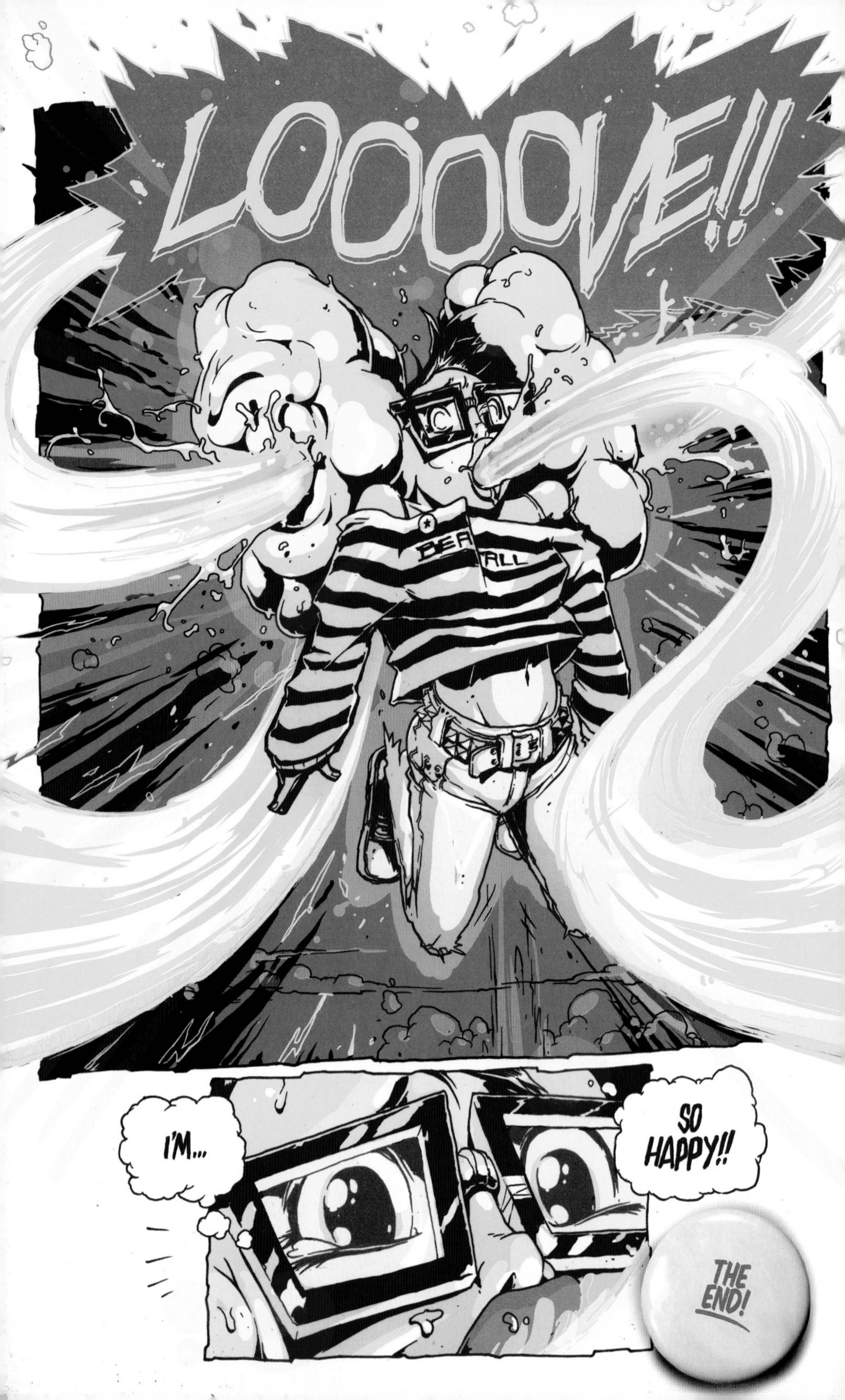
LOOOOVE!!
BE A
ALL
I'M...
SO HAPPY!!
THE END!

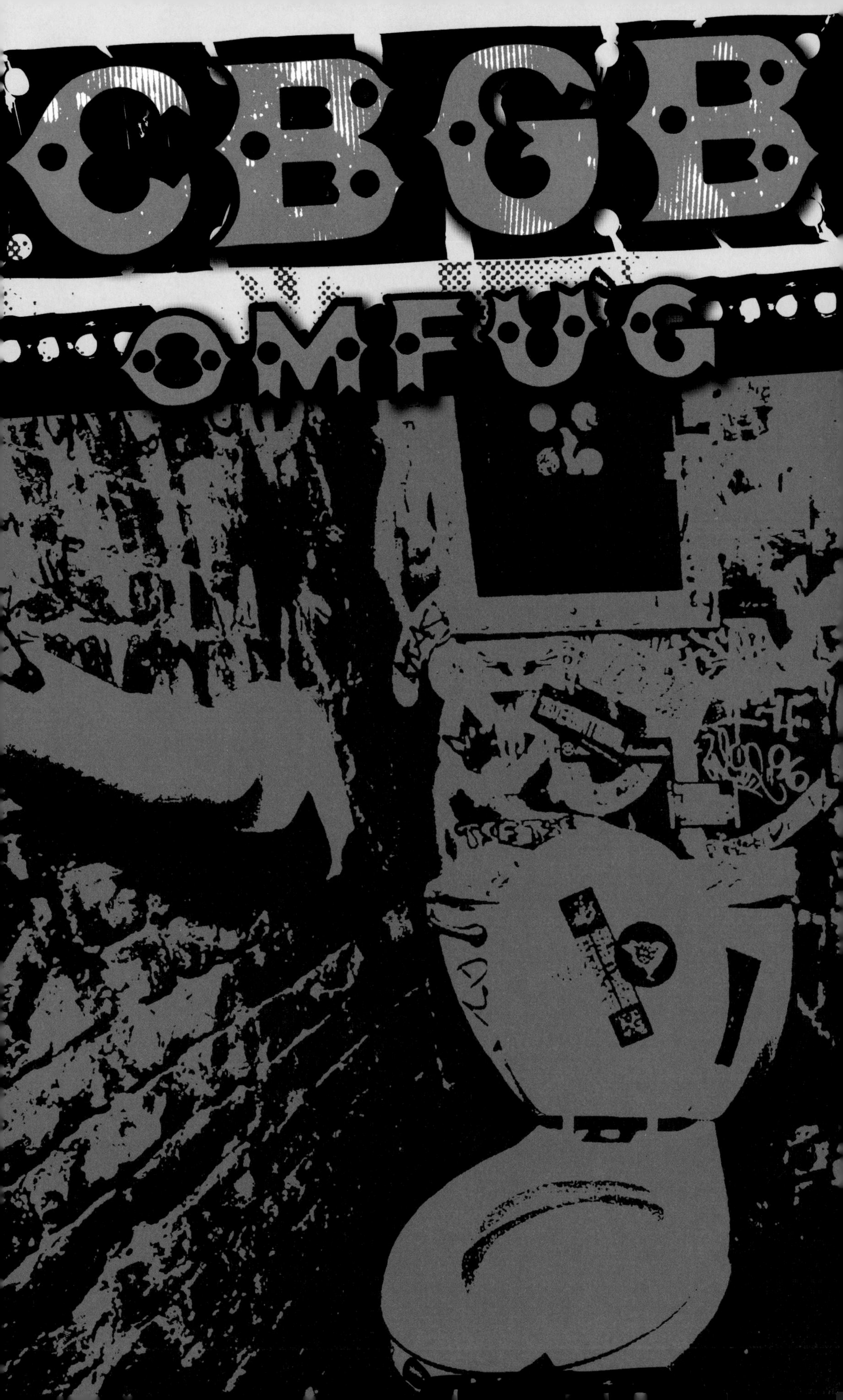
CBGB
OMFUG

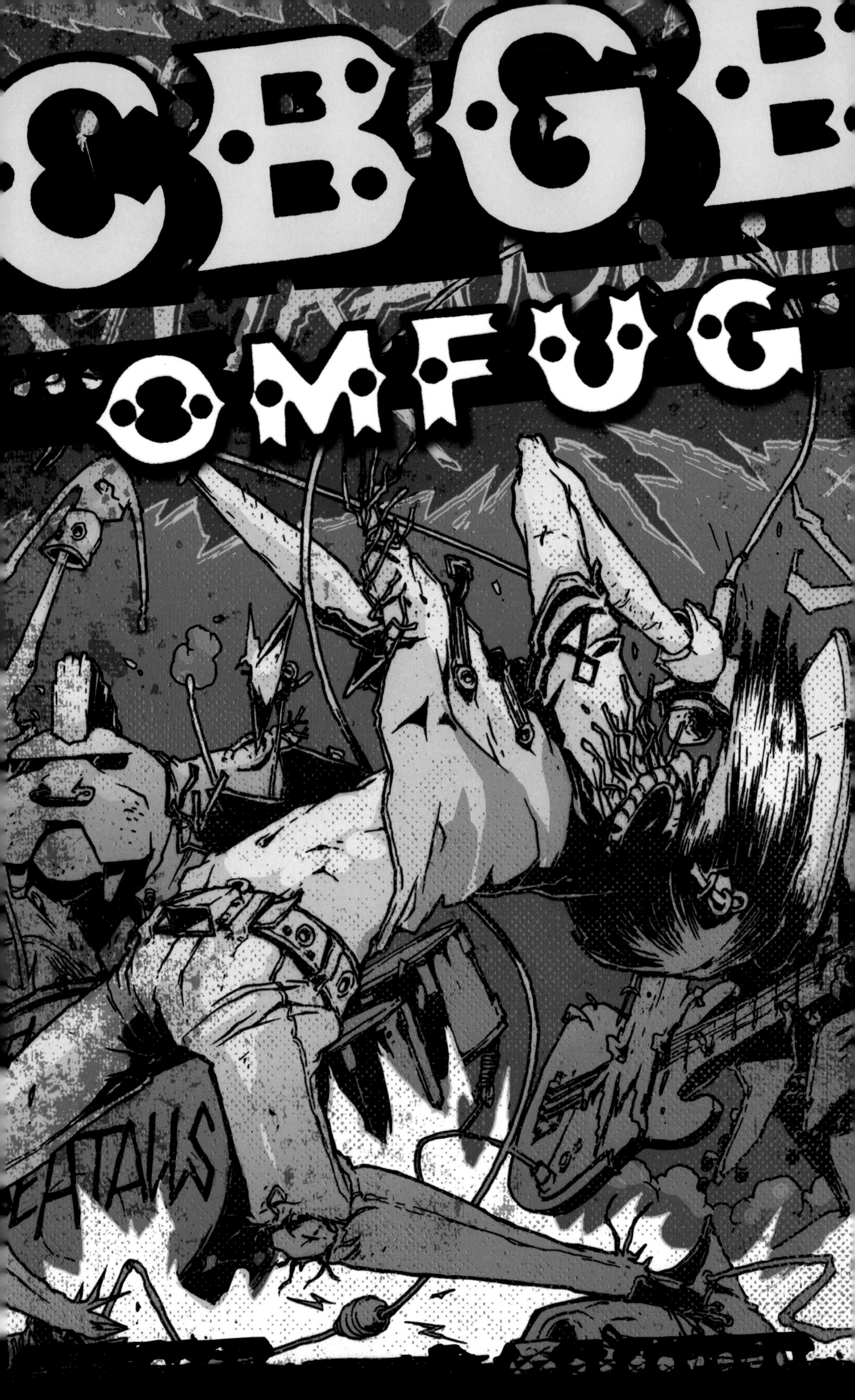
CBGB
OMFUG

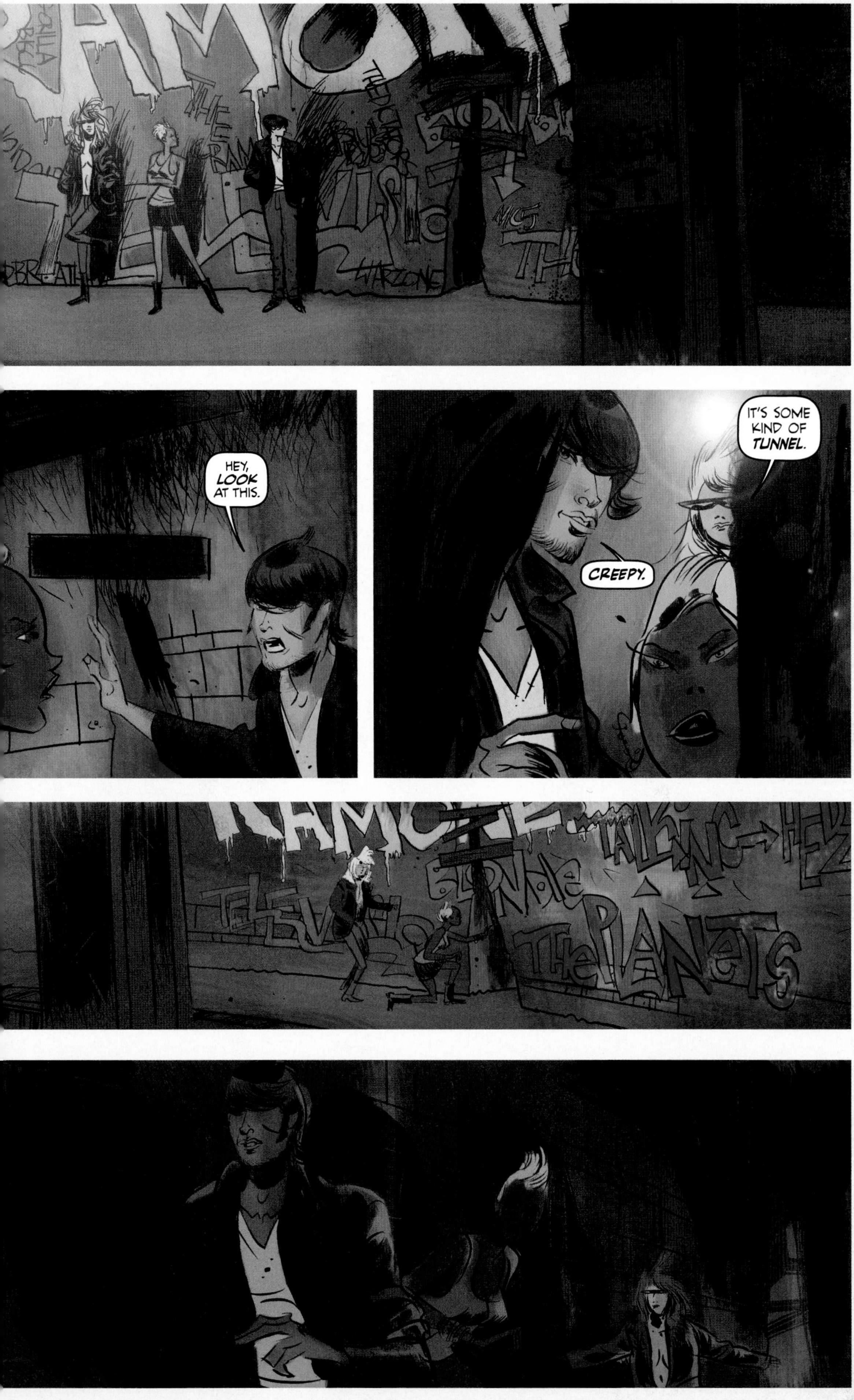
HEY, LOOK AT THIS.
IT'S SOME KIND OF TUNNEL.
CREEPY.

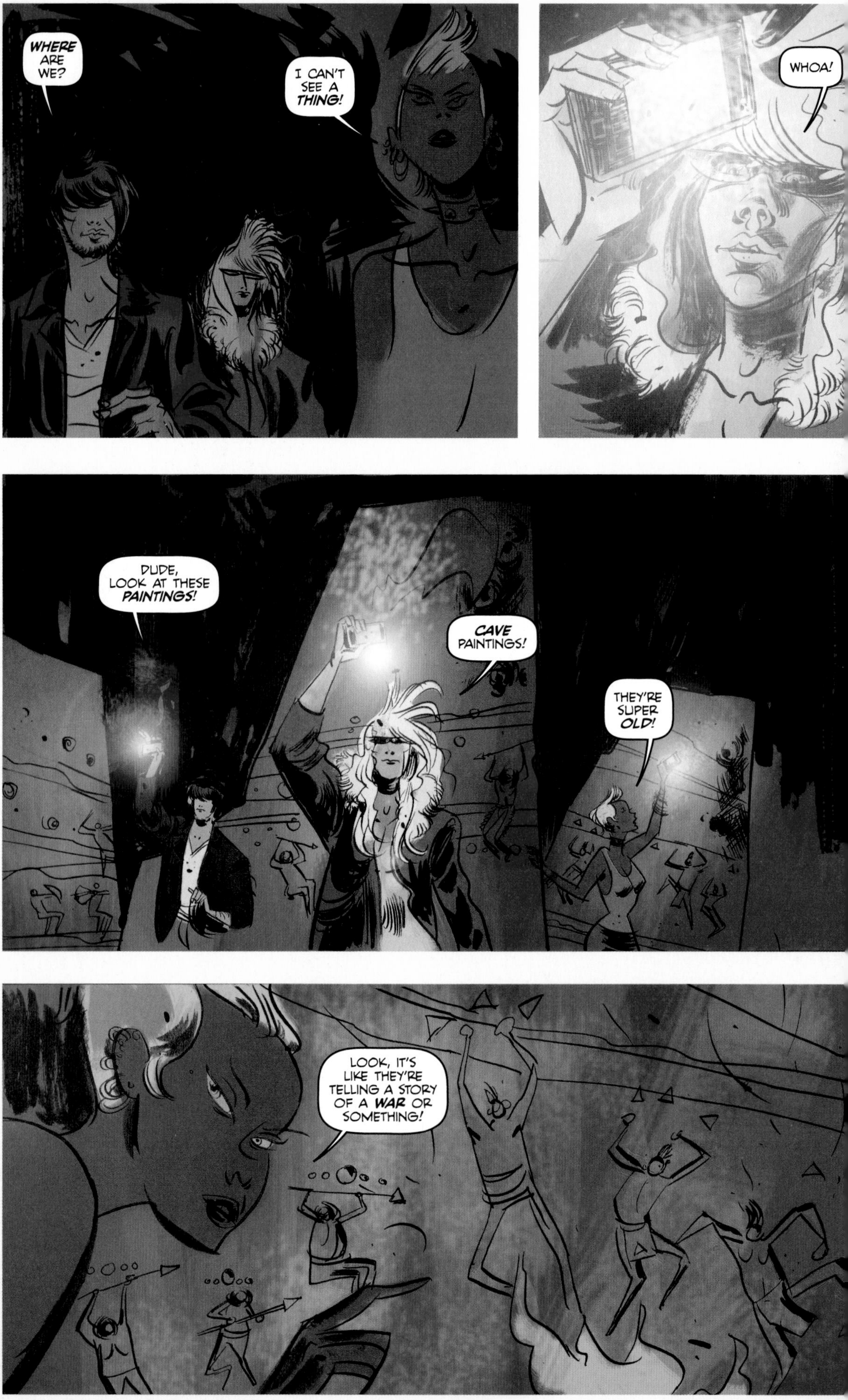
WHERE ARE WE?
I CAN'T SEE A THING!
WHOA!
DUDE, LOOK AT THESE PAINTINGS!
CAVE PAINTINGS!
THEY'RE SUPER OLD!
LOOK, IT'S LIKE THEY'RE TELLING A STORY OF A WAR OR SOMETHING!

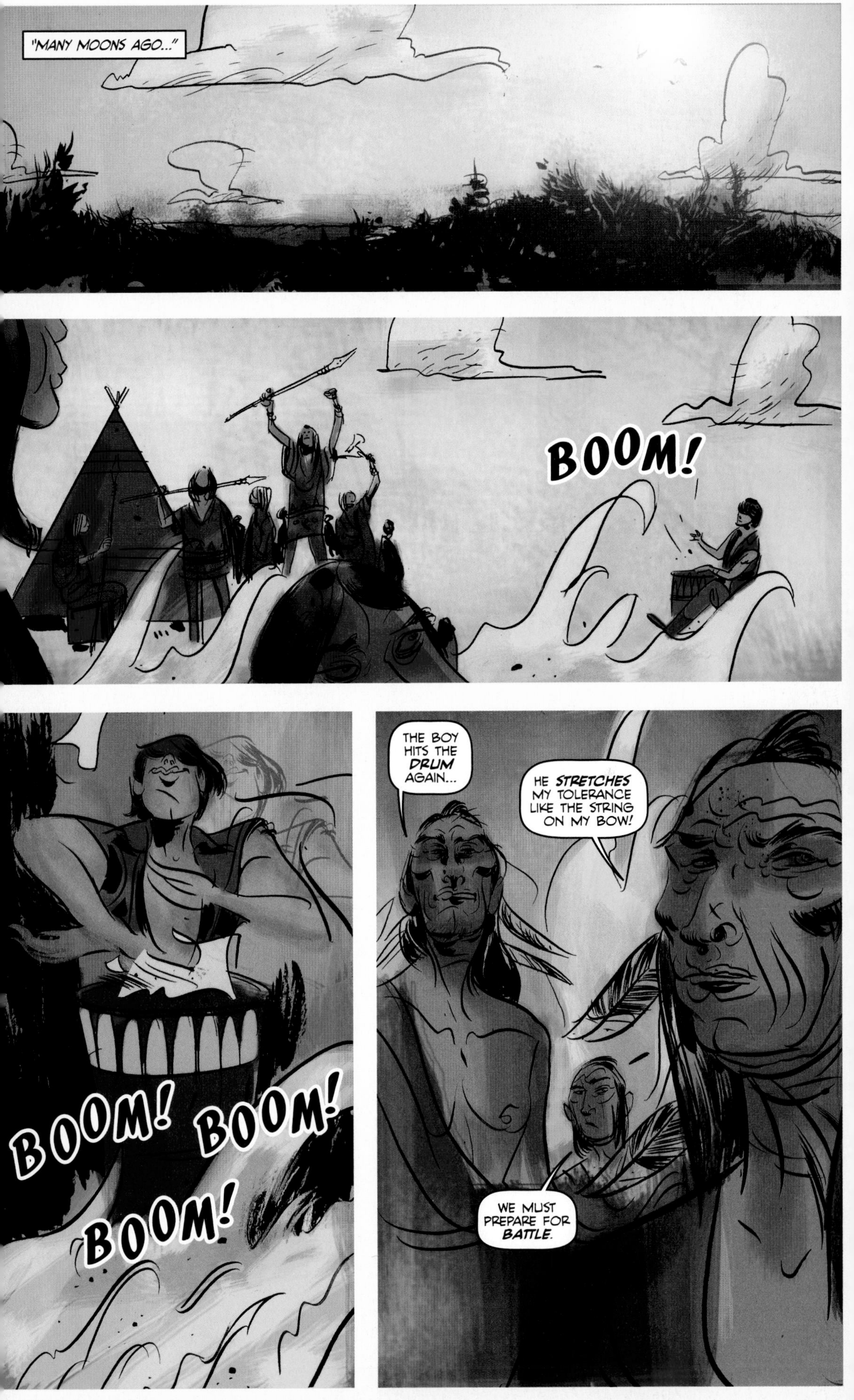
"MANY MOONS AGO..."
BOOM!
BOOM! BOOM!
BOOM!
THE BOY HITS THE *DRUM* AGAIN...
HE *STRETCHES* MY TOLERANCE LIKE THE STRING ON MY BOW!
WE MUST PREPARE FOR *BATTLE*.

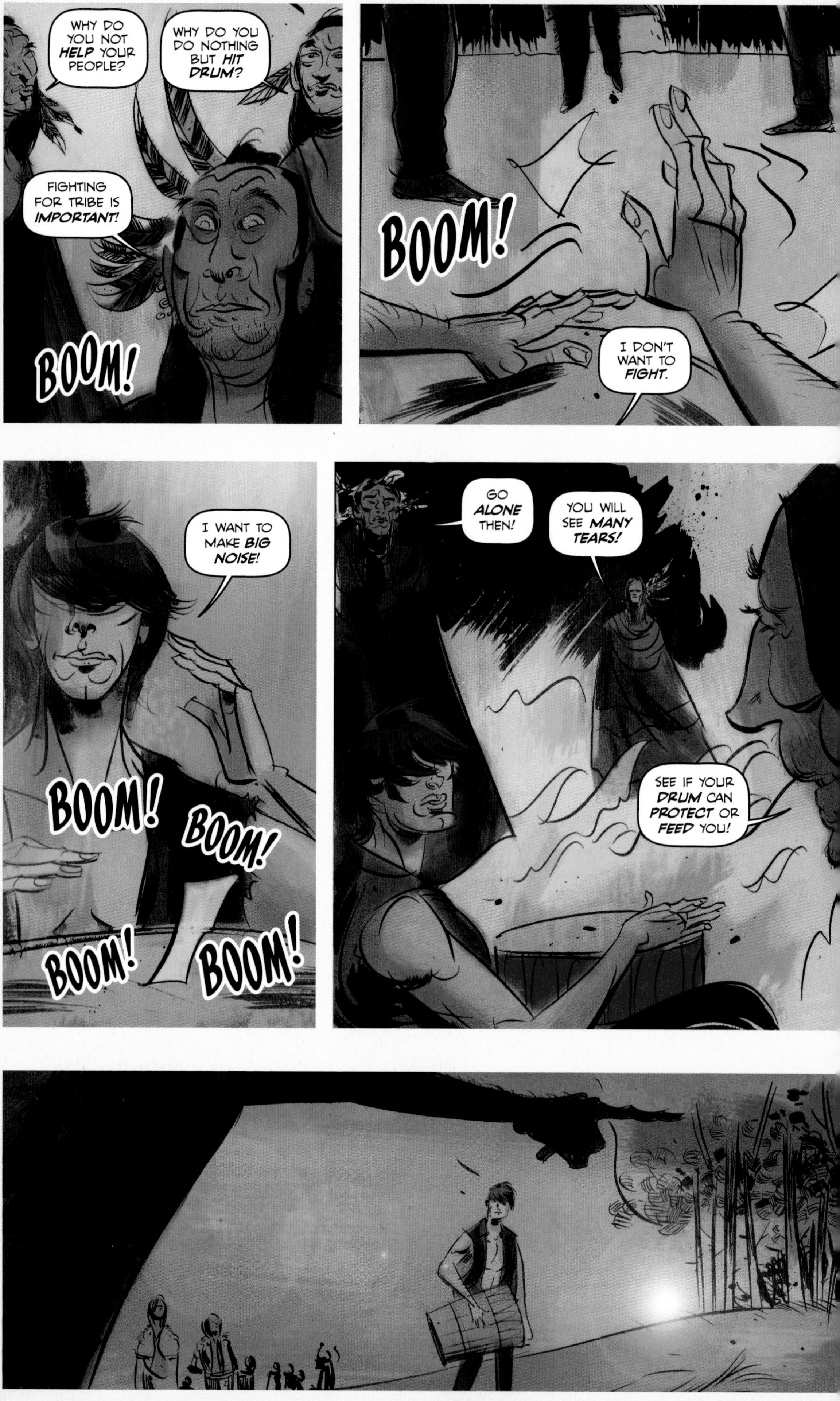
WHY DO YOU NOT HELP YOUR PEOPLE?
WHY DO YOU DO NOTHING BUT HIT DRUM?
FIGHTING FOR TRIBE IS IMPORTANT!
BOOM!
BOOM!
I DON'T WANT TO FIGHT.
I WANT TO MAKE BIG NOISE!
BOOM!
BOOM!
BOOM!
BOOM!
GO ALONE THEN!
YOU WILL SEE MANY TEARS!
SEE IF YOUR DRUM CAN PROTECT OR FEED YOU!

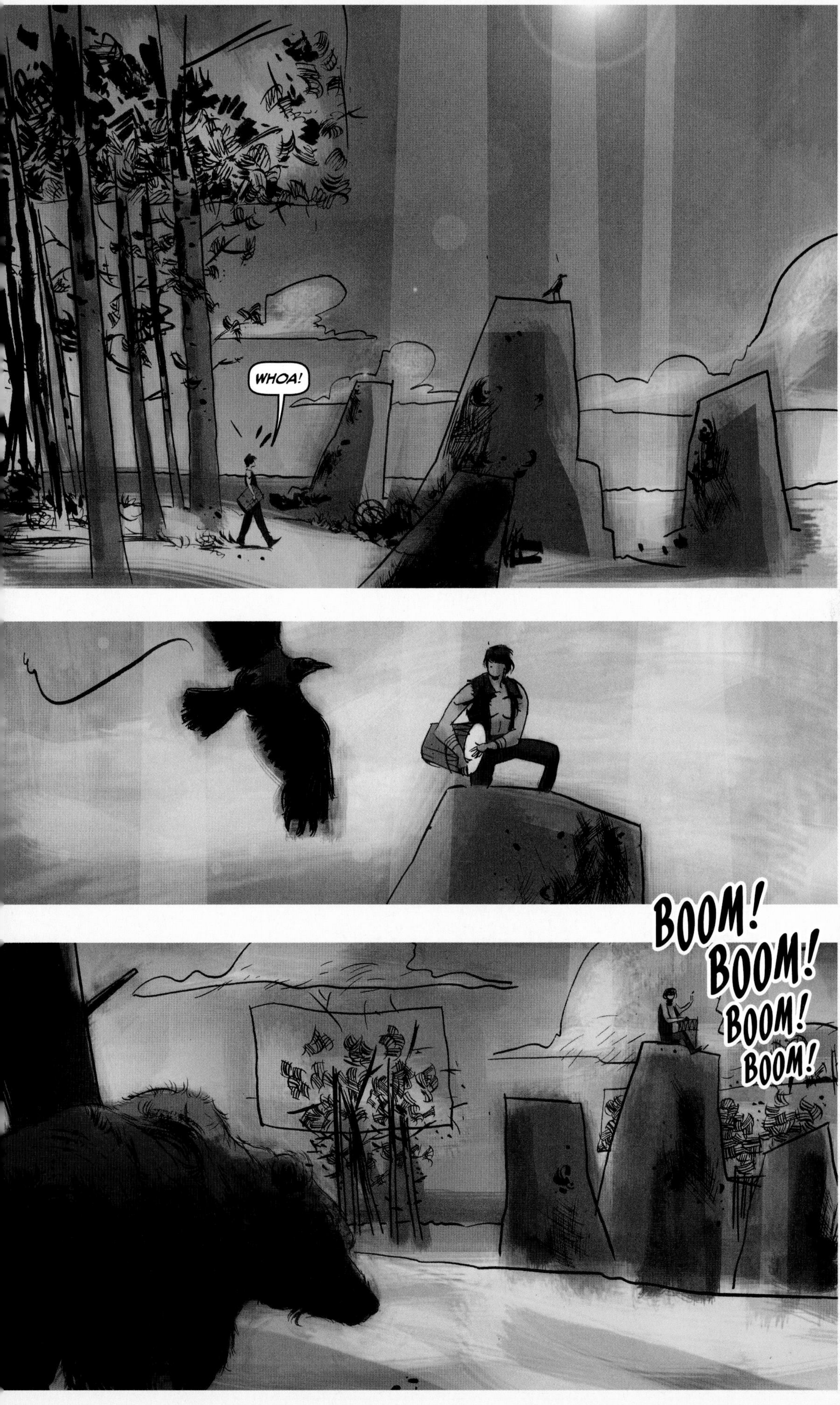
WHOA!
BOOM!
BOOM!
BOOM!
BOOM!

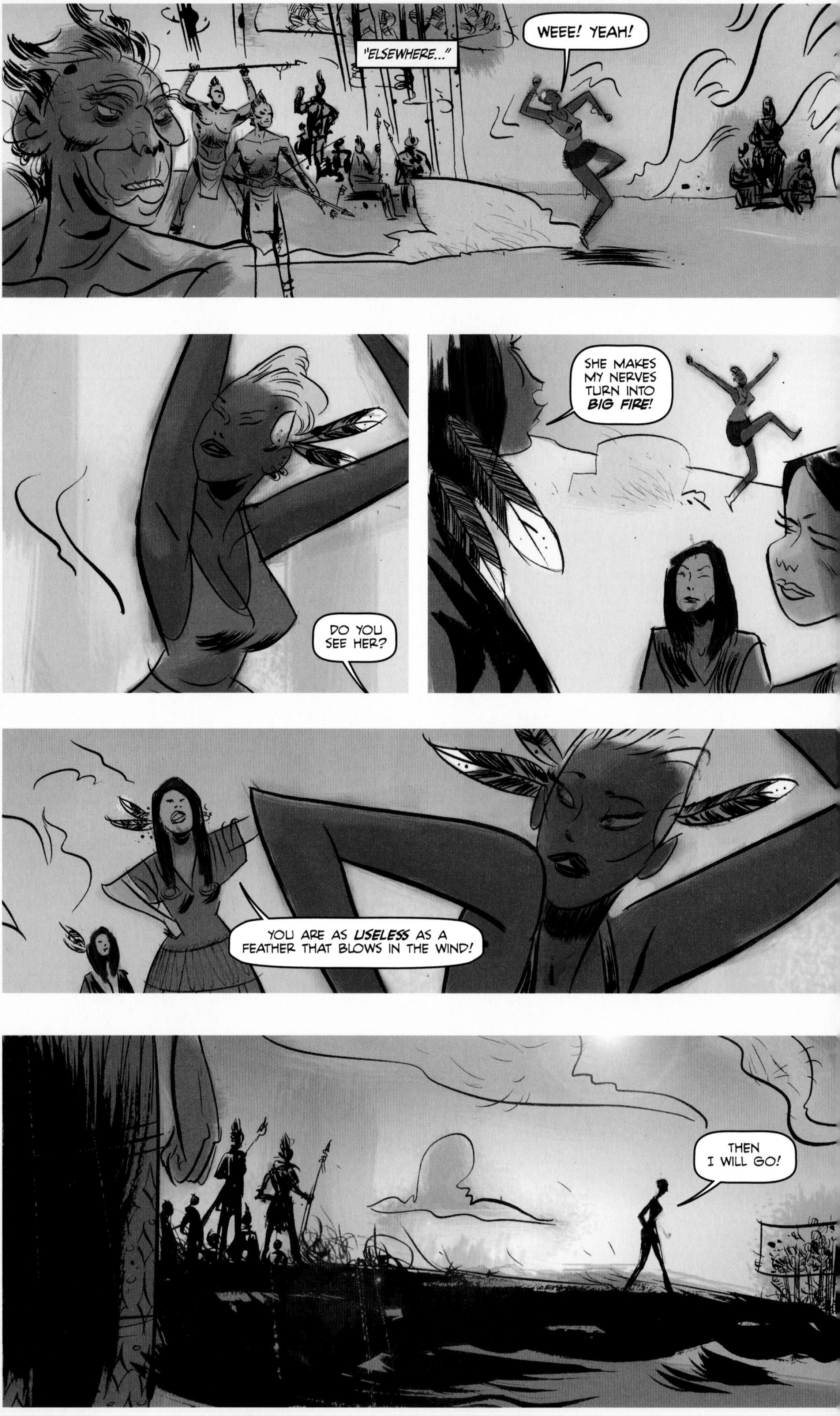
"ELSEWHERE..."
WEEE! YEAH!
DO YOU SEE HER?
SHE MAKES MY NERVES TURN INTO BIG FIRE!
YOU ARE AS USELESS AS A FEATHER THAT BLOWS IN THE WIND!
THEN I WILL GO!

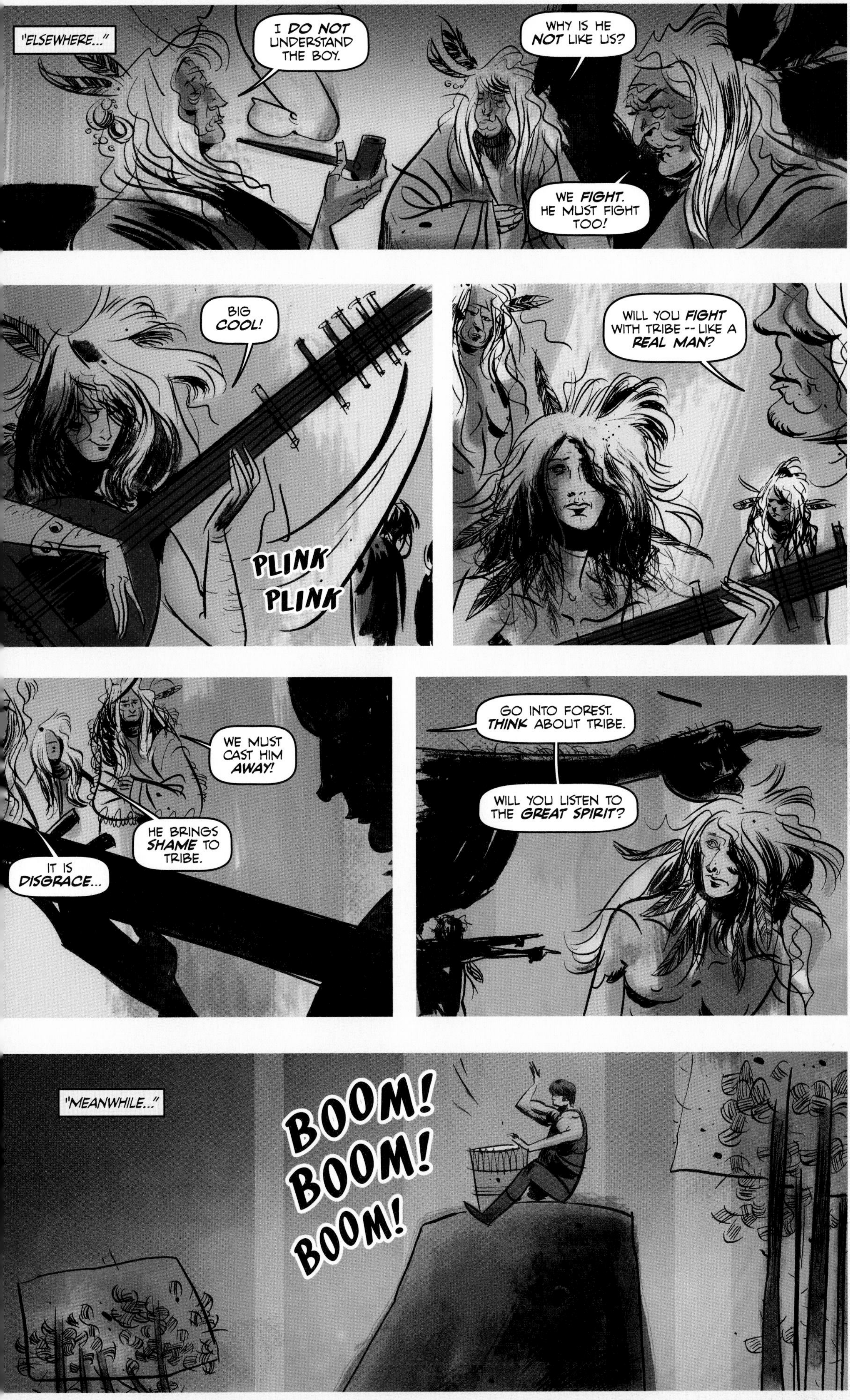

"ELSEWHERE..."
I DO NOT UNDERSTAND THE BOY.
WHY IS HE NOT LIKE US?
WE FIGHT. HE MUST FIGHT TOO!
BIG COOL!
PLINK PLINK
WILL YOU FIGHT WITH TRIBE -- LIKE A REAL MAN?
WE MUST CAST HIM AWAY!
HE BRINGS SHAME TO TRIBE.
IT IS DISGRACE...
GO INTO FOREST. THINK ABOUT TRIBE.
WILL YOU LISTEN TO THE GREAT SPIRIT?
"MEANWHILE..."
BOOM! BOOM! BOOM!

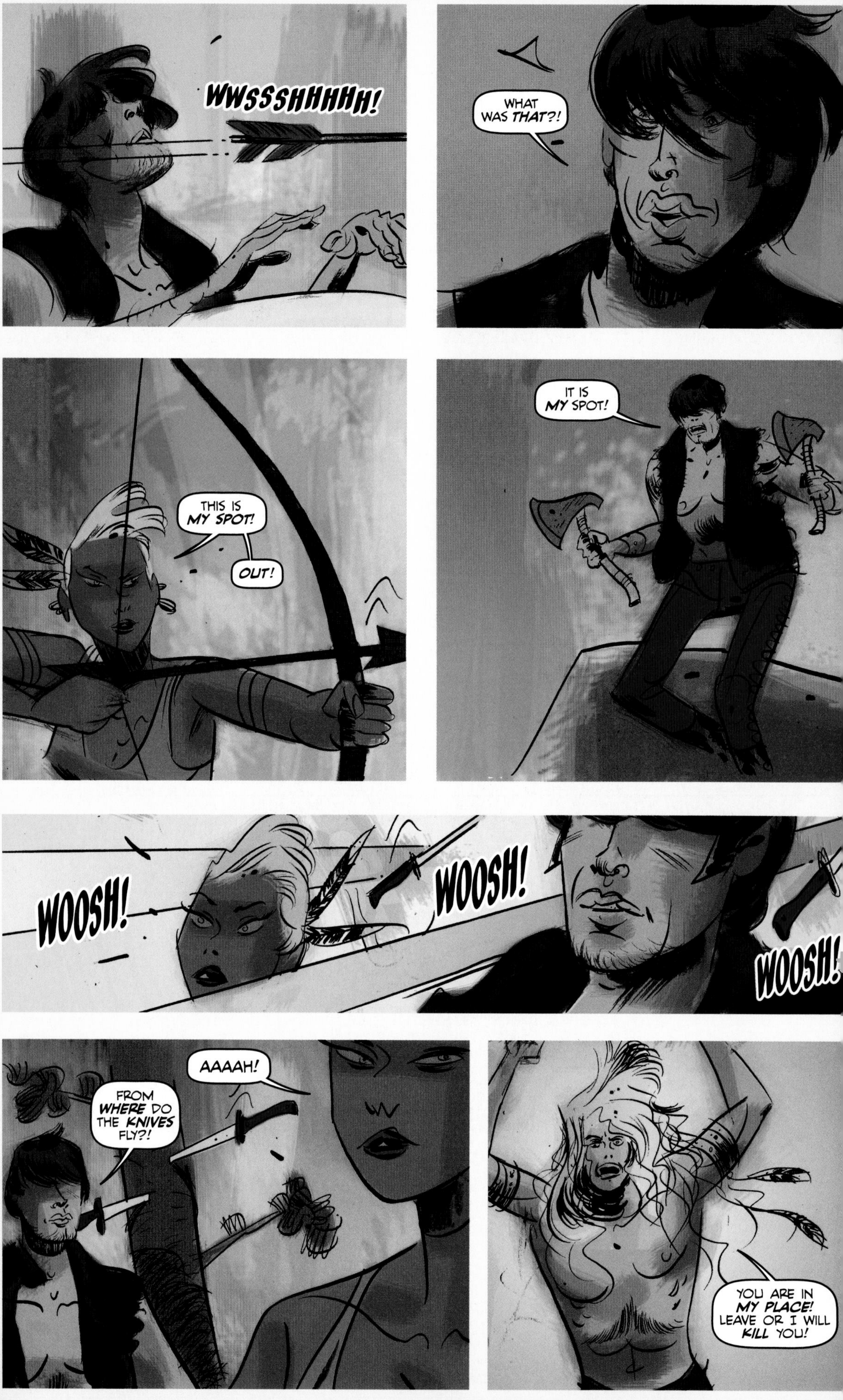
WWSSSHHHHH!
WHAT WAS THAT?!
THIS IS MY SPOT!
OUT!
IT IS MY SPOT!
WOOSH!
WOOSH!
WOOSH!
AAAAH!
FROM WHERE DO THE KNIVES FLY?!
YOU ARE IN MY PLACE! LEAVE OR I WILL KILL YOU!

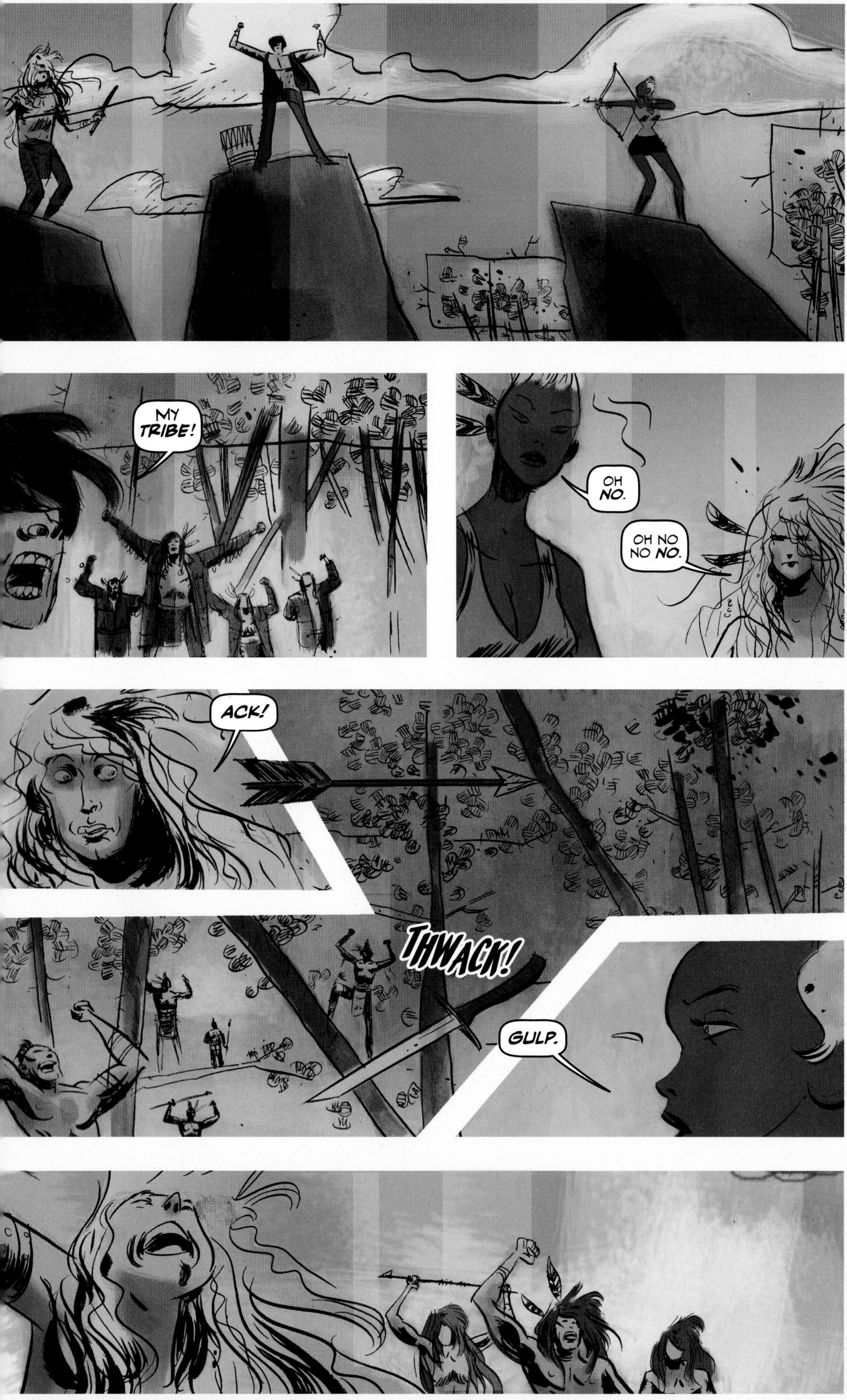
MY TRIBE!
OH NO.
OH NO NO NO.
ACK!
THWACK!
GULP.

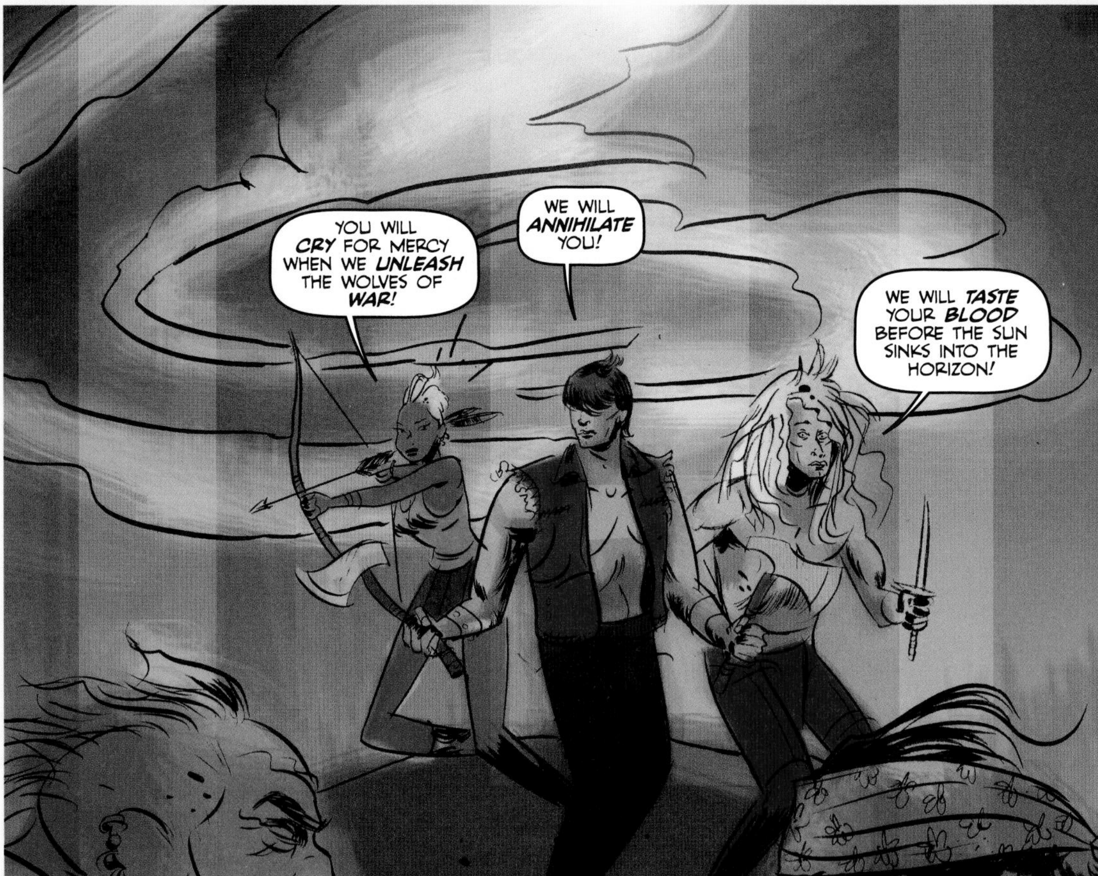
YOU WILL CRY FOR MERCY WHEN WE UNLEASH THE WOLVES OF WAR!
WE WILL ANNIHILATE YOU!
WE WILL TASTE YOUR BLOOD BEFORE THE SUN SINKS INTO THE HORIZON!

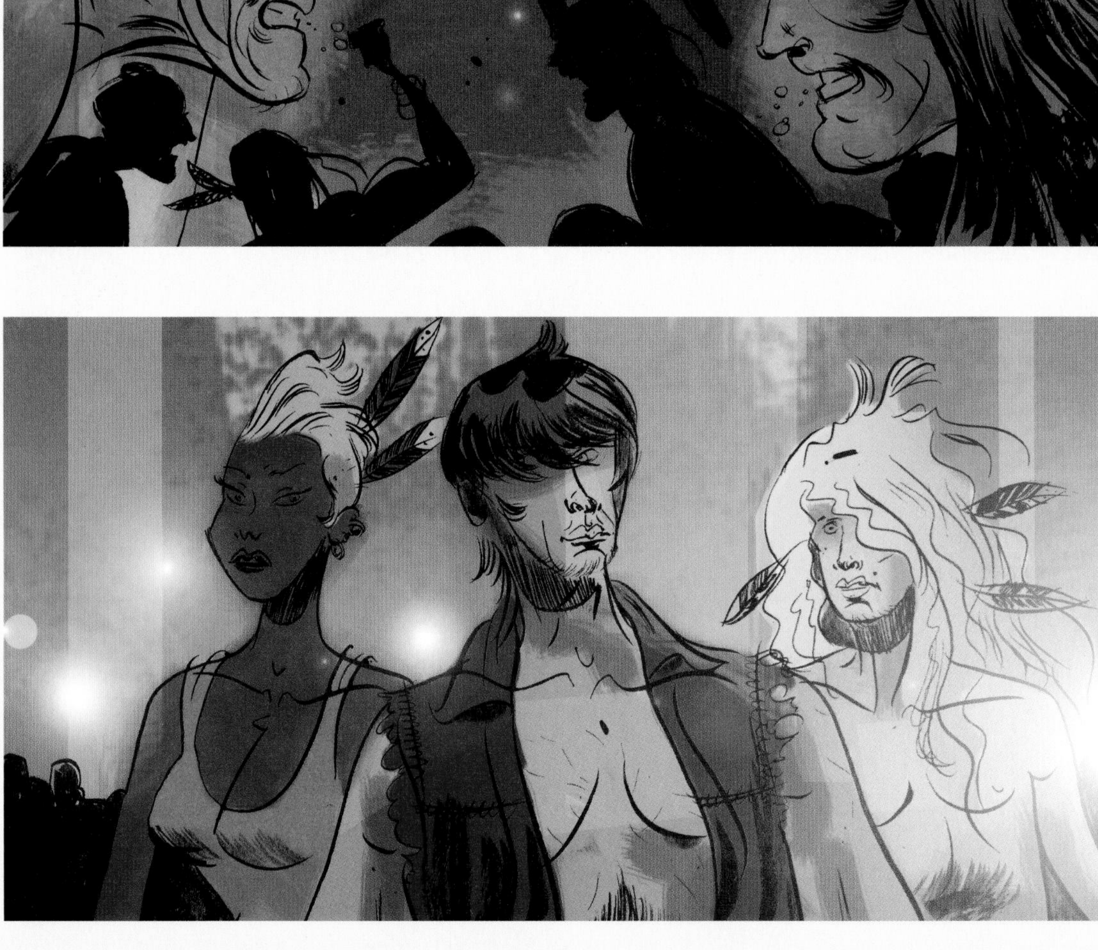

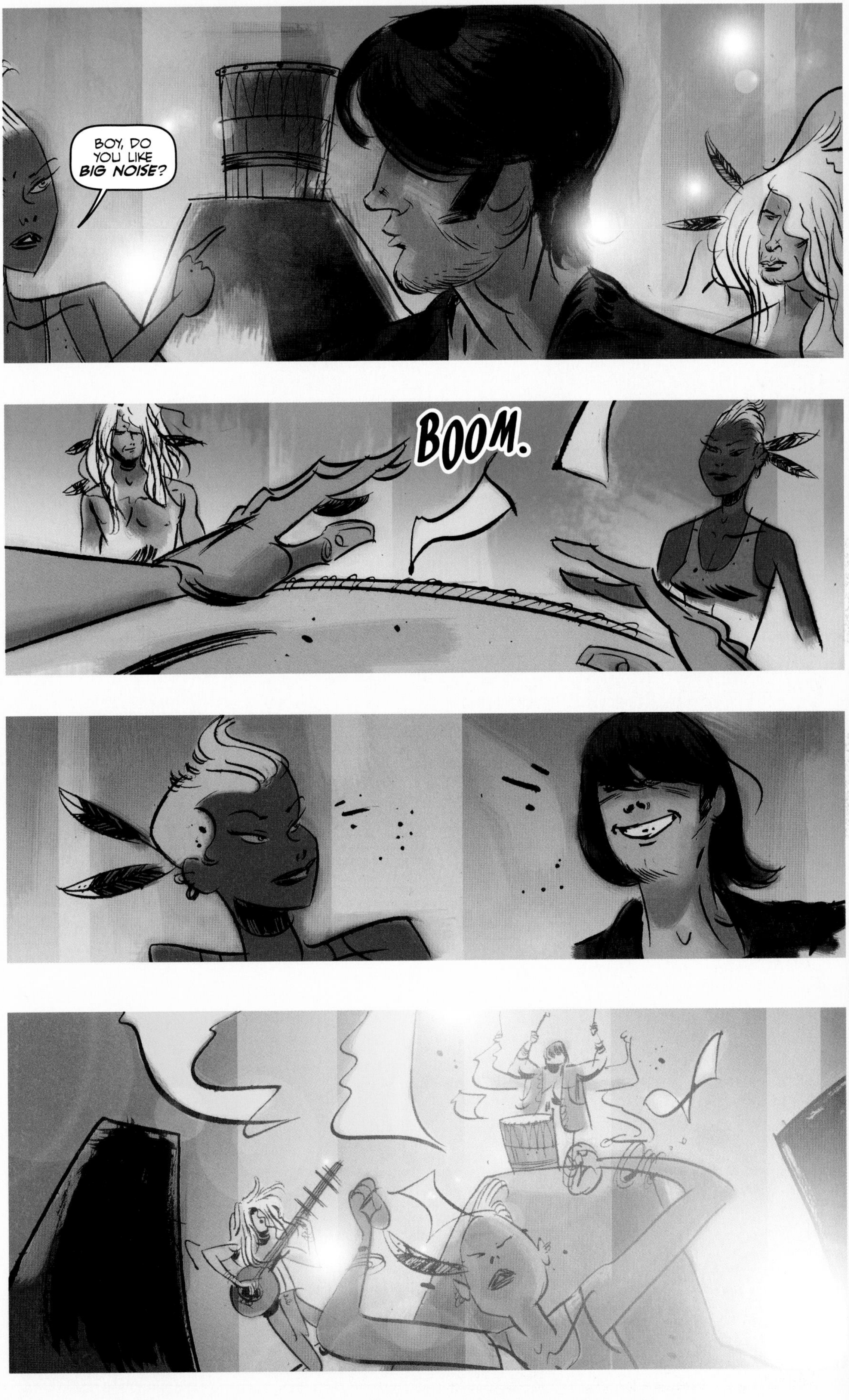
BOY, DO YOU LIKE BIG NOISE?
BOOM.

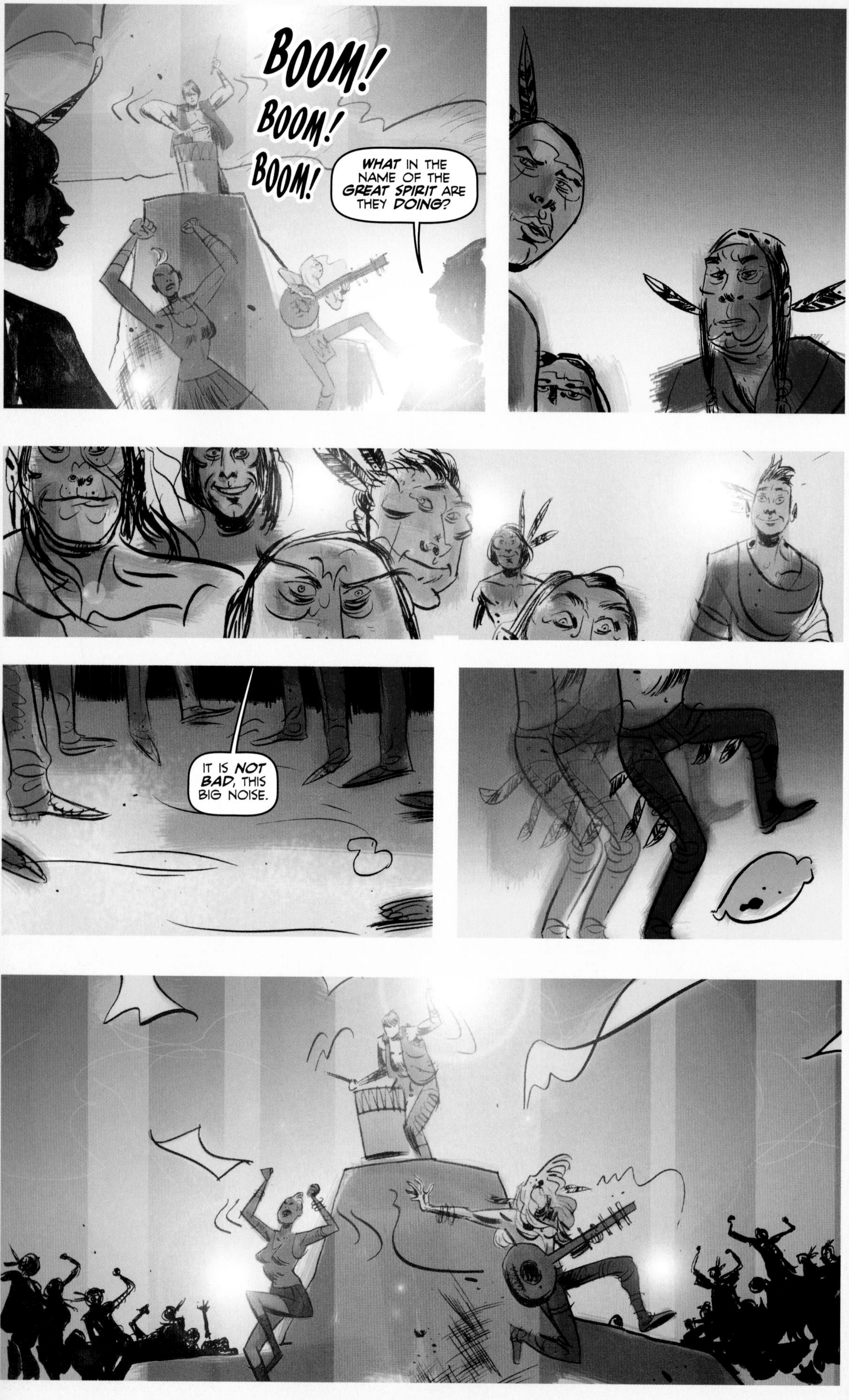
BOOM!
BOOM!
BOOM!
WHAT IN THE NAME OF THE GREAT SPIRIT ARE THEY DOING?
IT IS NOT BAD, THIS BIG NOISE.

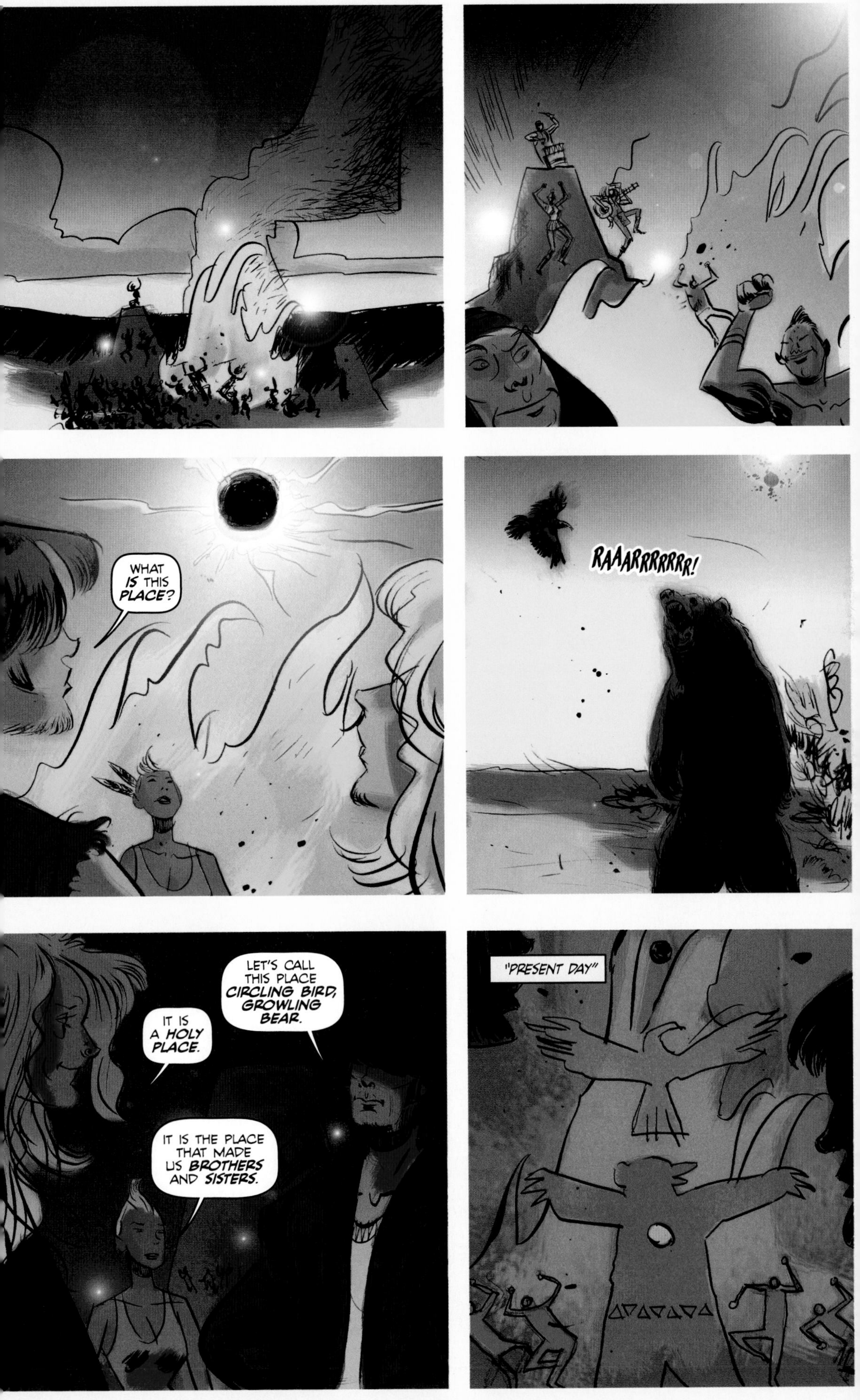
WHAT IS THIS PLACE?
RAAARRRRRR!
IT IS A HOLY PLACE.
LET'S CALL THIS PLACE CIRCLING BIRD, GROWLING BEAR.
IT IS THE PLACE THAT MADE US BROTHERS AND SISTERS.
"PRESENT DAY"

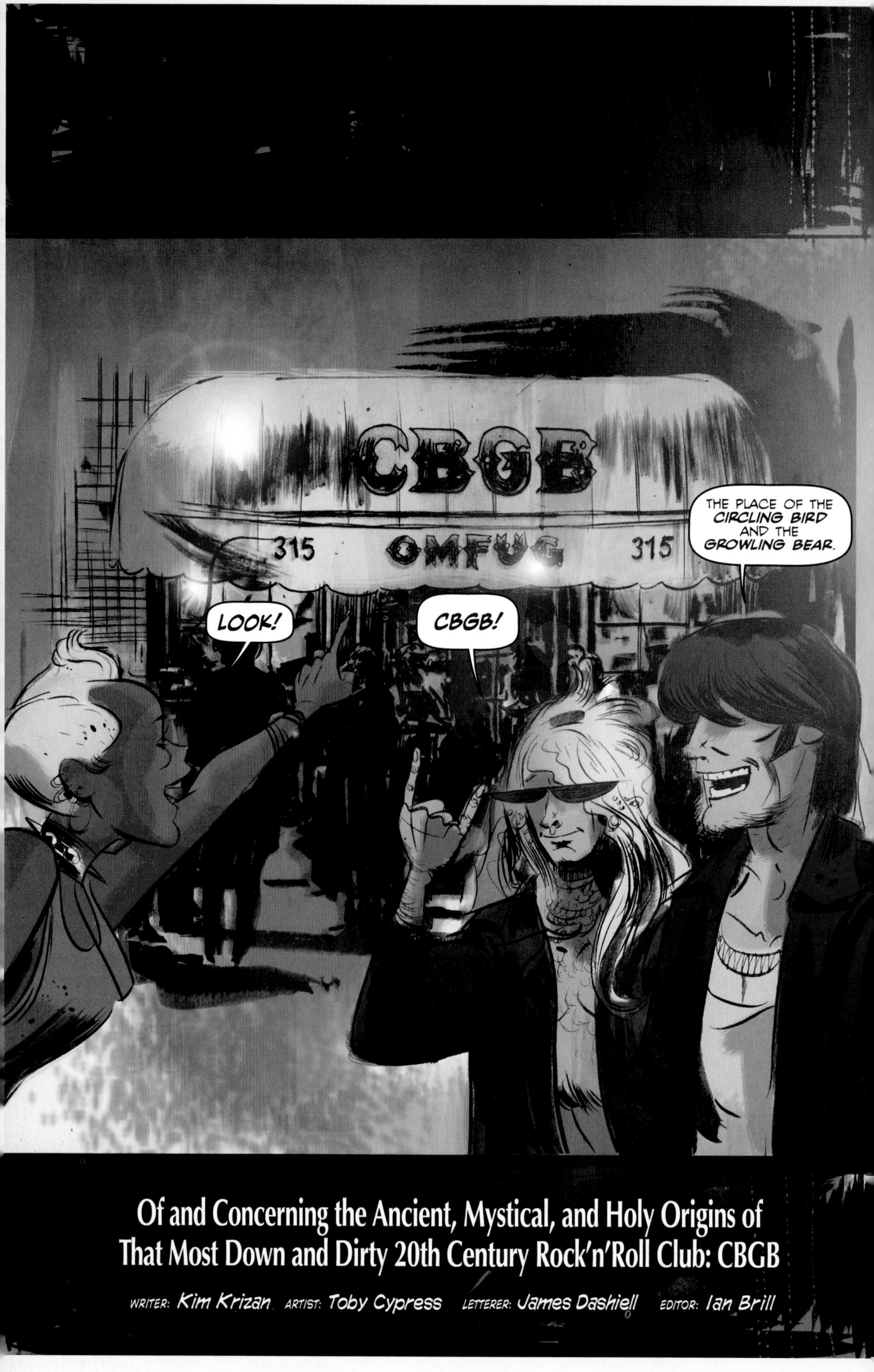
CBGB
315
OMFUG
315
LOOK!
CBGB!
THE PLACE OF THE CIRCLING BIRD AND THE GROWLING BEAR.

Of and Concerning the Ancient, Mystical, and Holy Origins of That Most Down and Dirty 20th Century Rock'n'Roll Club: CBGB

WRITER: Kim Krizan ARTIST: Toby Cypress LETTERER: James Dashiell EDITOR: Ian Brill

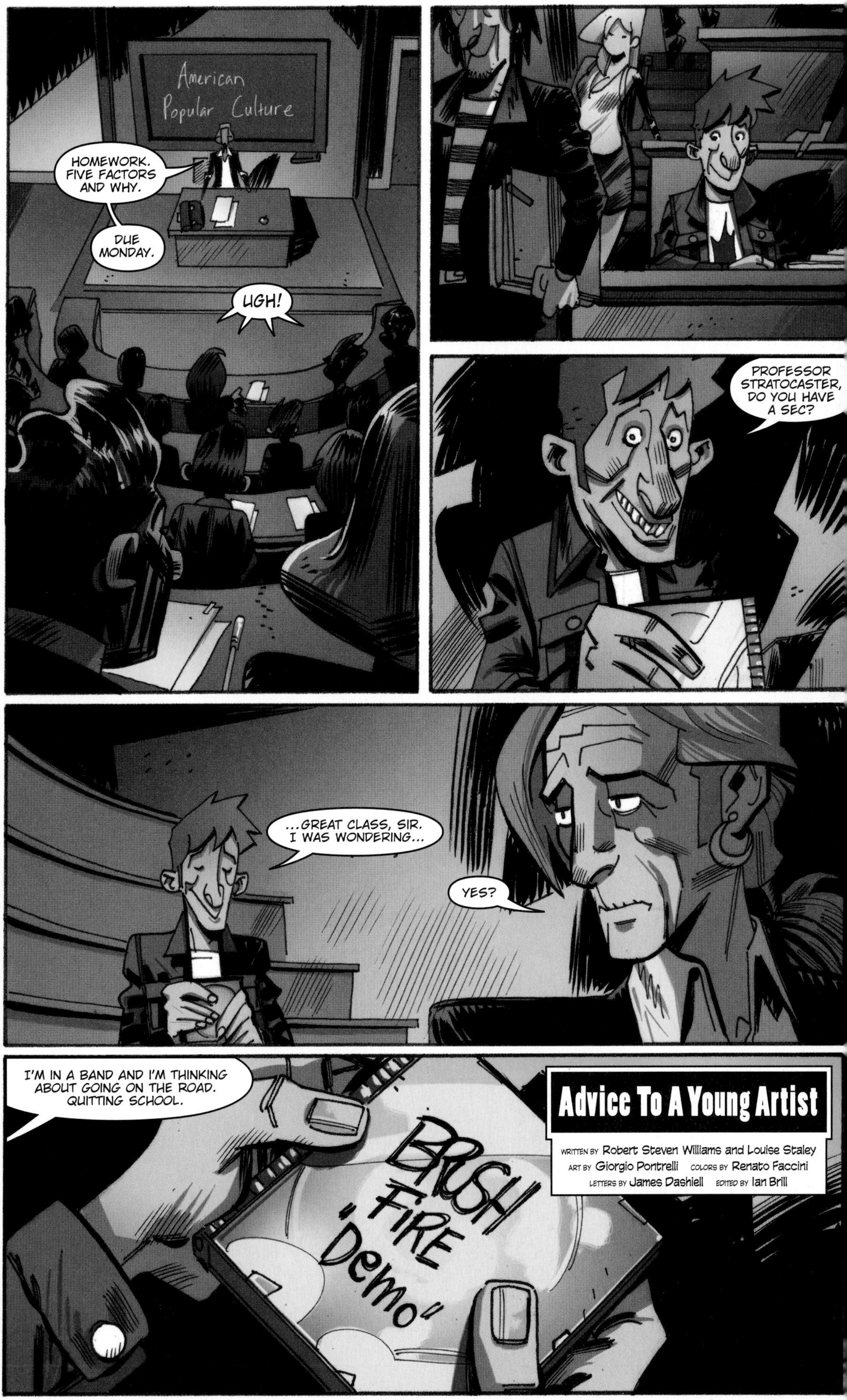
American Popular Culture
HOMEWORK. FIVE FACTORS AND WHY.
DUE MONDAY.
UGH!
PROFESSOR STRATOCASTER, DO YOU HAVE A SEC?
...GREAT CLASS, SIR. I WAS WONDERING...
YES?
I'M IN A BAND AND I'M THINKING ABOUT GOING ON THE ROAD. QUITTING SCHOOL.
BRUSH "FIRE" "Demo"
Advice To A Young Artist
WRITTEN BY Robert Steven Williams and Louise Staley
ART BY Giorgio Pontrelli COLORS BY Renato Faccini
LETTERS BY James Dashiell EDITED BY Ian Brill

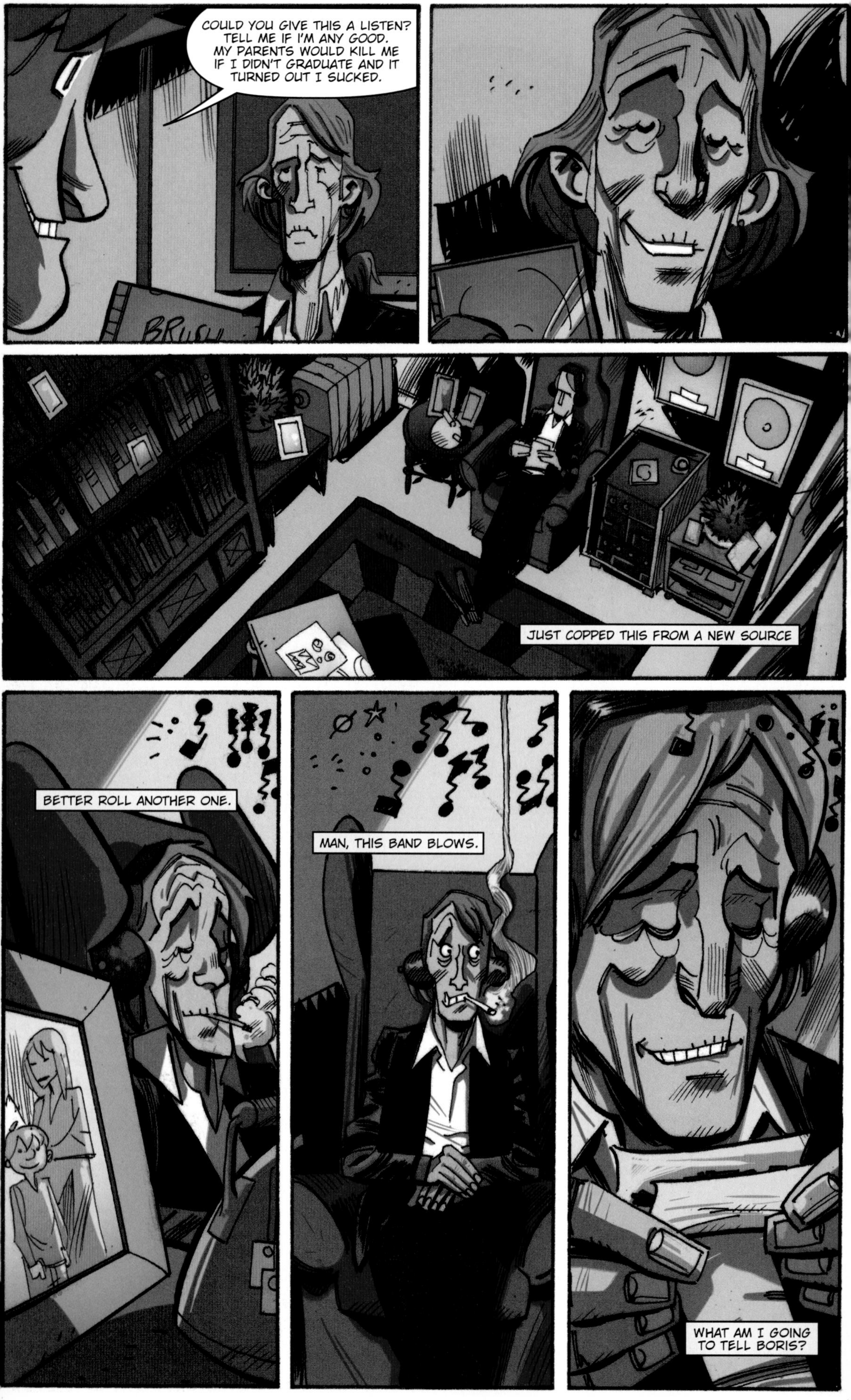
COULD YOU GIVE THIS A LISTEN? TELL ME IF I'M ANY GOOD. MY PARENTS WOULD KILL ME IF I DIDN'T GRADUATE AND IT TURNED OUT I SUCKED.
JUST COPPED THIS FROM A NEW SOURCE
BETTER ROLL ANOTHER ONE.
MAN, THIS BAND BLOWS.
WHAT AM I GOING TO TELL BORIS?

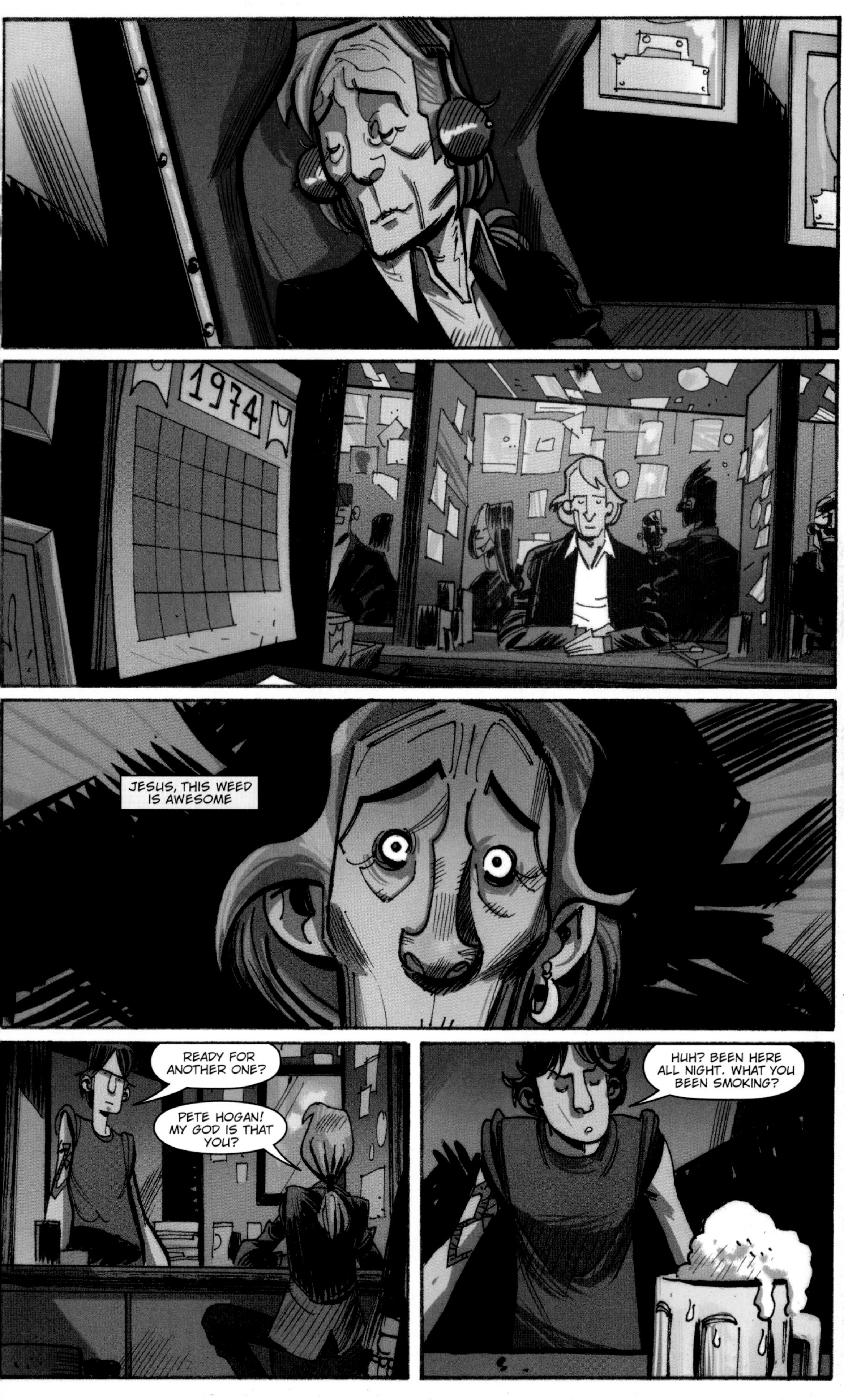
1974
JESUS, THIS WEED IS AWESOME
READY FOR ANOTHER ONE?
PETE HOGAN! MY GOD IS THAT YOU?
HUH? BEEN HERE ALL NIGHT. WHAT YOU BEEN SMOKING?

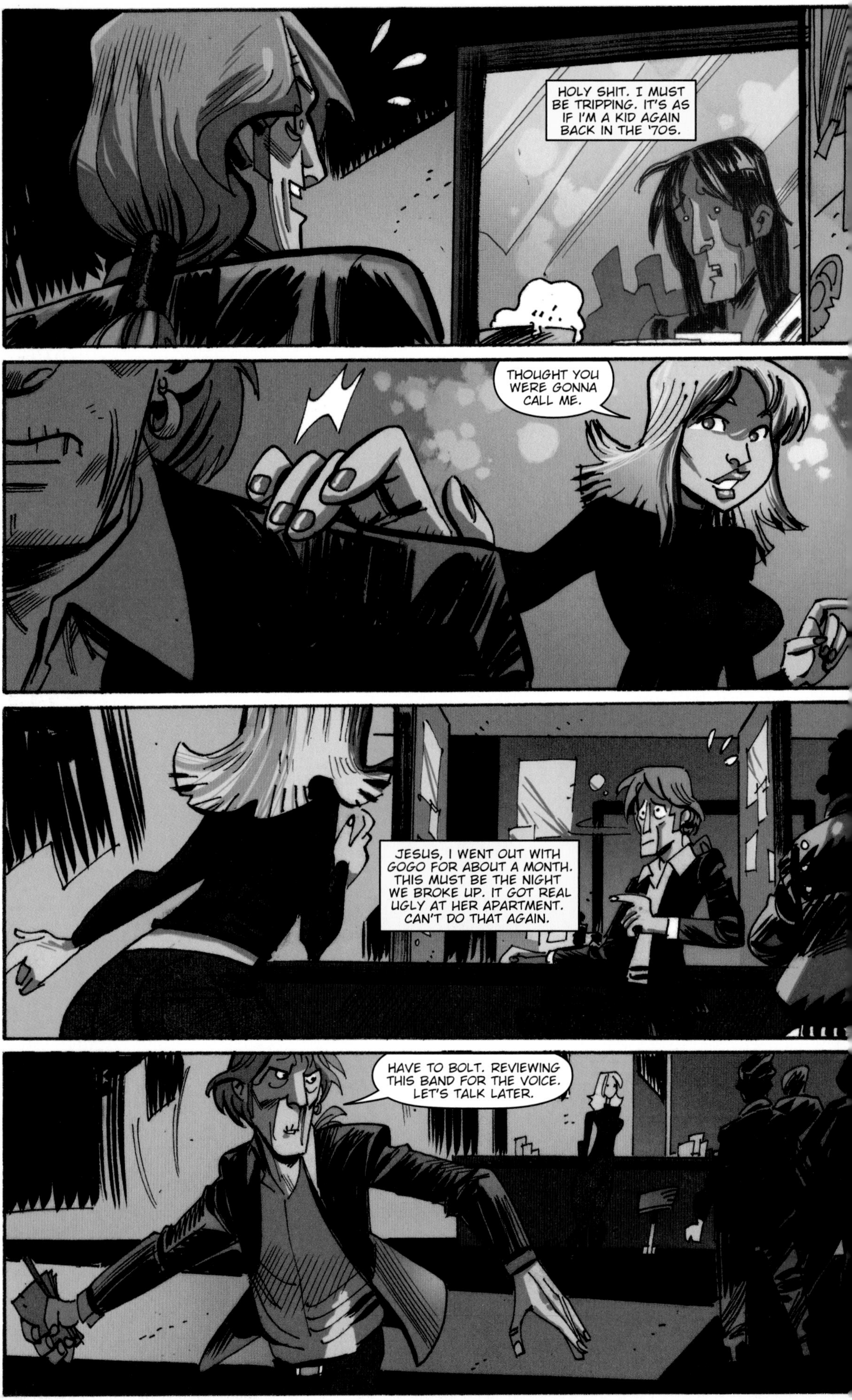
HOLY SHIT. I MUST BE TRIPPING. IT'S AS IF I'M A KID AGAIN BACK IN THE '70S.
THOUGHT YOU WERE GONNA CALL ME.
JESUS, I WENT OUT WITH GOGO FOR ABOUT A MONTH. THIS MUST BE THE NIGHT WE BROKE UP. IT GOT REAL UGLY AT HER APARTMENT. CAN'T DO THAT AGAIN.
HAVE TO BOLT. REVIEWING THIS BAND FOR THE VOICE. LET'S TALK LATER.

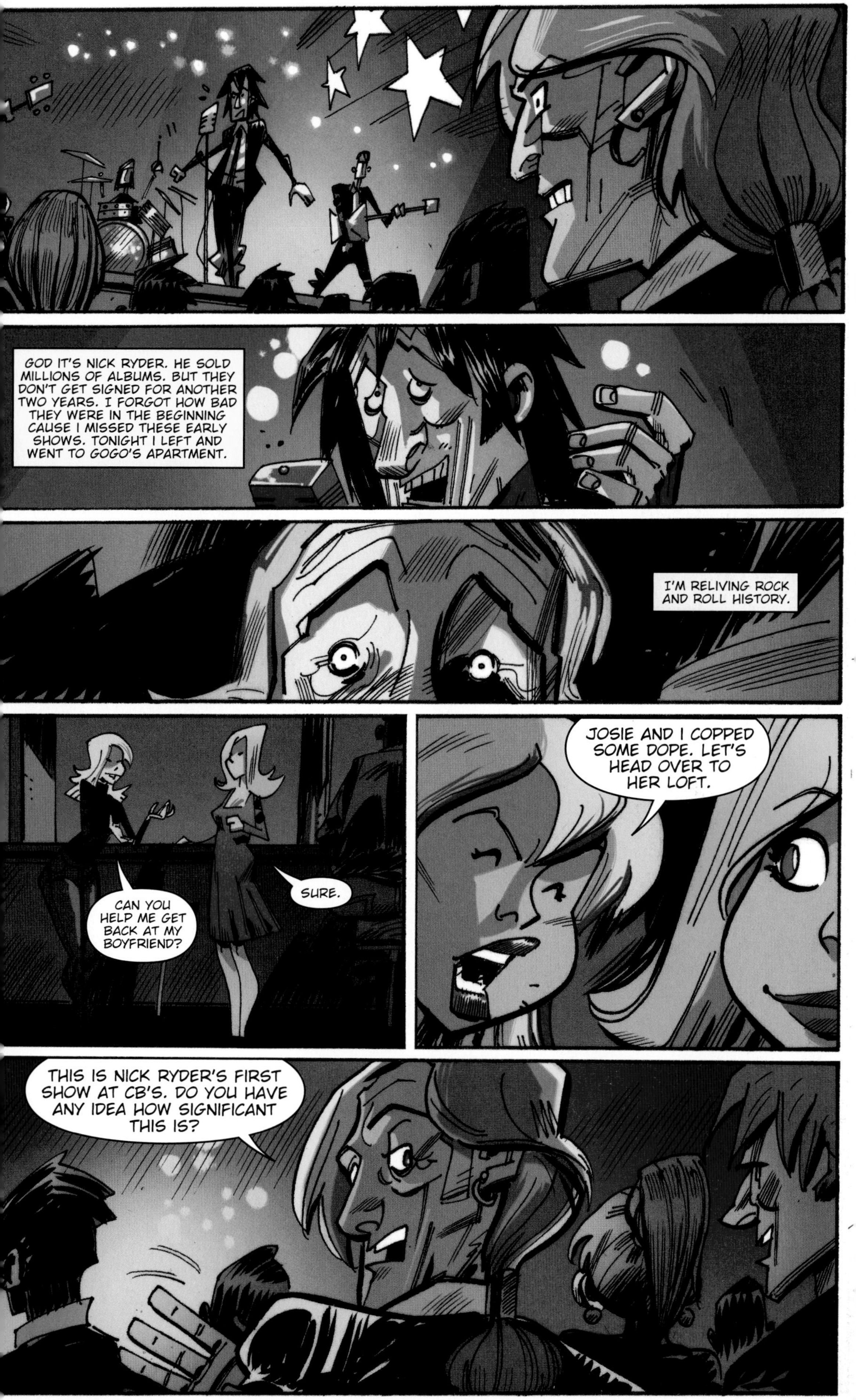
GOD IT'S NICK RYDER. HE SOLD MILLIONS OF ALBUMS. BUT THEY DON'T GET SIGNED FOR ANOTHER TWO YEARS. I FORGOT HOW BAD THEY WERE IN THE BEGINNING CAUSE I MISSED THESE EARLY SHOWS. TONIGHT I LEFT AND WENT TO GOGO'S APARTMENT.
I'M RELIVING ROCK AND ROLL HISTORY.
CAN YOU HELP ME GET BACK AT MY BOYFRIEND?
SURE.
JOSIE AND I COPPED SOME DOPE. LET'S HEAD OVER TO HER LOFT.
THIS IS NICK RYDER'S FIRST SHOW AT CB'S. DO YOU HAVE ANY IDEA HOW SIGNIFICANT THIS IS?

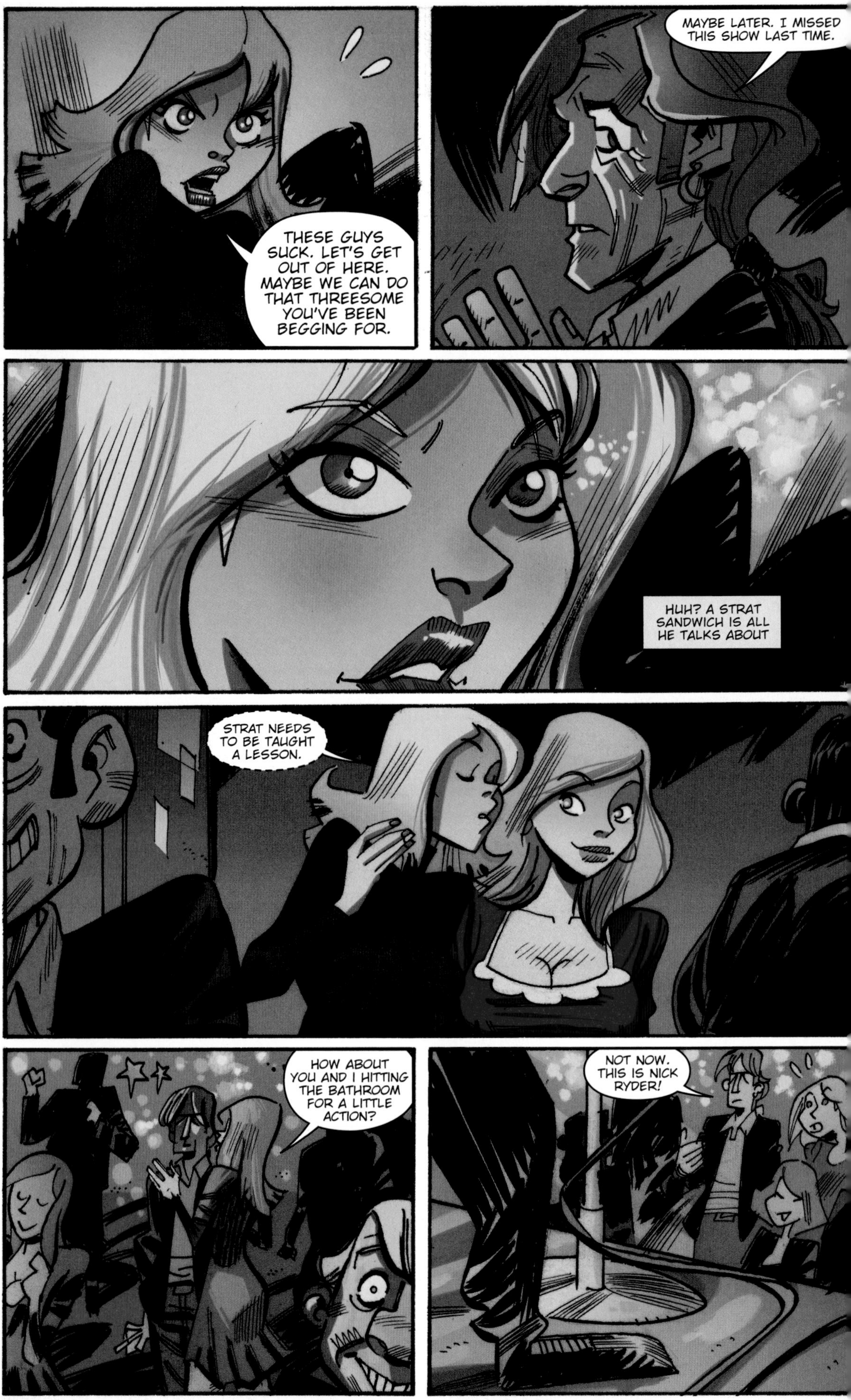
THESE GUYS SUCK. LET'S GET OUT OF HERE. MAYBE WE CAN DO THAT THREESOME YOU'VE BEEN BEGGING FOR.
MAYBE LATER. I MISSED THIS SHOW LAST TIME.
HUH? A STRAT SANDWICH IS ALL HE TALKS ABOUT
STRAT NEEDS TO BE TAUGHT A LESSON.
HOW ABOUT YOU AND I HITTING THE BATHROOM FOR A LITTLE ACTION?
NOT NOW. THIS IS NICK RYDER!

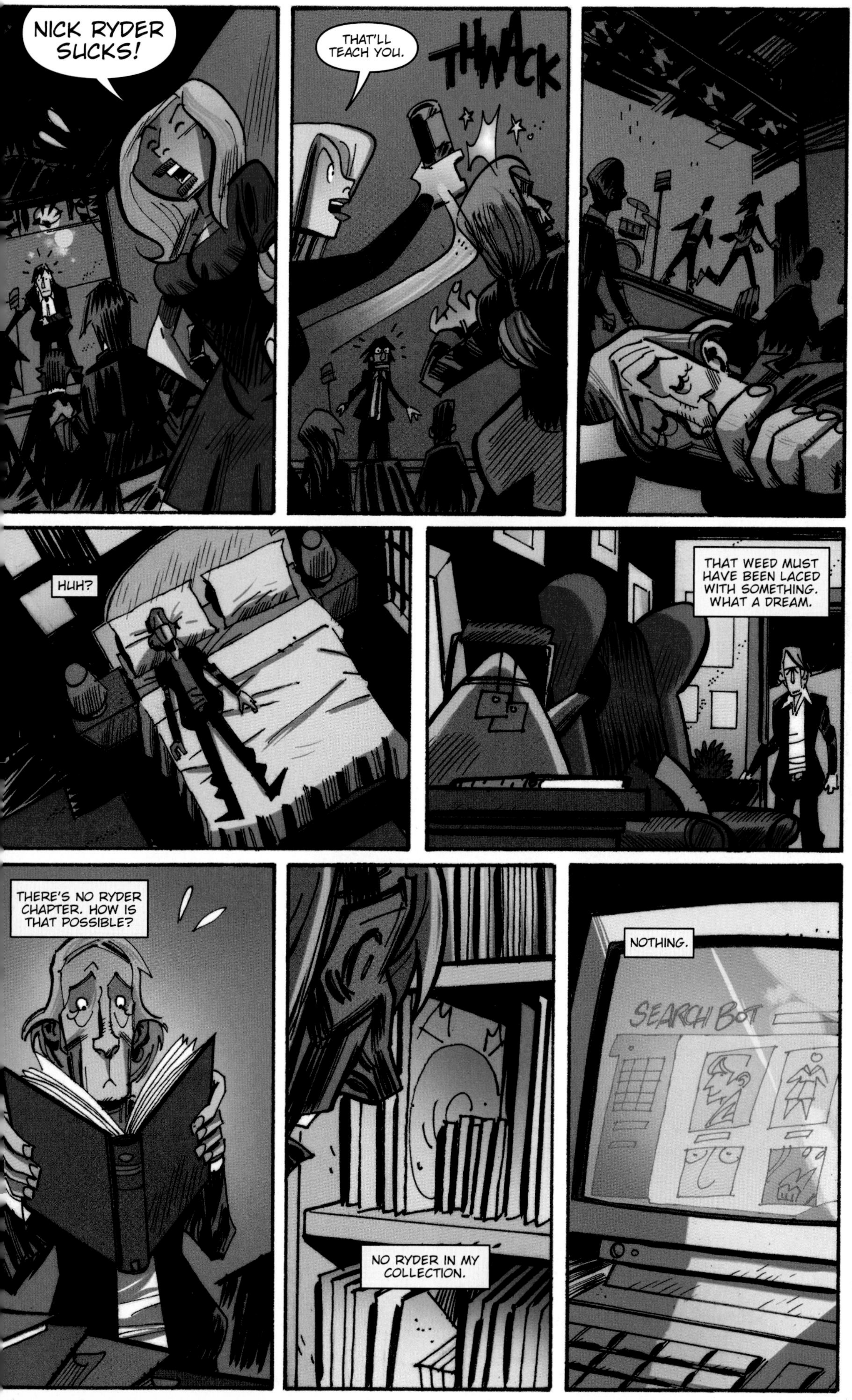
NICK RYDER SUCKS!
THAT'LL TEACH YOU.
THWACK
HUH?
THAT WEED MUST HAVE BEEN LACED WITH SOMETHING. WHAT A DREAM.
THERE'S NO RYDER CHAPTER. HOW IS THAT POSSIBLE?
NO RYDER IN MY COLLECTION.
NOTHING.
SEARCH BOT

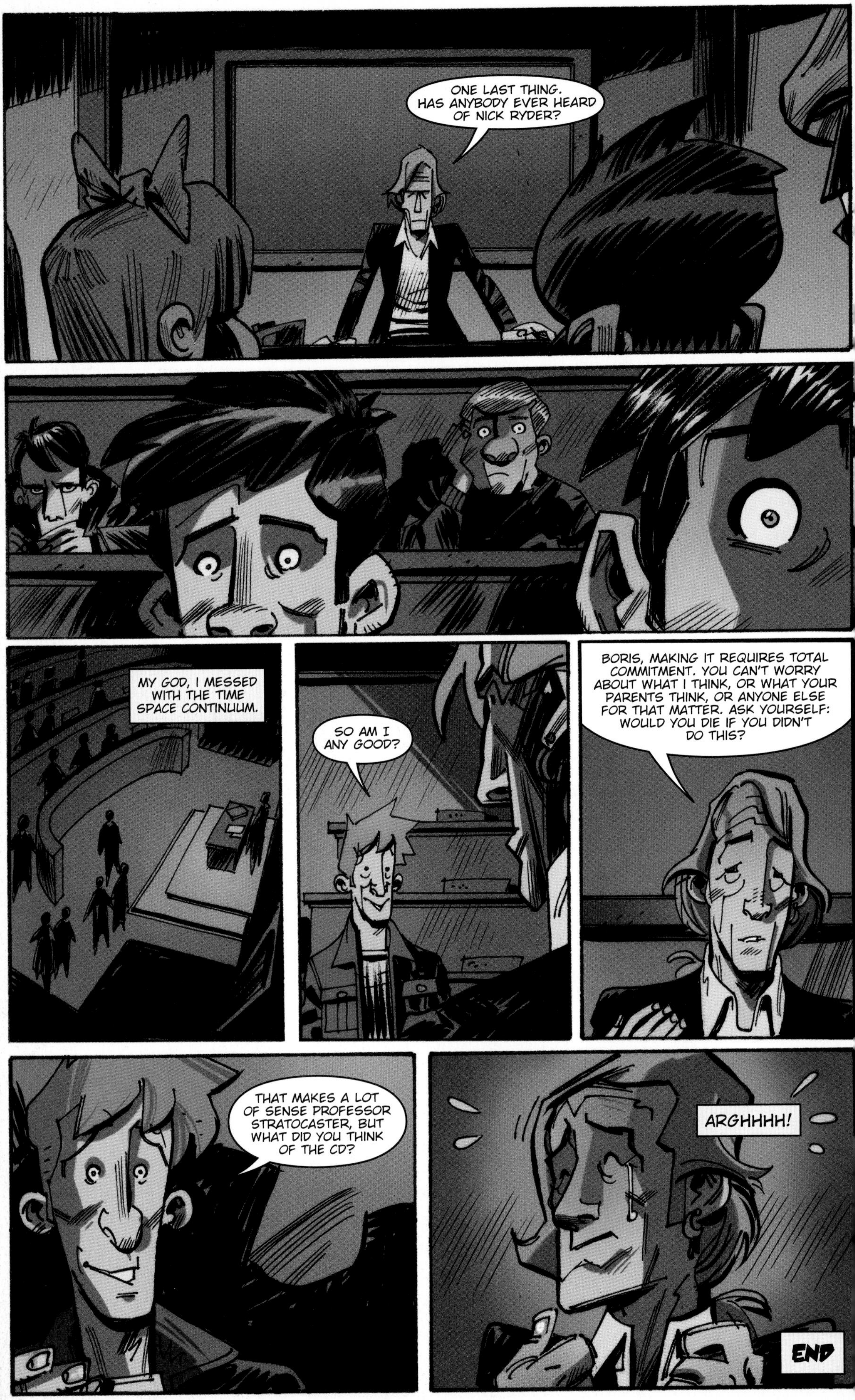
ONE LAST THING. HAS ANYBODY EVER HEARD OF NICK RYDER?
MY GOD, I MESSED WITH THE TIME SPACE CONTINUUM.
SO AM I ANY GOOD?
BORIS, MAKING IT REQUIRES TOTAL COMMITMENT. YOU CAN'T WORRY ABOUT WHAT I THINK, OR WHAT YOUR PARENTS THINK, OR ANYONE ELSE FOR THAT MATTER. ASK YOURSELF: WOULD YOU DIE IF YOU DIDN'T DO THIS?
THAT MAKES A LOT OF SENSE PROFESSOR STRATOCASTER, BUT WHAT DID YOU THINK OF THE CD?
ARGHHHH!
END

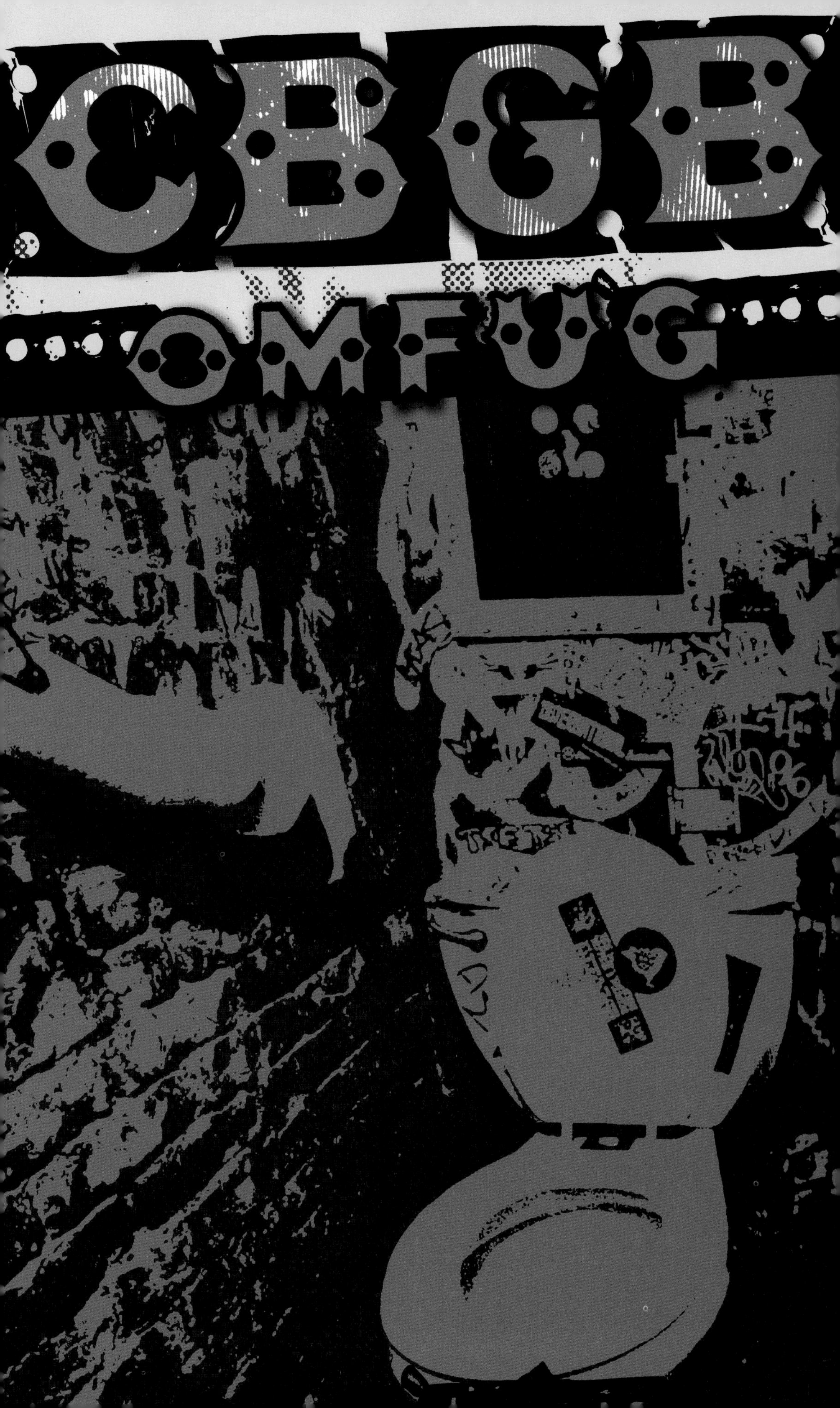
CBGB
OMFUG

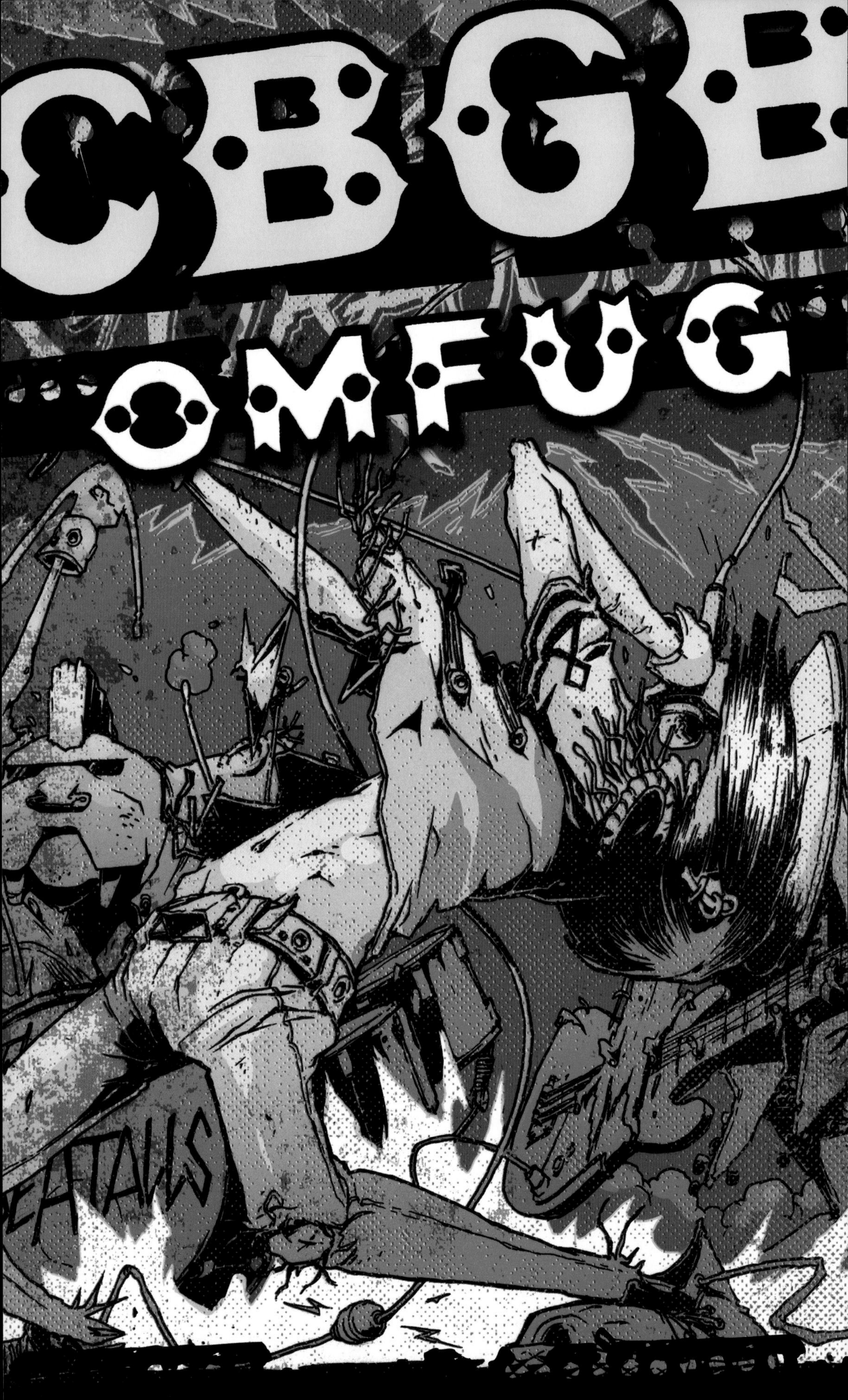
C.B.G.B.
O.M.F.U.G.

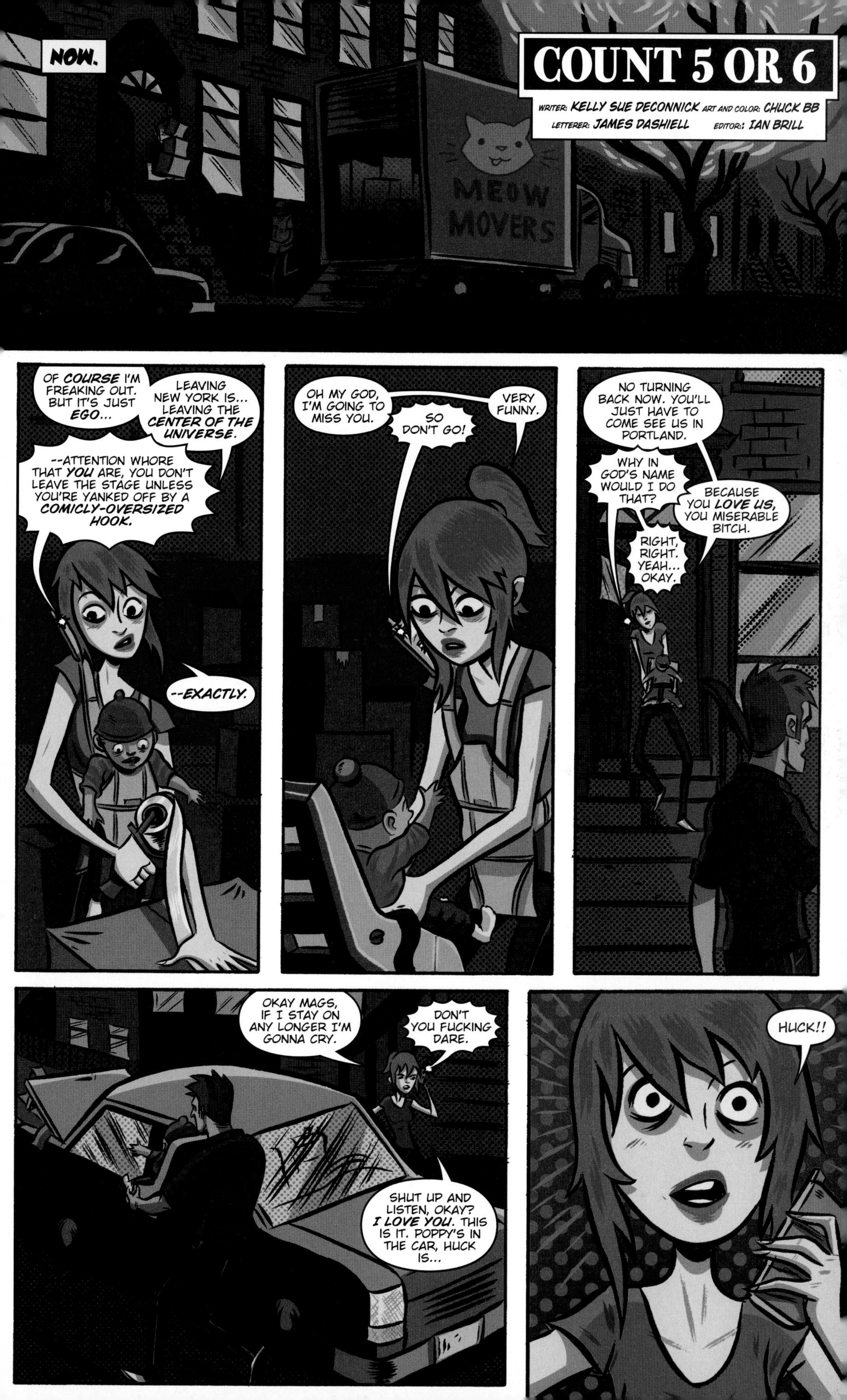

NOW.
COUNT 5 OR 6
WRITER: KELLY SUE DECONNICK ART AND COLOR: CHUCK BB
LETTERER: JAMES DASHIELL EDITOR: IAN BRILL
MEOW MOVERS
OF COURSE I'M FREAKING OUT. BUT IT'S JUST EGO...
LEAVING NEW YORK IS... LEAVING THE CENTER OF THE UNIVERSE.
--ATTENTION WHORE THAT YOU ARE, YOU DON'T LEAVE THE STAGE UNLESS YOU'RE YANKED OFF BY A COMICLY-OVERSIZED HOOK.
--EXACTLY.
OH MY GOD, I'M GOING TO MISS YOU.
SO DON'T GO!
VERY FUNNY.
NO TURNING BACK NOW. YOU'LL JUST HAVE TO COME SEE US IN PORTLAND.
WHY IN GOD'S NAME WOULD I DO THAT?
BECAUSE YOU LOVE US, YOU MISERABLE BITCH.
RIGHT, RIGHT. YEAH... OKAY.
OKAY MAGS, IF I STAY ON ANY LONGER I'M GONNA CRY.
DON'T YOU FUCKING DARE.
SHUT UP AND LISTEN, OKAY? I LOVE YOU. THIS IS IT. POPPY'S IN THE CAR, HUCK IS...
HUCK!!

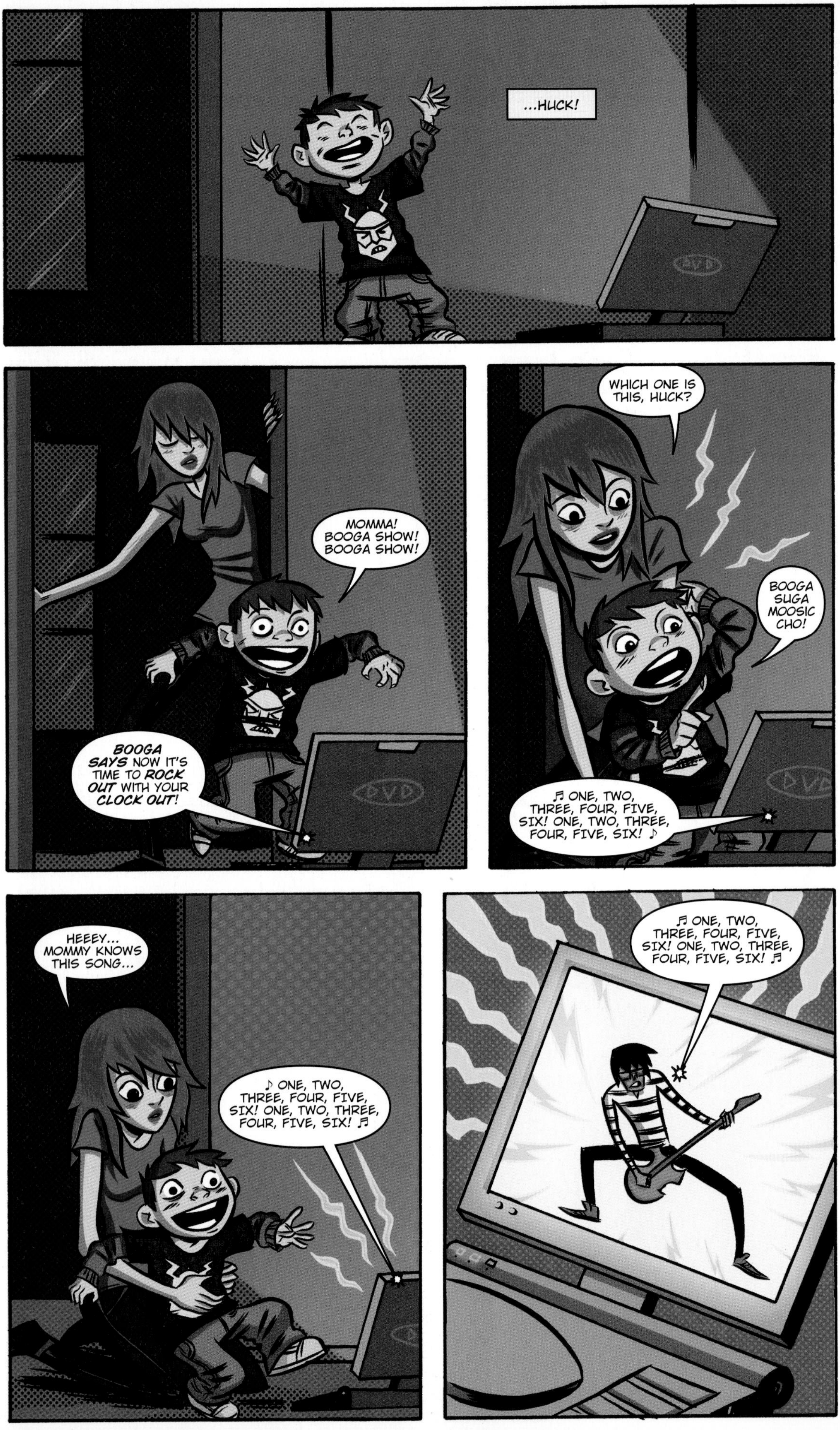
...HUCK!
MOMMA! BOOGA SHOW! BOOGA SHOW!
BOOGA SAYS NOW IT'S TIME TO ROCK OUT WITH YOUR CLOCK OUT!
WHICH ONE IS THIS, HUCK?
BOOGA SUGA MOOSIC CHO!
♬ ONE, TWO, THREE, FOUR, FIVE, SIX! ONE, TWO, THREE, FOUR, FIVE, SIX! ♪
HEEEY... MOMMY KNOWS THIS SONG...
♪ ONE, TWO, THREE, FOUR, FIVE, SIX! ONE, TWO, THREE, FOUR, FIVE, SIX! ♬
♬ ONE, TWO, THREE, FOUR, FIVE, SIX! ONE, TWO, THREE, FOUR, FIVE, SIX! ♬

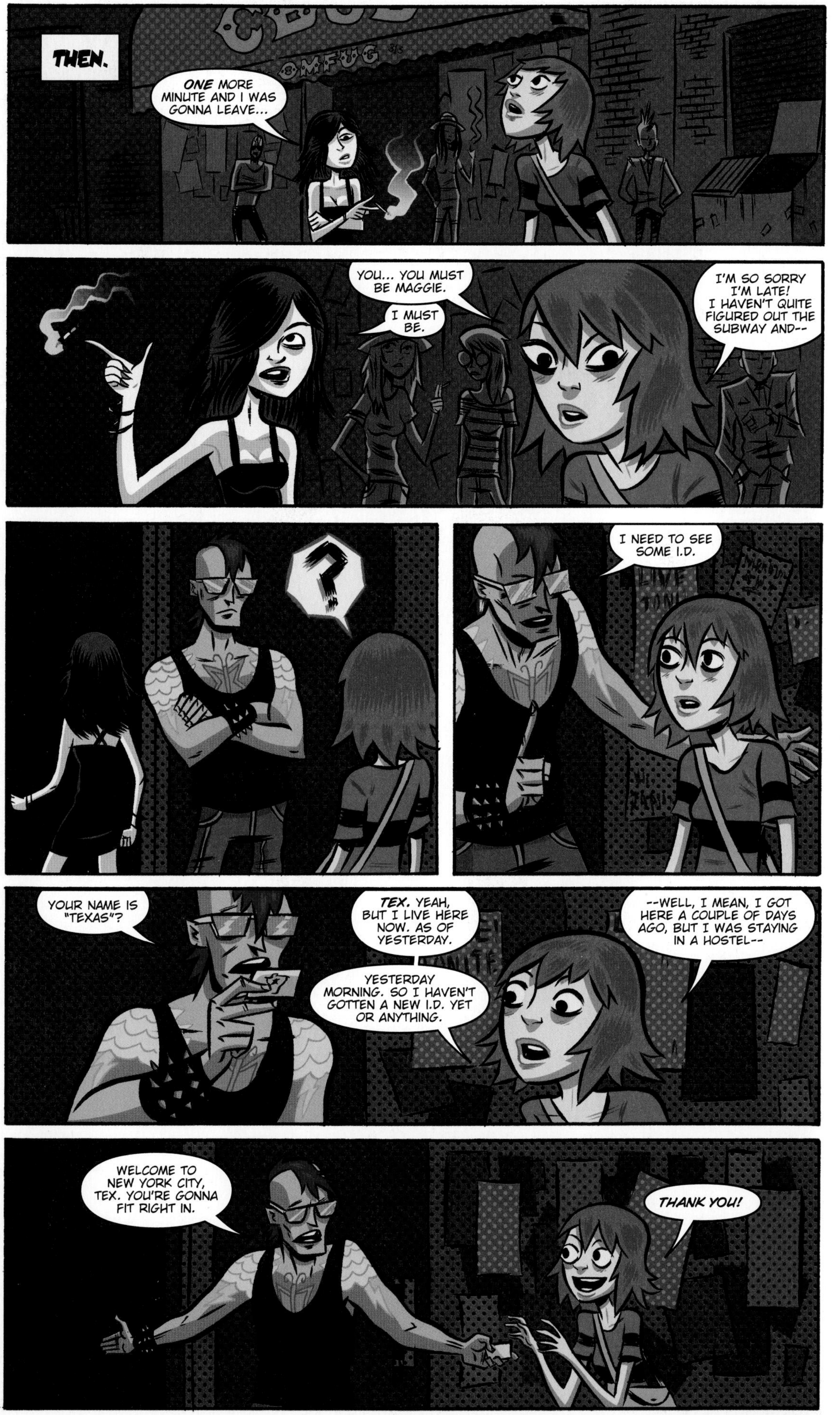
THEN.
OMFUG
ONE MORE MINUTE AND I WAS GONNA LEAVE...
YOU... YOU MUST BE MAGGIE.
I MUST BE.
I'M SO SORRY I'M LATE! I HAVEN'T QUITE FIGURED OUT THE SUBWAY AND--
?
I NEED TO SEE SOME I.D.
YOUR NAME IS "TEXAS"?
TEX. YEAH, BUT I LIVE HERE NOW. AS OF YESTERDAY.
YESTERDAY MORNING. SO I HAVEN'T GOTTEN A NEW I.D. YET OR ANYTHING.
--WELL, I MEAN, I GOT HERE A COUPLE OF DAYS AGO, BUT I WAS STAYING IN A HOSTEL--
WELCOME TO NEW YORK CITY, TEX. YOU'RE GONNA FIT RIGHT IN.
THANK YOU!

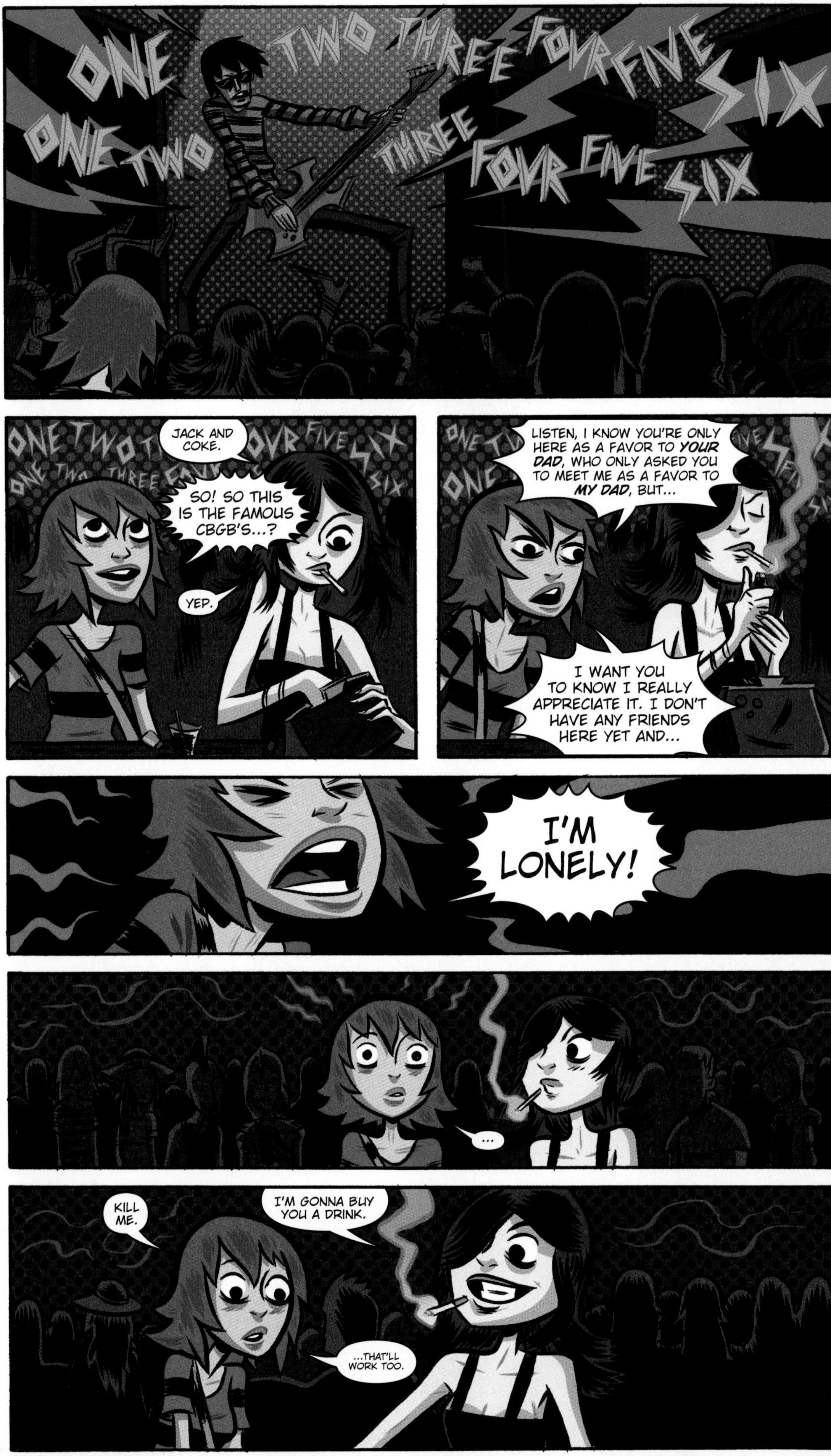

ONE TWO THREE FOUR FIVE SIX
ONE TWO THREE FOUR FIVE SIX
JACK AND COKE.
SO! SO THIS IS THE FAMOUS CBGB'S...?
YEP.
LISTEN, I KNOW YOU'RE ONLY HERE AS A FAVOR TO YOUR DAD, WHO ONLY ASKED YOU TO MEET ME AS A FAVOR TO MY DAD, BUT...
I WANT YOU TO KNOW I REALLY APPRECIATE IT. I DON'T HAVE ANY FRIENDS HERE YET AND...
I'M LONELY!
...
KILL ME.
I'M GONNA BUY YOU A DRINK.
...THAT'LL WORK TOO.

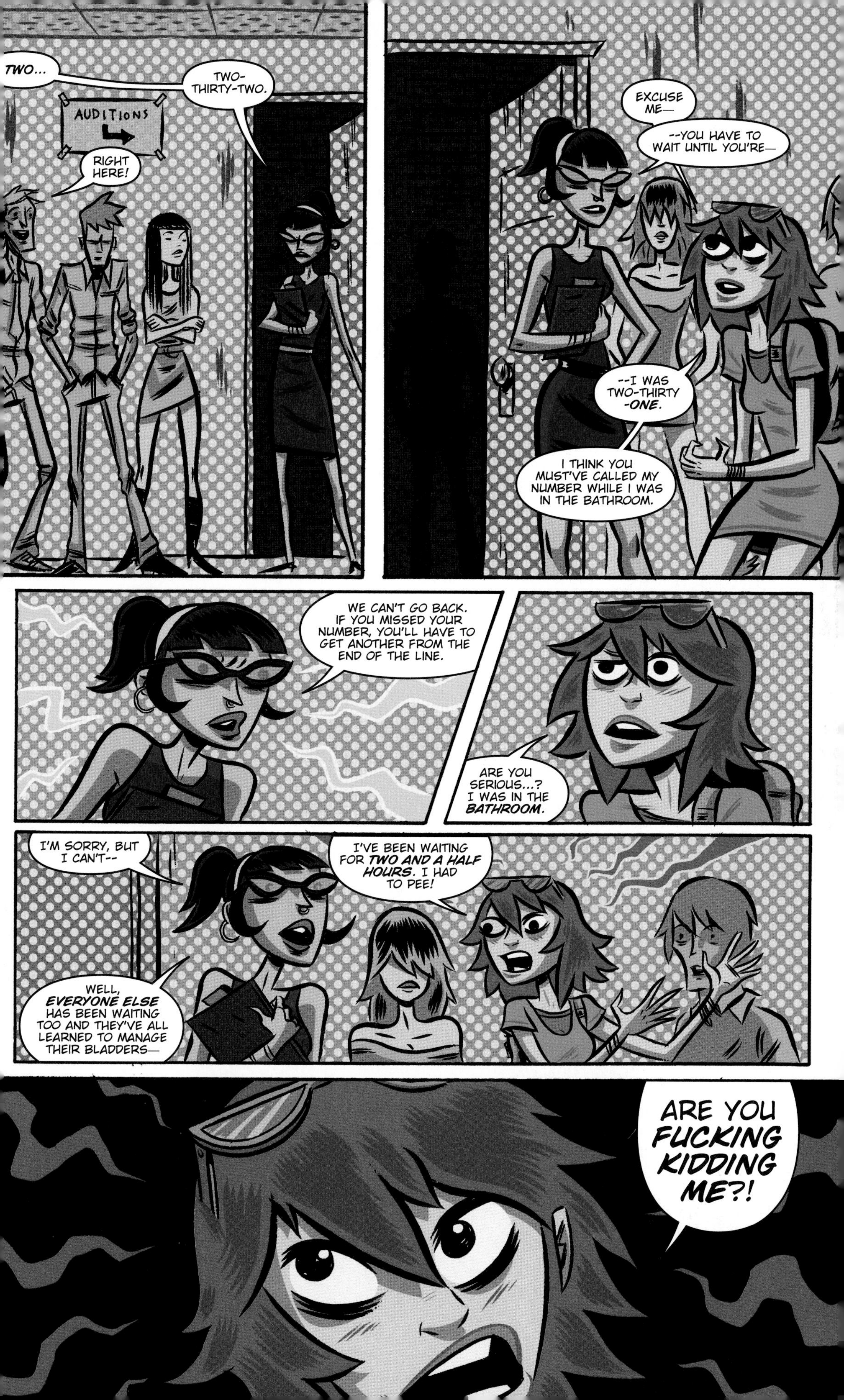
TWO...
TWO-THIRTY-TWO.
AUDITIONS
RIGHT HERE!
EXCUSE ME—
--YOU HAVE TO WAIT UNTIL YOU'RE—
--I WAS TWO-THIRTY *-ONE.*
I THINK YOU MUST'VE CALLED MY NUMBER WHILE I WAS IN THE BATHROOM.
WE CAN'T GO BACK. IF YOU MISSED YOUR NUMBER, YOU'LL HAVE TO GET ANOTHER FROM THE END OF THE LINE.
ARE YOU SERIOUS...? I WAS IN THE *BATHROOM.*
I'M SORRY, BUT I CAN'T--
I'VE BEEN WAITING FOR *TWO AND A HALF HOURS.* I HAD TO PEE!
WELL, *EVERYONE ELSE* HAS BEEN WAITING TOO AND THEY'VE ALL LEARNED TO MANAGE THEIR BLADDERS—
ARE YOU *FUCKING KIDDING ME?!*

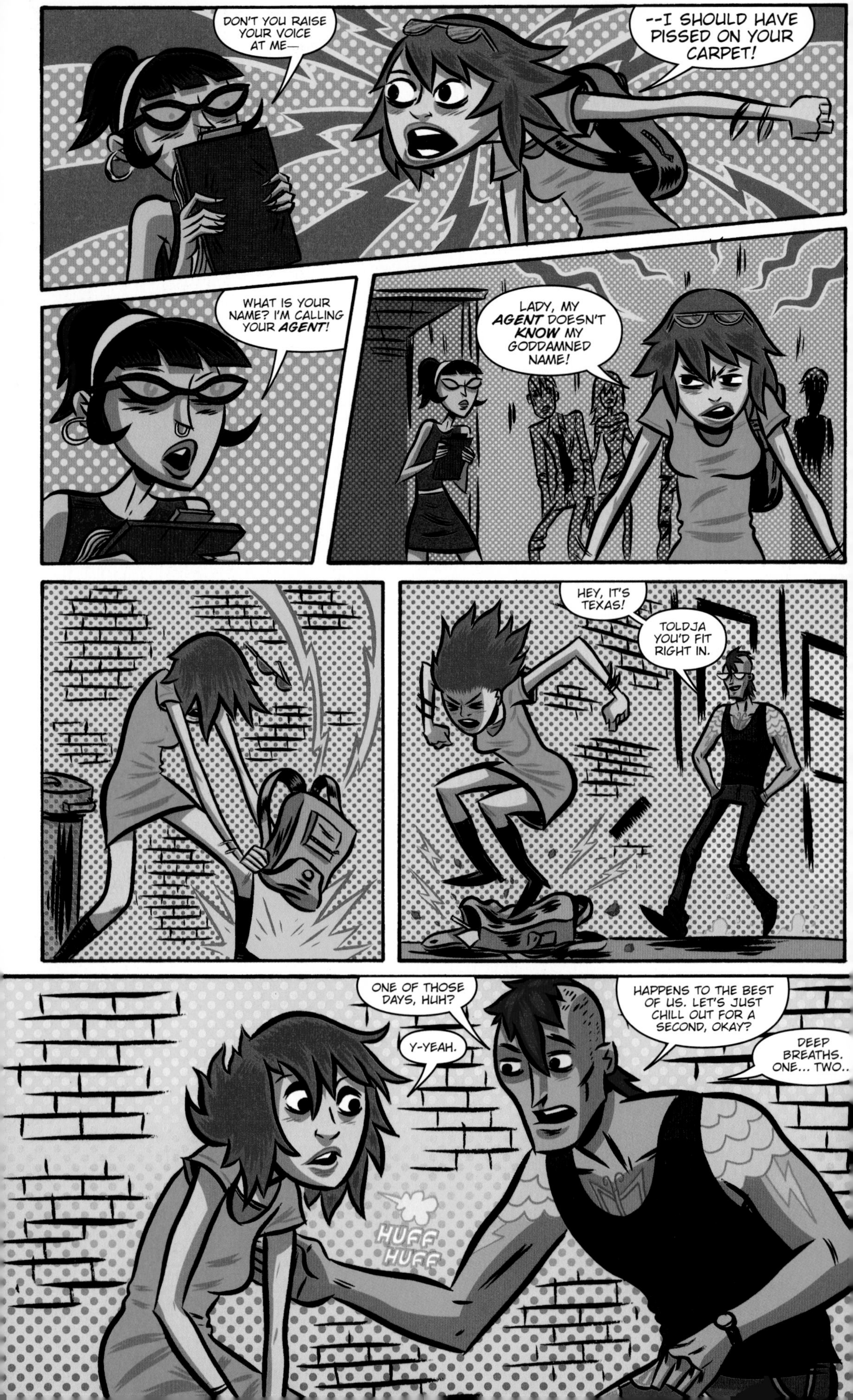

DON'T YOU RAISE YOUR VOICE AT ME—
--I SHOULD HAVE PISSED ON YOUR CARPET!
WHAT IS YOUR NAME? I'M CALLING YOUR AGENT!
LADY, MY AGENT DOESN'T KNOW MY GODDAMNED NAME!
HEY, IT'S TEXAS!
TOLDJA YOU'D FIT RIGHT IN.
ONE OF THOSE DAYS, HUH?
Y-YEAH.
HAPPENS TO THE BEST OF US. LET'S JUST CHILL OUT FOR A SECOND, OKAY?
DEEP BREATHS. ONE... TWO...
HUFF HUFF

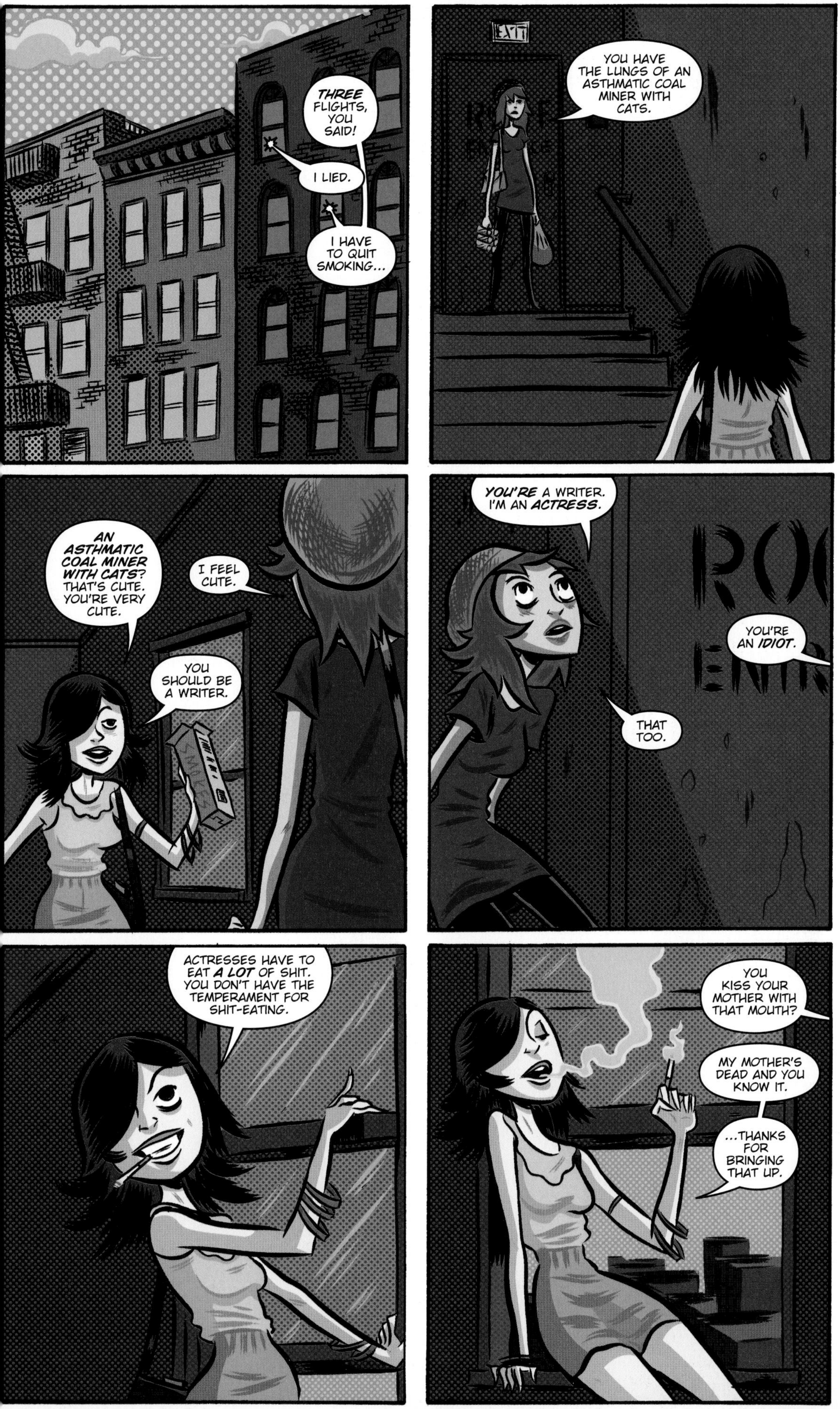
THREE FLIGHTS, YOU SAID!
I LIED.
I HAVE TO QUIT SMOKING...
YOU HAVE THE LUNGS OF AN ASTHMATIC COAL MINER WITH CATS.
AN ASTHMATIC COAL MINER WITH CATS? THAT'S CUTE. YOU'RE VERY CUTE.
I FEEL CUTE.
YOU SHOULD BE A WRITER.
YOU'RE A WRITER. I'M AN ACTRESS.
YOU'RE AN IDIOT.
THAT TOO.
ACTRESSES HAVE TO EAT A LOT OF SHIT. YOU DON'T HAVE THE TEMPERAMENT FOR SHIT-EATING.
YOU KISS YOUR MOTHER WITH THAT MOUTH?
MY MOTHER'S DEAD AND YOU KNOW IT.
...THANKS FOR BRINGING THAT UP.

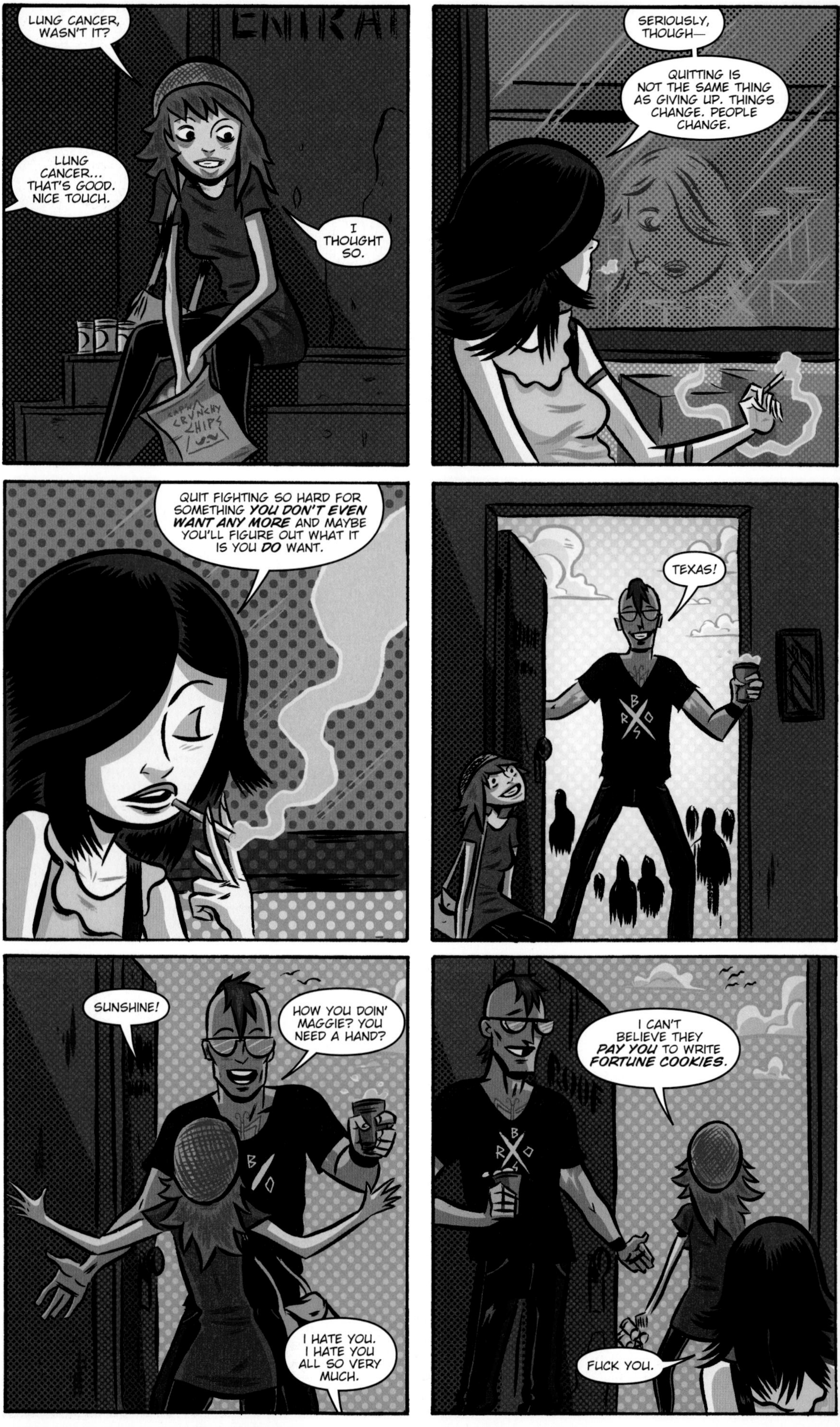
LUNG CANCER, WASN'T IT?
LUNG CANCER... THAT'S GOOD. NICE TOUCH.
I THOUGHT SO.
SERIOUSLY, THOUGH—
QUITTING IS NOT THE SAME THING AS GIVING UP. THINGS CHANGE. PEOPLE CHANGE.
QUIT FIGHTING SO HARD FOR SOMETHING YOU DON'T EVEN WANT ANY MORE AND MAYBE YOU'LL FIGURE OUT WHAT IT IS YOU DO WANT.
TEXAS!
SUNSHINE!
HOW YOU DOIN' MAGGIE? YOU NEED A HAND?
I HATE YOU. I HATE YOU ALL SO VERY MUCH.
I CAN'T BELIEVE THEY PAY YOU TO WRITE FORTUNE COOKIES.
FUCK YOU.

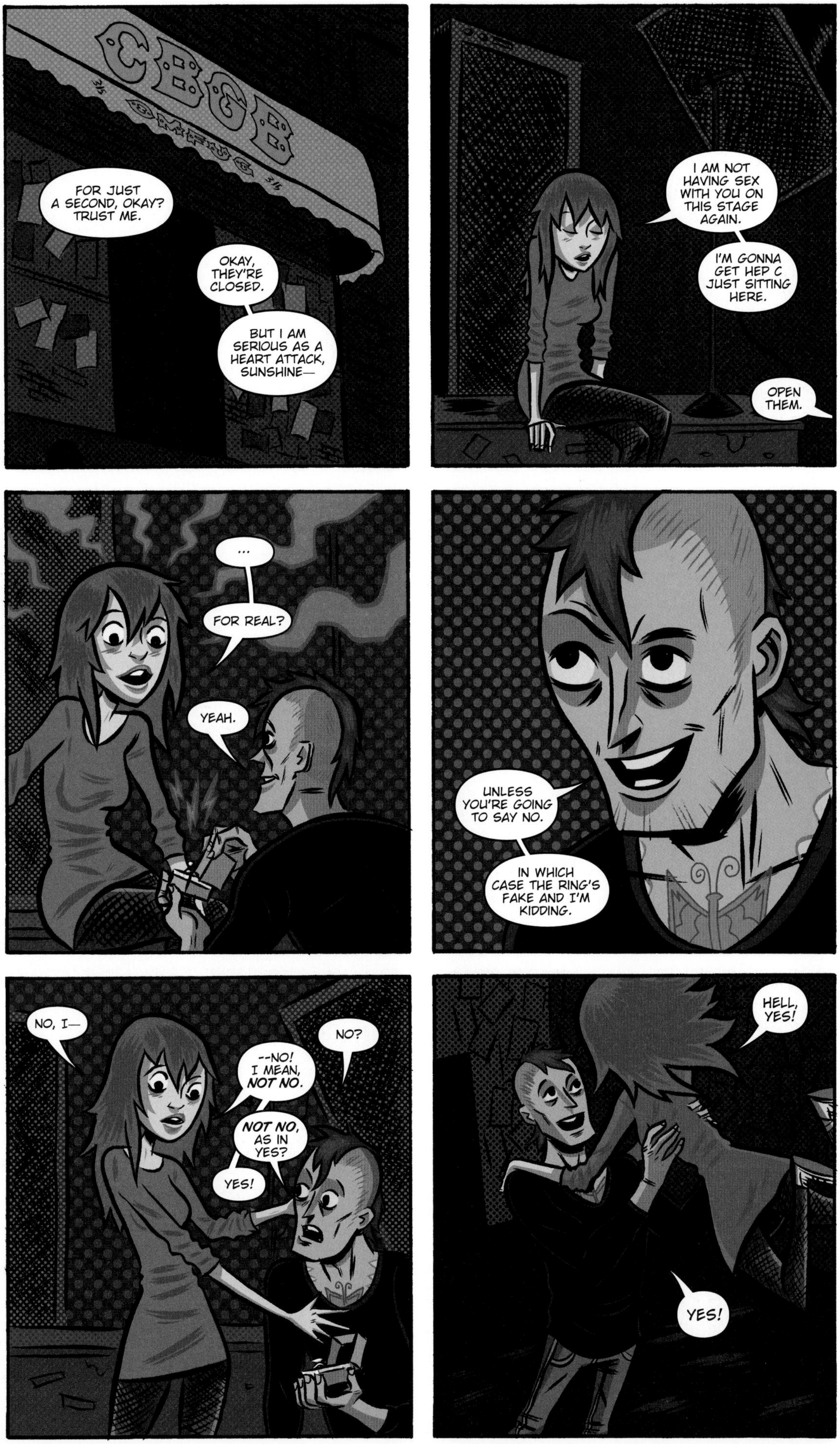
CBGB
FOR JUST A SECOND, OKAY? TRUST ME.
OKAY, THEY'RE CLOSED.
BUT I AM SERIOUS AS A HEART ATTACK, SUNSHINE—
I AM NOT HAVING SEX WITH YOU ON THIS STAGE AGAIN.
I'M GONNA GET HEP C JUST SITTING HERE.
OPEN THEM.
...
FOR REAL?
YEAH.
UNLESS YOU'RE GOING TO SAY NO.
IN WHICH CASE THE RING'S FAKE AND I'M KIDDING.
NO, I—
NO?
--NO! I MEAN, NOT NO.
NOT NO, AS IN YES?
YES!
HELL, YES!
YES!

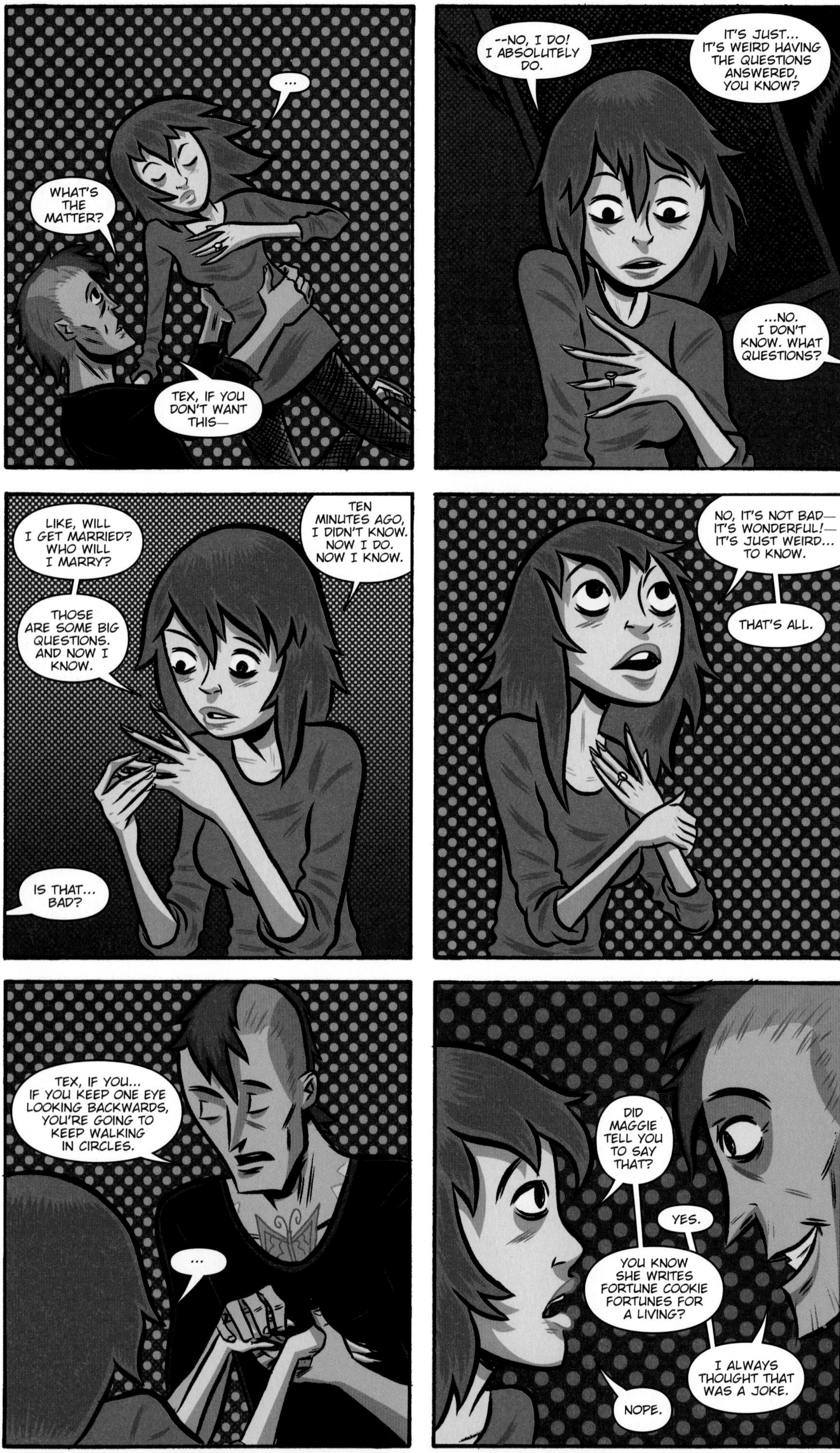
...
WHAT'S THE MATTER?
TEX, IF YOU DON'T WANT THIS—
--NO, I DO! I ABSOLUTELY DO.
IT'S JUST... IT'S WEIRD HAVING THE QUESTIONS ANSWERED, YOU KNOW?
...NO. I DON'T KNOW. WHAT QUESTIONS?
LIKE, WILL I GET MARRIED? WHO WILL I MARRY?
THOSE ARE SOME BIG QUESTIONS. AND NOW I KNOW.
TEN MINUTES AGO, I DIDN'T KNOW. NOW I DO. NOW I KNOW.
IS THAT... BAD?
NO, IT'S NOT BAD— IT'S WONDERFUL!— IT'S JUST WEIRD... TO KNOW.
THAT'S ALL.
TEX, IF YOU... IF YOU KEEP ONE EYE LOOKING BACKWARDS, YOU'RE GOING TO KEEP WALKING IN CIRCLES.
...
DID MAGGIE TELL YOU TO SAY THAT?
YES.
YOU KNOW SHE WRITES FORTUNE COOKIE FORTUNES FOR A LIVING?
I ALWAYS THOUGHT THAT WAS A JOKE.
NOPE.

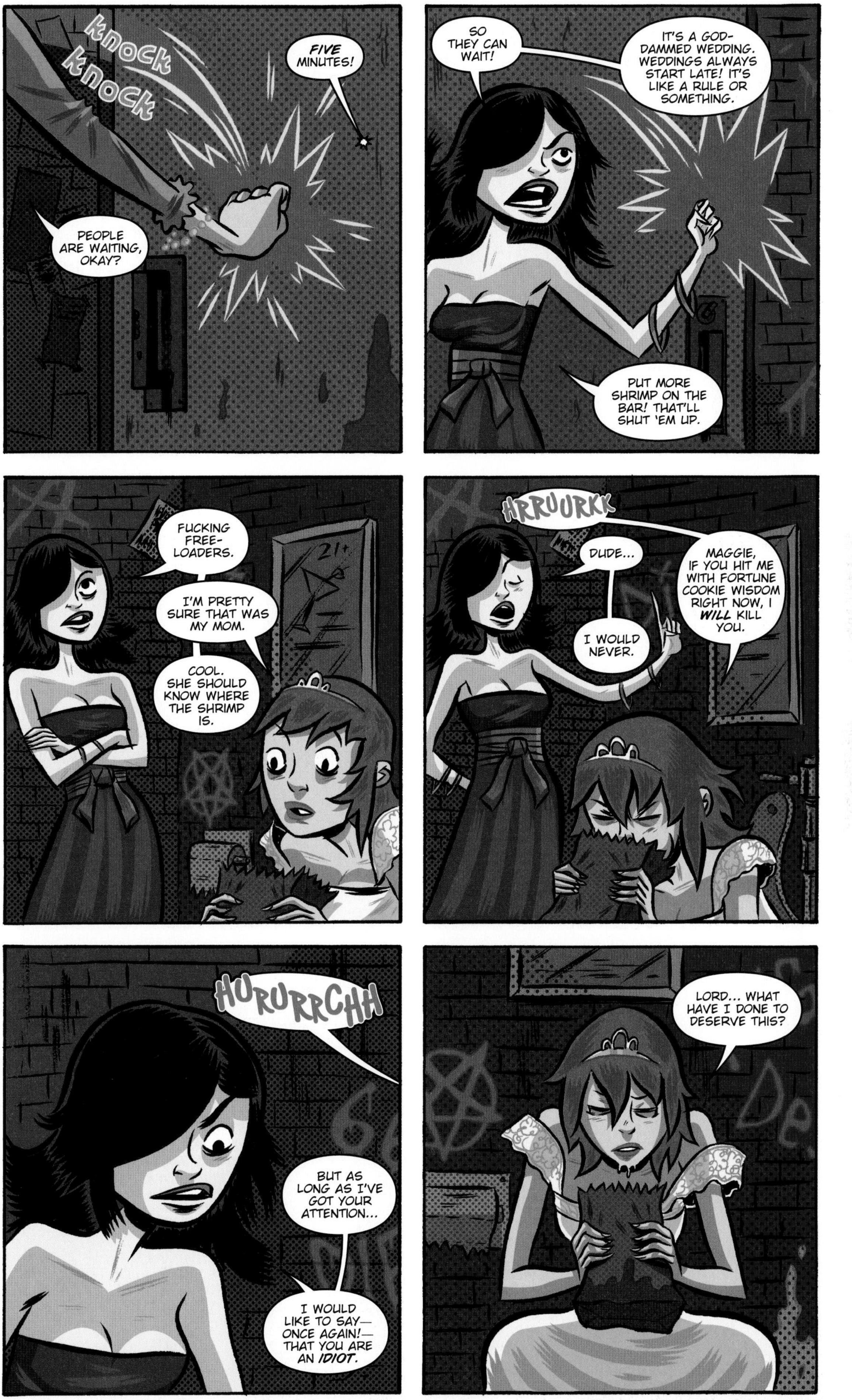
knock knock
FIVE MINUTES!
PEOPLE ARE WAITING, OKAY?
SO THEY CAN WAIT!
IT'S A GOD-DAMMED WEDDING. WEDDINGS ALWAYS START LATE! IT'S LIKE A RULE OR SOMETHING.
PUT MORE SHRIMP ON THE BAR! THAT'LL SHUT 'EM UP.
FUCKING FREE-LOADERS.
I'M PRETTY SURE THAT WAS MY MOM.
COOL. SHE SHOULD KNOW WHERE THE SHRIMP IS.
HRRUURKK
DUDE...
MAGGIE, IF YOU HIT ME WITH FORTUNE COOKIE WISDOM RIGHT NOW, I WILL KILL YOU.
I WOULD NEVER.
HURURRCHH
BUT AS LONG AS I'VE GOT YOUR ATTENTION...
I WOULD LIKE TO SAY—ONCE AGAIN!—THAT YOU ARE AN IDIOT.
LORD... WHAT HAVE I DONE TO DESERVE THIS?

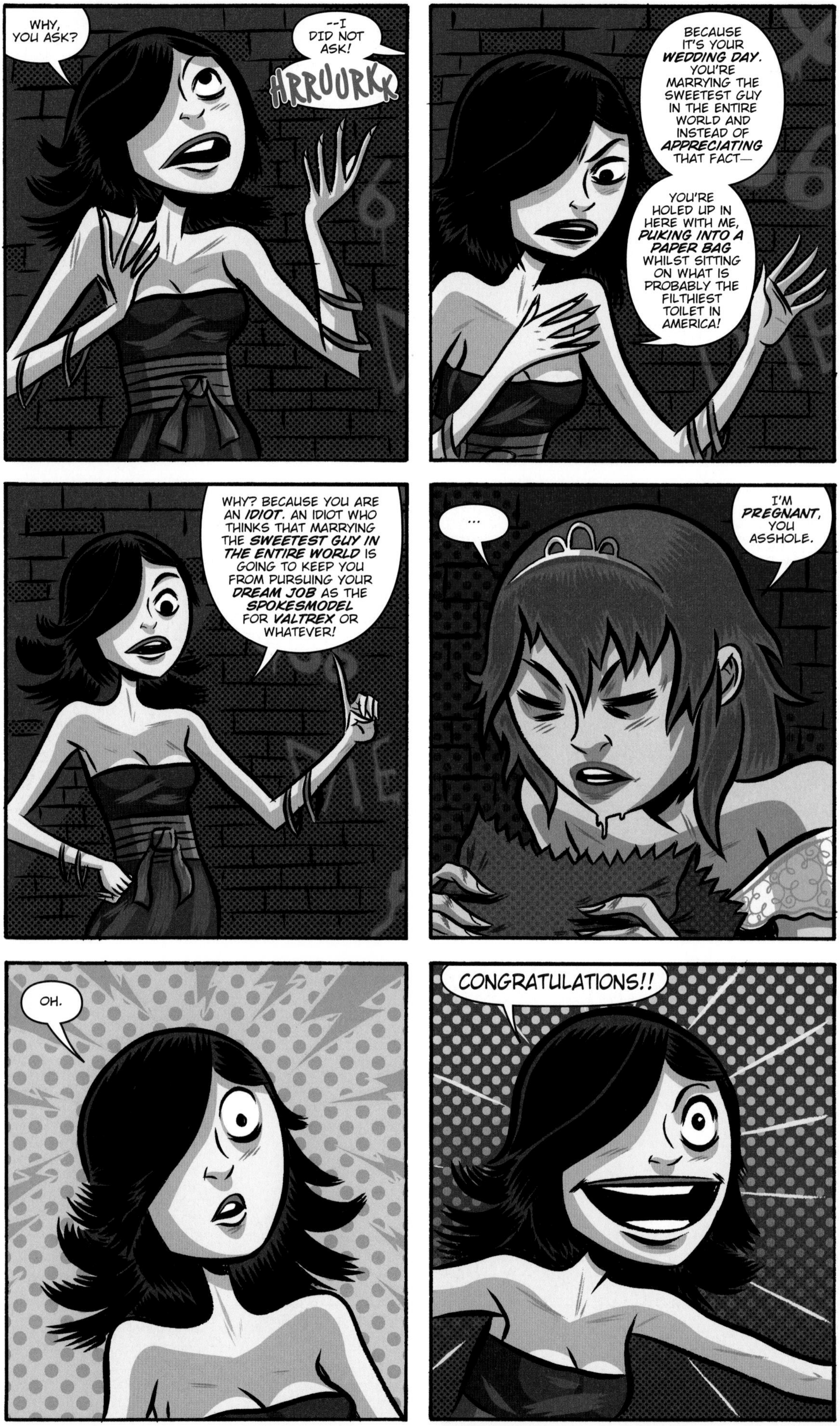
WHY, YOU ASK?
--I DID NOT ASK!
HRRUURKK
BECAUSE IT'S YOUR WEDDING DAY. YOU'RE MARRYING THE SWEETEST GUY IN THE ENTIRE WORLD AND INSTEAD OF APPRECIATING THAT FACT—
YOU'RE HOLED UP IN HERE WITH ME, PUKING INTO A PAPER BAG WHILST SITTING ON WHAT IS PROBABLY THE FILTHIEST TOILET IN AMERICA!
WHY? BECAUSE YOU ARE AN IDIOT. AN IDIOT WHO THINKS THAT MARRYING THE SWEETEST GUY IN THE ENTIRE WORLD IS GOING TO KEEP YOU FROM PURSUING YOUR DREAM JOB AS THE SPOKESMODEL FOR VALTREX OR WHATEVER!
...
I'M PREGNANT, YOU ASSHOLE.
OH.
CONGRATULATIONS!!

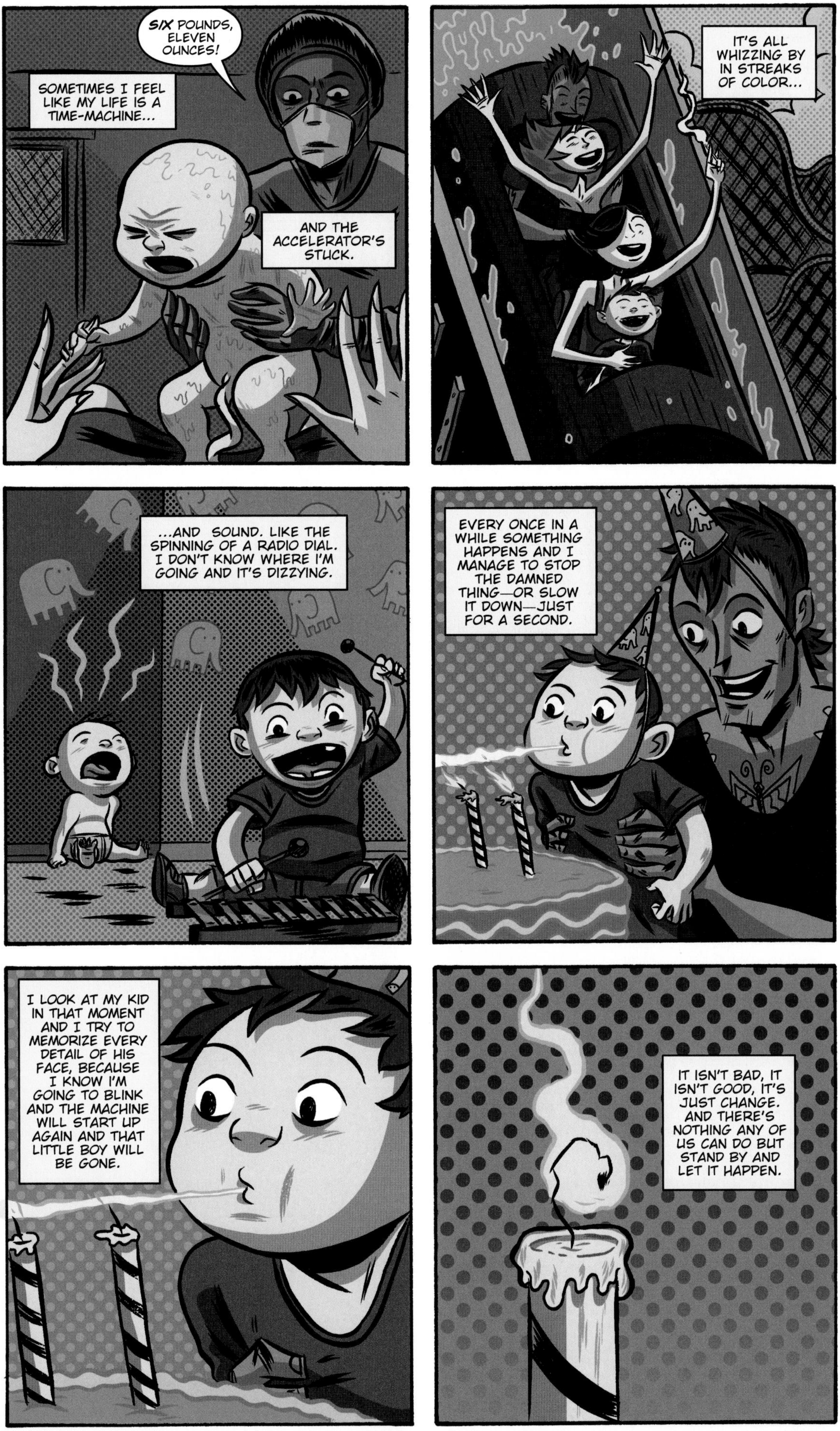
SIX POUNDS, ELEVEN OUNCES!
SOMETIMES I FEEL LIKE MY LIFE IS A TIME-MACHINE...
AND THE ACCELERATOR'S STUCK.
IT'S ALL WHIZZING BY IN STREAKS OF COLOR...
...AND SOUND. LIKE THE SPINNING OF A RADIO DIAL. I DON'T KNOW WHERE I'M GOING AND IT'S DIZZYING.
EVERY ONCE IN A WHILE SOMETHING HAPPENS AND I MANAGE TO STOP THE DAMNED THING—OR SLOW IT DOWN—JUST FOR A SECOND.
I LOOK AT MY KID IN THAT MOMENT AND I TRY TO MEMORIZE EVERY DETAIL OF HIS FACE, BECAUSE I KNOW I'M GOING TO BLINK AND THE MACHINE WILL START UP AGAIN AND THAT LITTLE BOY WILL BE GONE.
IT ISN'T BAD, IT ISN'T GOOD, IT'S JUST CHANGE. AND THERE'S NOTHING ANY OF US CAN DO BUT STAND BY AND LET IT HAPPEN.

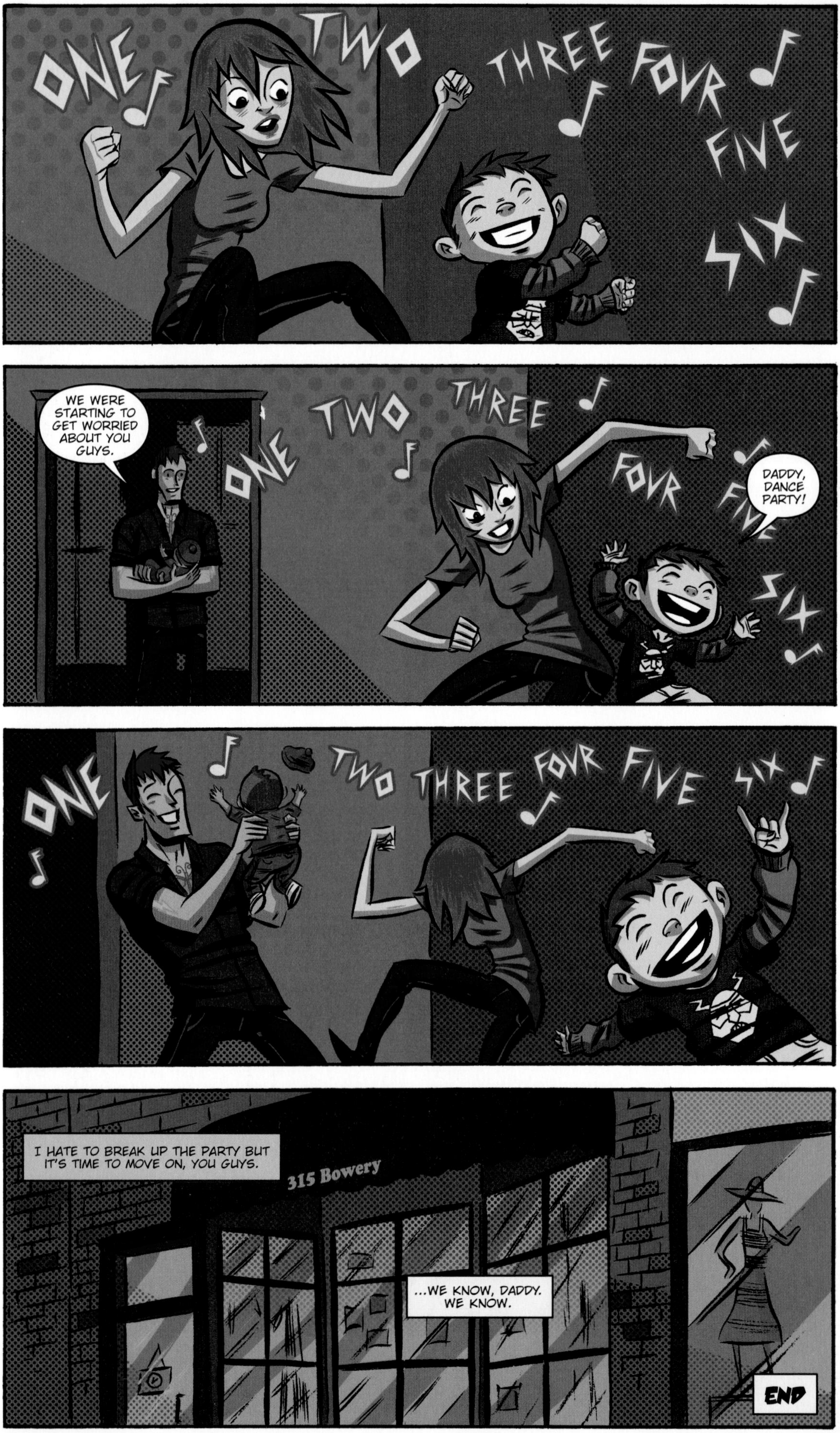
ONE TWO THREE FOUR FIVE SIX
WE WERE STARTING TO GET WORRIED ABOUT YOU GUYS.
ONE TWO THREE FOUR FIVE SIX
DADDY, DANCE PARTY!
ONE TWO THREE FOUR FIVE SIX
I HATE TO BREAK UP THE PARTY BUT IT'S TIME TO MOVE ON, YOU GUYS.
315 Bowery
...WE KNOW, DADDY. WE KNOW.
END

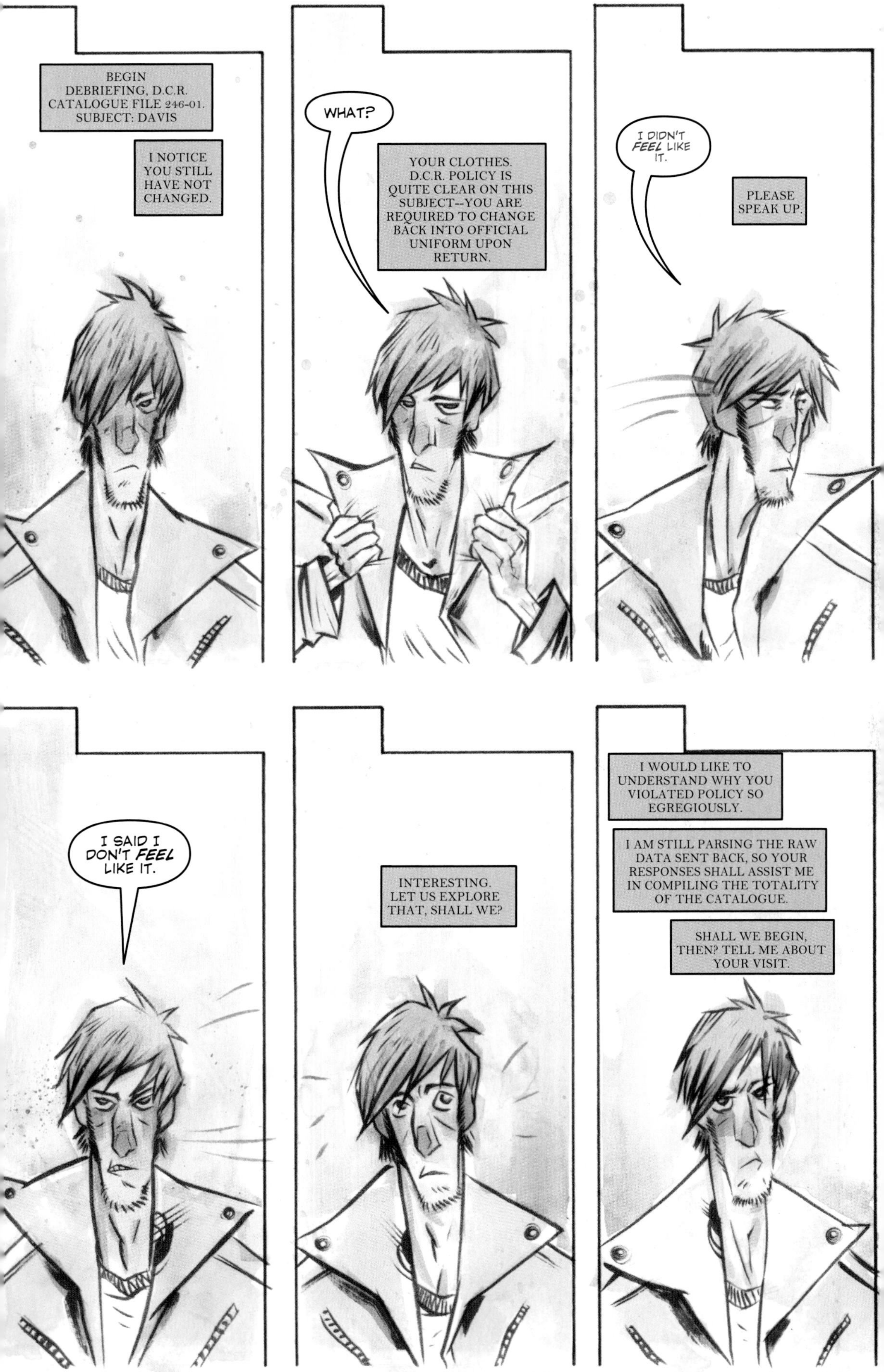
BEGIN DEBRIEFING, D.C.R. CATALOGUE FILE 246-01. SUBJECT: DAVIS
I NOTICE YOU STILL HAVE NOT CHANGED.
WHAT?
YOUR CLOTHES. D.C.R. POLICY IS QUITE CLEAR ON THIS SUBJECT--YOU ARE REQUIRED TO CHANGE BACK INTO OFFICIAL UNIFORM UPON RETURN.
I DIDN'T FEEL LIKE IT.
PLEASE SPEAK UP.
I SAID I DON'T FEEL LIKE IT.
INTERESTING. LET US EXPLORE THAT, SHALL WE?
I WOULD LIKE TO UNDERSTAND WHY YOU VIOLATED POLICY SO EGREGIOUSLY.
I AM STILL PARSING THE RAW DATA SENT BACK, SO YOUR RESPONSES SHALL ASSIST ME IN COMPILING THE TOTALITY OF THE CATALOGUE.
SHALL WE BEGIN, THEN? TELL ME ABOUT YOUR VISIT.

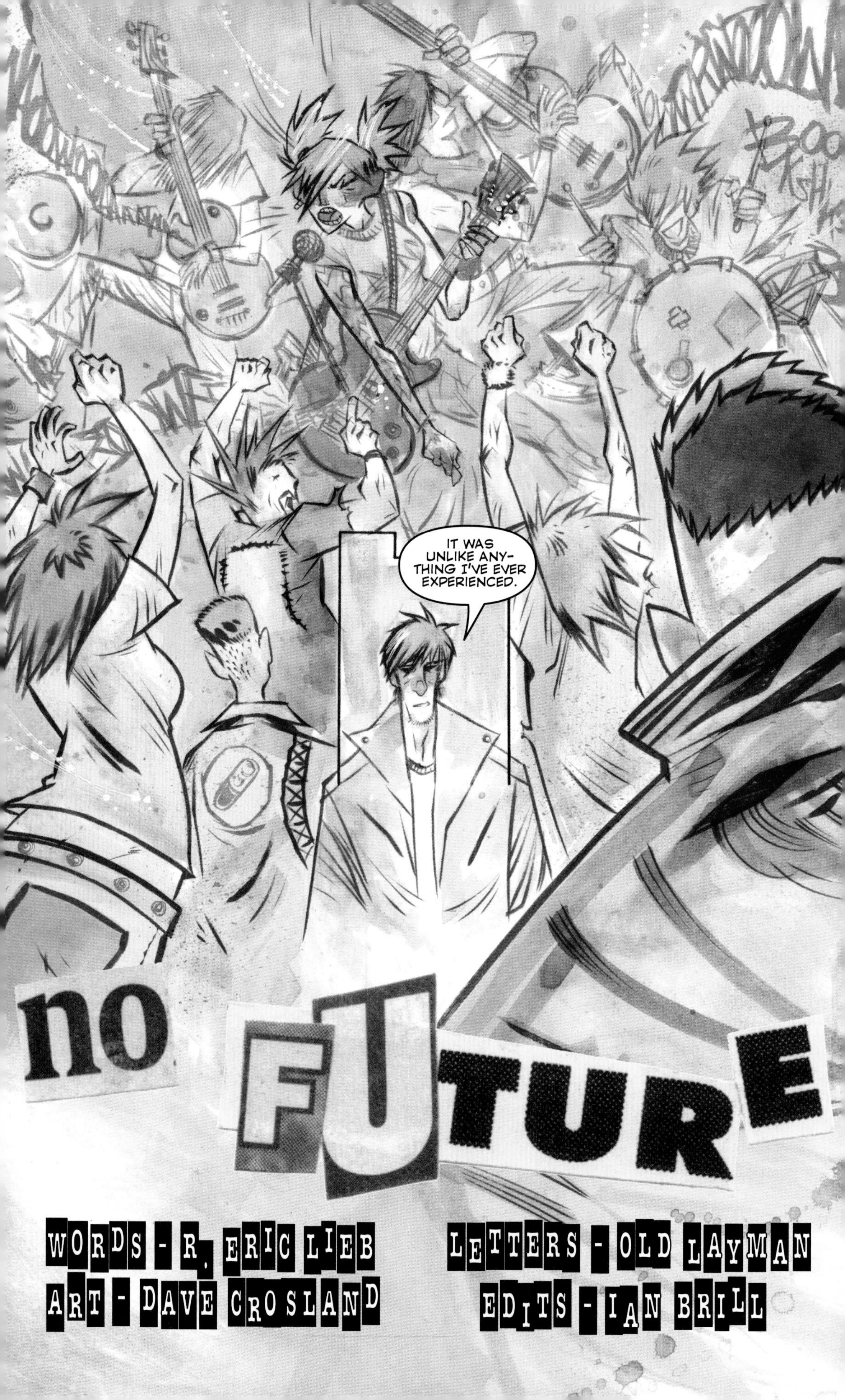
IT WAS UNLIKE ANY-THING I'VE EVER EXPERIENCED.
no FUTURE
WORDS - R. ERIC LIEB
ART - DAVE CROSLAND
LETTERS - OLD LAYMAN
EDITS - IAN BRILL

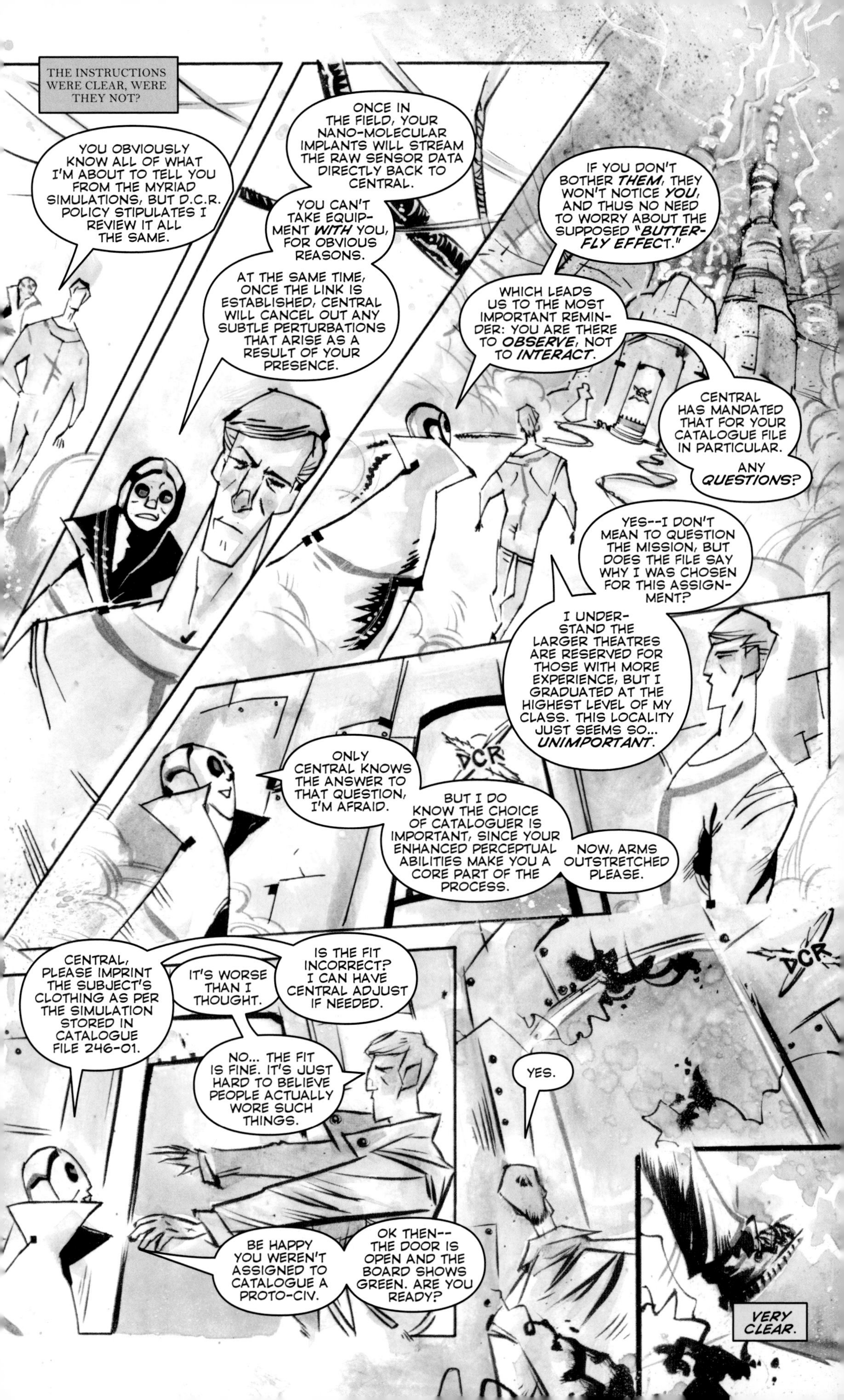
THE INSTRUCTIONS WERE CLEAR, WERE THEY NOT?
YOU OBVIOUSLY KNOW ALL OF WHAT I'M ABOUT TO TELL YOU FROM THE MYRIAD SIMULATIONS, BUT D.C.R. POLICY STIPULATES I REVIEW IT ALL THE SAME.
ONCE IN THE FIELD, YOUR NANO-MOLECULAR IMPLANTS WILL STREAM THE RAW SENSOR DATA DIRECTLY BACK TO CENTRAL.
YOU CAN'T TAKE EQUIPMENT *WITH* YOU, FOR OBVIOUS REASONS.
AT THE SAME TIME, ONCE THE LINK IS ESTABLISHED, CENTRAL WILL CANCEL OUT ANY SUBTLE PERTURBATIONS THAT ARISE AS A RESULT OF YOUR PRESENCE.
IF YOU DON'T BOTHER *THEM*, THEY WON'T NOTICE *YOU*, AND THUS NO NEED TO WORRY ABOUT THE SUPPOSED "*BUTTERFLY EFFECT*."
WHICH LEADS US TO THE MOST IMPORTANT REMINDER: YOU ARE THERE TO *OBSERVE*, NOT TO *INTERACT*.
CENTRAL HAS MANDATED THAT FOR YOUR CATALOGUE FILE IN PARTICULAR.
ANY *QUESTIONS*?
YES--I DON'T MEAN TO QUESTION THE MISSION, BUT DOES THE FILE SAY WHY I WAS CHOSEN FOR THIS ASSIGNMENT?
I UNDERSTAND THE LARGER THEATRES ARE RESERVED FOR THOSE WITH MORE EXPERIENCE, BUT I GRADUATED AT THE HIGHEST LEVEL OF MY CLASS. THIS LOCALITY JUST SEEMS SO... *UNIMPORTANT*.
DCR
ONLY CENTRAL KNOWS THE ANSWER TO THAT QUESTION, I'M AFRAID.
BUT I DO KNOW THE CHOICE OF CATALOGUER IS IMPORTANT, SINCE YOUR ENHANCED PERCEPTUAL ABILITIES MAKE YOU A CORE PART OF THE PROCESS.
NOW, ARMS OUTSTRETCHED PLEASE.
CENTRAL, PLEASE IMPRINT THE SUBJECT'S CLOTHING AS PER THE SIMULATION STORED IN CATALOGUE FILE 246-01.
IT'S WORSE THAN I THOUGHT.
IS THE FIT INCORRECT? I CAN HAVE CENTRAL ADJUST IF NEEDED.
NO... THE FIT IS FINE. IT'S JUST HARD TO BELIEVE PEOPLE ACTUALLY WORE SUCH THINGS.
BE HAPPY YOU WEREN'T ASSIGNED TO CATALOGUE A PROTO-CIV.
OK THEN-- THE DOOR IS OPEN AND THE BOARD SHOWS GREEN. ARE YOU READY?
DCR
YES.
VERY CLEAR.

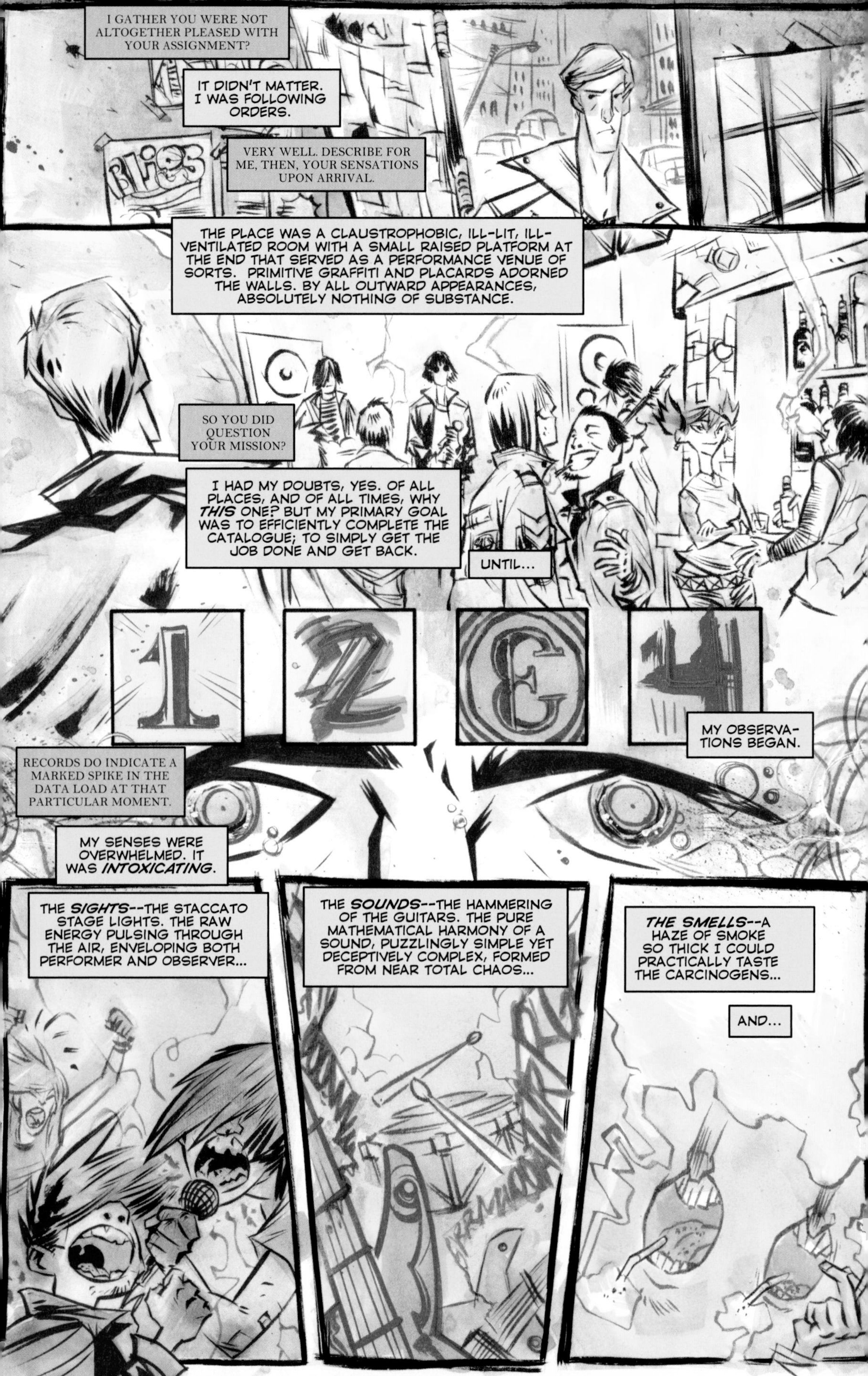
I GATHER YOU WERE NOT ALTOGETHER PLEASED WITH YOUR ASSIGNMENT?
IT DIDN'T MATTER. I WAS FOLLOWING ORDERS.
VERY WELL. DESCRIBE FOR ME, THEN, YOUR SENSATIONS UPON ARRIVAL.
THE PLACE WAS A CLAUSTROPHOBIC, ILL-LIT, ILL-VENTILATED ROOM WITH A SMALL RAISED PLATFORM AT THE END THAT SERVED AS A PERFORMANCE VENUE OF SORTS. PRIMITIVE GRAFFITI AND PLACARDS ADORNED THE WALLS. BY ALL OUTWARD APPEARANCES, ABSOLUTELY NOTHING OF SUBSTANCE.
SO YOU DID QUESTION YOUR MISSION?
I HAD MY DOUBTS, YES. OF ALL PLACES, AND OF ALL TIMES, WHY *THIS* ONE? BUT MY PRIMARY GOAL WAS TO EFFICIENTLY COMPLETE THE CATALOGUE; TO SIMPLY GET THE JOB DONE AND GET BACK.
UNTIL...
1
2
3
4
MY OBSERVATIONS BEGAN.
RECORDS DO INDICATE A MARKED SPIKE IN THE DATA LOAD AT THAT PARTICULAR MOMENT.
MY SENSES WERE OVERWHELMED. IT WAS *INTOXICATING*.
THE *SIGHTS*--THE STACCATO STAGE LIGHTS. THE RAW ENERGY PULSING THROUGH THE AIR, ENVELOPING BOTH PERFORMER AND OBSERVER...
THE *SOUNDS*--THE HAMMERING OF THE GUITARS. THE PURE MATHEMATICAL HARMONY OF A SOUND, PUZZLINGLY SIMPLE YET DECEPTIVELY COMPLEX, FORMED FROM NEAR TOTAL CHAOS...
THE SMELLS--A HAZE OF SMOKE SO THICK I COULD PRACTICALLY TASTE THE CARCINOGENS...
AND...

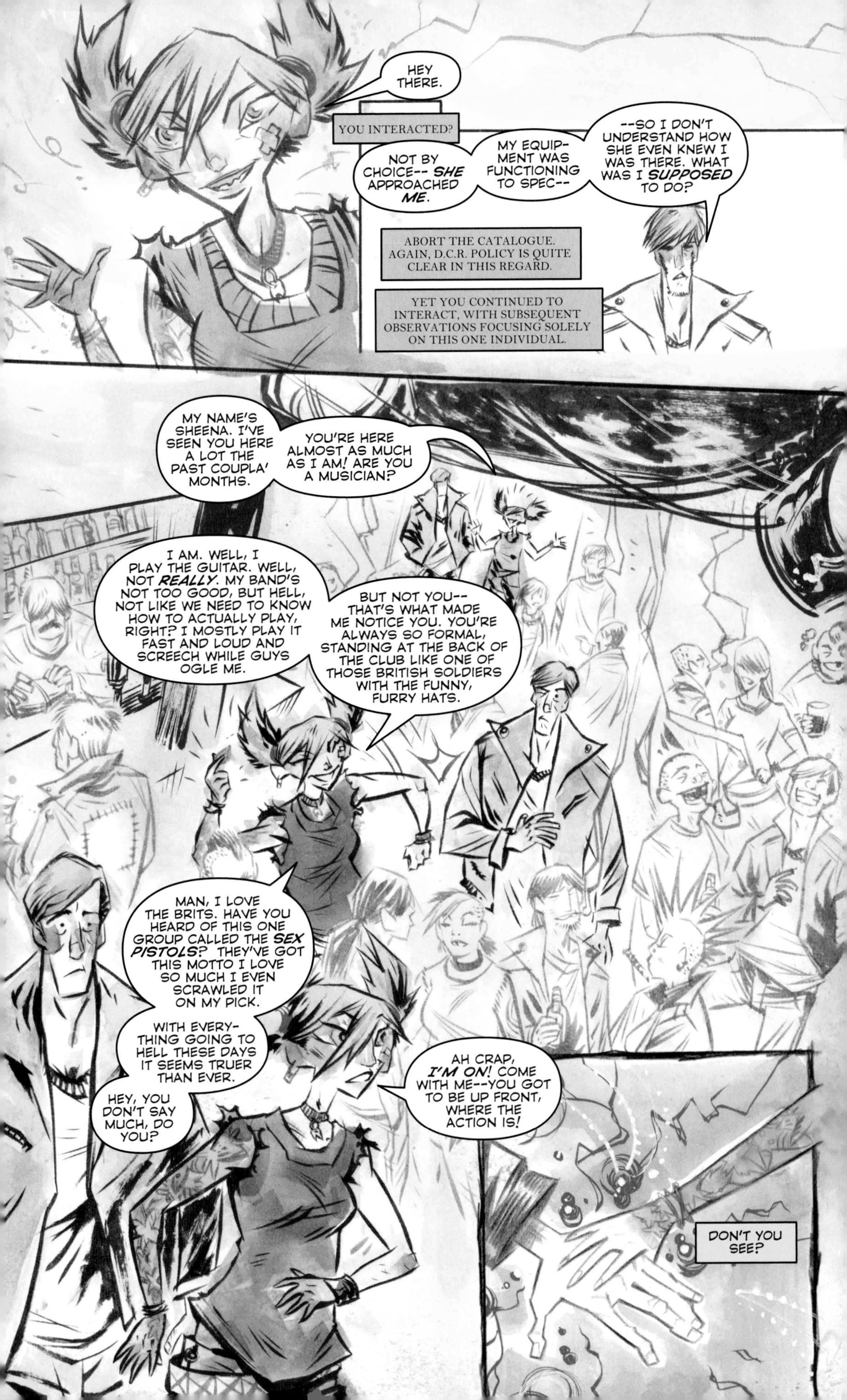
HEY THERE.
YOU INTERACTED?
NOT BY CHOICE-- SHE APPROACHED ME.
MY EQUIPMENT WAS FUNCTIONING TO SPEC--
--SO I DON'T UNDERSTAND HOW SHE EVEN KNEW I WAS THERE. WHAT WAS I SUPPOSED TO DO?
ABORT THE CATALOGUE. AGAIN, D.C.R. POLICY IS QUITE CLEAR IN THIS REGARD.
YET YOU CONTINUED TO INTERACT, WITH SUBSEQUENT OBSERVATIONS FOCUSING SOLELY ON THIS ONE INDIVIDUAL.
MY NAME'S SHEENA. I'VE SEEN YOU HERE A LOT THE PAST COUPLA' MONTHS.
YOU'RE HERE ALMOST AS MUCH AS I AM! ARE YOU A MUSICIAN?
I AM. WELL, I PLAY THE GUITAR. WELL, NOT REALLY. MY BAND'S NOT TOO GOOD, BUT HELL, NOT LIKE WE NEED TO KNOW HOW TO ACTUALLY PLAY, RIGHT? I MOSTLY PLAY IT FAST AND LOUD AND SCREECH WHILE GUYS OGLE ME.
BUT NOT YOU-- THAT'S WHAT MADE ME NOTICE YOU. YOU'RE ALWAYS SO FORMAL, STANDING AT THE BACK OF THE CLUB LIKE ONE OF THOSE BRITISH SOLDIERS WITH THE FUNNY, FURRY HATS.
MAN, I LOVE THE BRITS. HAVE YOU HEARD OF THIS ONE GROUP CALLED THE SEX PISTOLS? THEY'VE GOT THIS MOTTO I LOVE SO MUCH I EVEN SCRAWLED IT ON MY PICK.
WITH EVERYTHING GOING TO HELL THESE DAYS IT SEEMS TRUER THAN EVER.
HEY, YOU DON'T SAY MUCH, DO YOU?
AH CRAP, I'M ON! COME WITH ME--YOU GOT TO BE UP FRONT, WHERE THE ACTION IS!
DON'T YOU SEE?

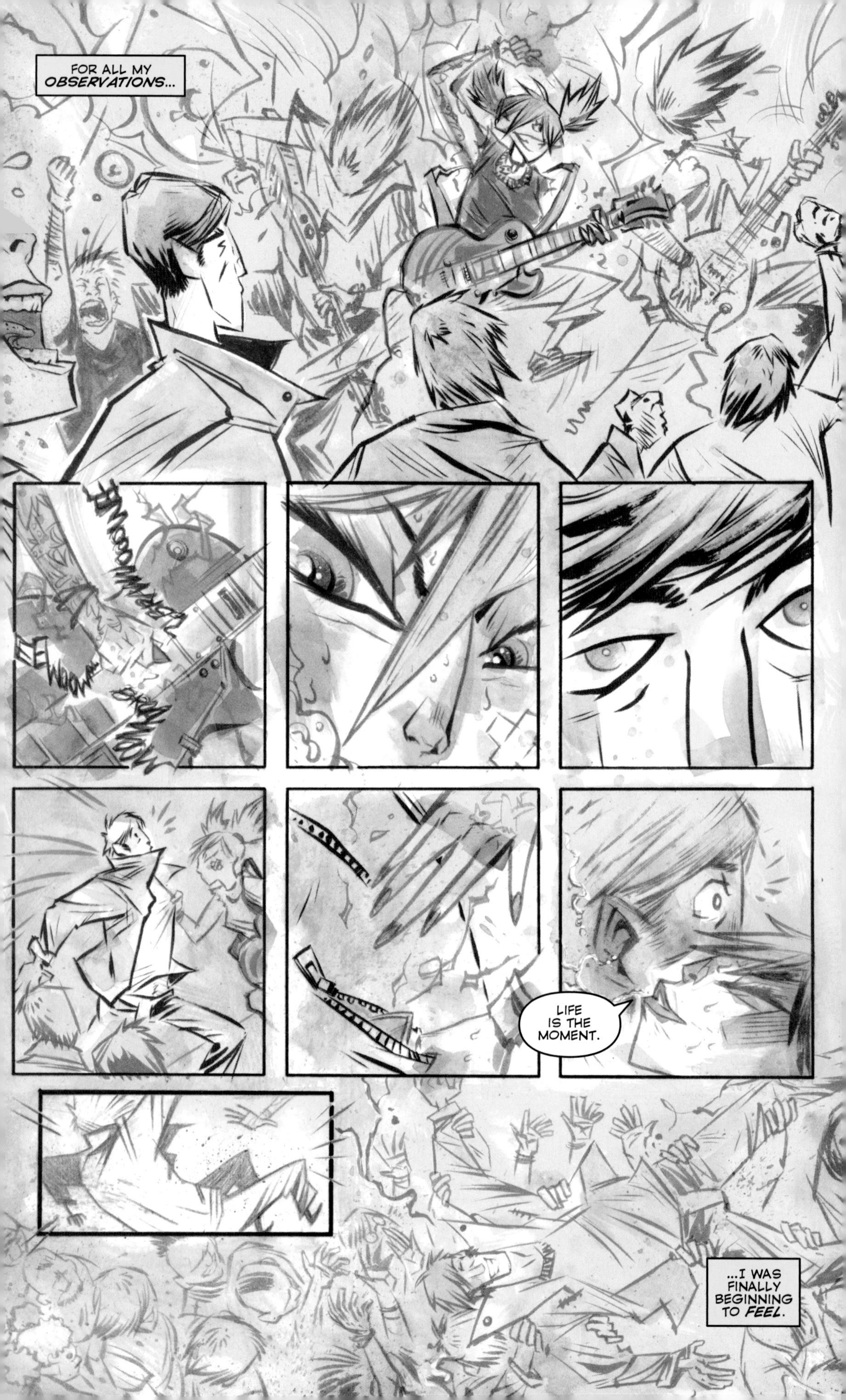
FOR ALL MY *OBSERVATIONS*...
LIFE IS THE MOMENT.
...I WAS FINALLY BEGINNING TO *FEEL*.

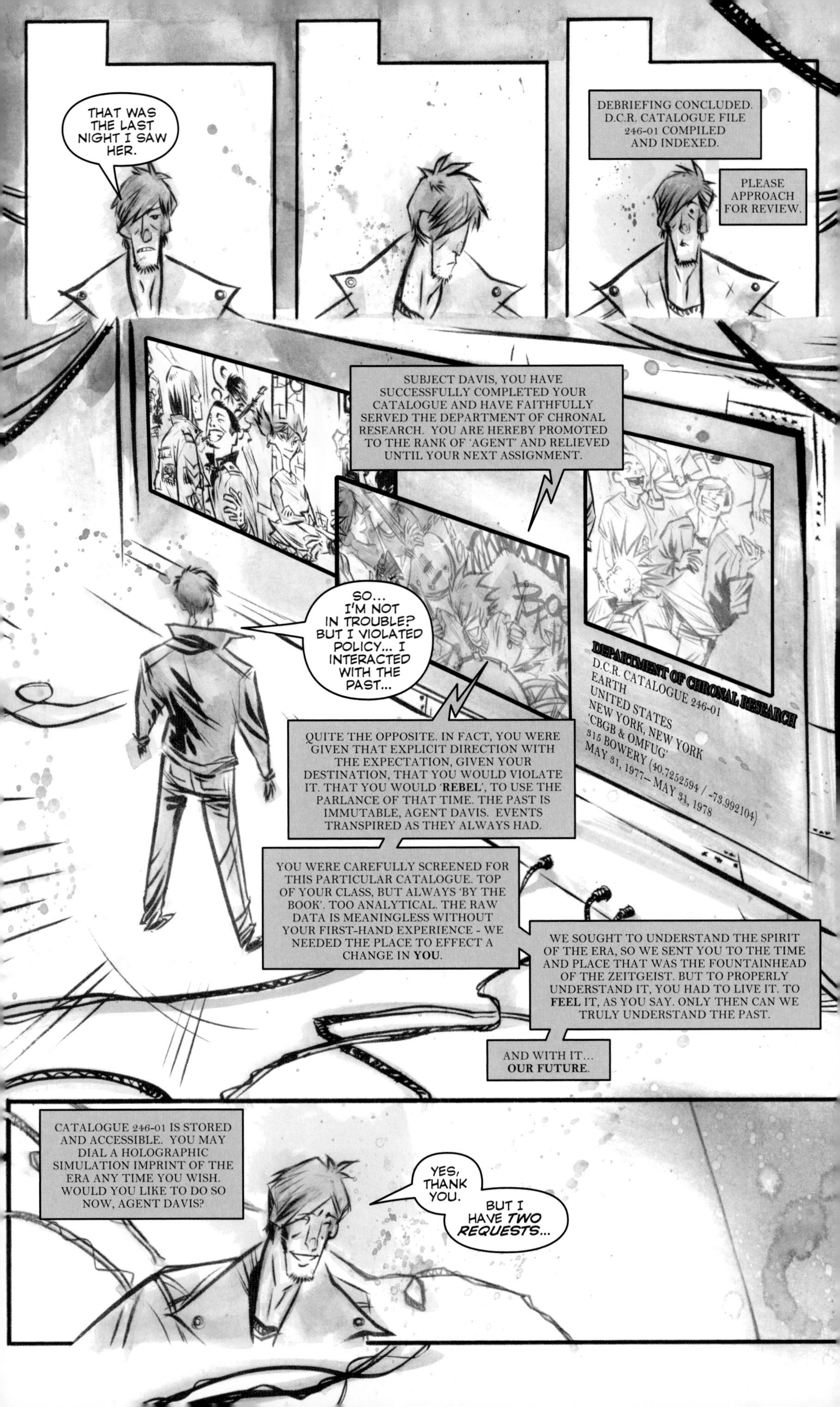
THAT WAS THE LAST NIGHT I SAW HER.
DEBRIEFING CONCLUDED. D.C.R. CATALOGUE FILE 246-01 COMPILED AND INDEXED.
PLEASE APPROACH FOR REVIEW.
SUBJECT DAVIS, YOU HAVE SUCCESSFULLY COMPLETED YOUR CATALOGUE AND HAVE FAITHFULLY SERVED THE DEPARTMENT OF CHRONAL RESEARCH. YOU ARE HEREBY PROMOTED TO THE RANK OF 'AGENT' AND RELIEVED UNTIL YOUR NEXT ASSIGNMENT.
SO... I'M NOT IN TROUBLE? BUT I VIOLATED POLICY... I INTERACTED WITH THE PAST...
DEPARTMENT OF CHRONAL RESEARCH
D.C.R. CATALOGUE 246-01
EARTH
UNITED STATES
NEW YORK, NEW YORK
'CBGB & OMFUG'
315 BOWERY (40.7252594 / -73.992104)
MAY 31, 1977– MAY 31, 1978
QUITE THE OPPOSITE. IN FACT, YOU WERE GIVEN THAT EXPLICIT DIRECTION WITH THE EXPECTATION, GIVEN YOUR DESTINATION, THAT YOU WOULD VIOLATE IT. THAT YOU WOULD '**REBEL**', TO USE THE PARLANCE OF THAT TIME. THE PAST IS IMMUTABLE, AGENT DAVIS. EVENTS TRANSPIRED AS THEY ALWAYS HAD.
YOU WERE CAREFULLY SCREENED FOR THIS PARTICULAR CATALOGUE. TOP OF YOUR CLASS, BUT ALWAYS 'BY THE BOOK'. TOO ANALYTICAL. THE RAW DATA IS MEANINGLESS WITHOUT YOUR FIRST-HAND EXPERIENCE - WE NEEDED THE PLACE TO EFFECT A CHANGE IN **YOU**.
WE SOUGHT TO UNDERSTAND THE SPIRIT OF THE ERA, SO WE SENT YOU TO THE TIME AND PLACE THAT WAS THE FOUNTAINHEAD OF THE ZEITGEIST. BUT TO PROPERLY UNDERSTAND IT, YOU HAD TO LIVE IT. TO **FEEL** IT, AS YOU SAY. ONLY THEN CAN WE TRULY UNDERSTAND THE PAST.
AND WITH IT... **OUR FUTURE**.
CATALOGUE 246-01 IS STORED AND ACCESSIBLE. YOU MAY DIAL A HOLOGRAPHIC SIMULATION IMPRINT OF THE ERA ANY TIME YOU WISH. WOULD YOU LIKE TO DO SO NOW, AGENT DAVIS?
YES, THANK YOU.
BUT I HAVE ***TWO REQUESTS***...

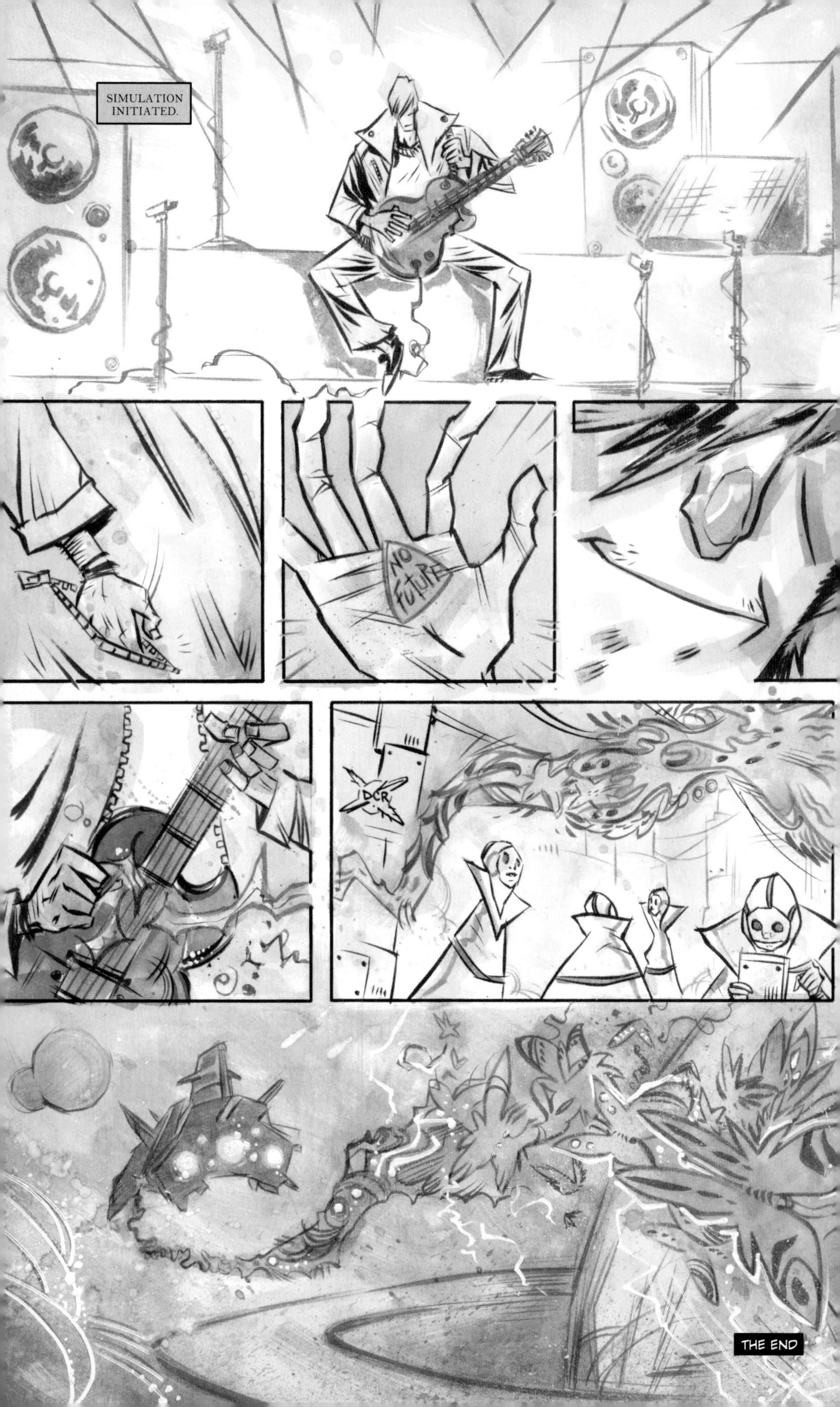
SIMULATION INITIATED.
NO FUTURE
DCR
THE END

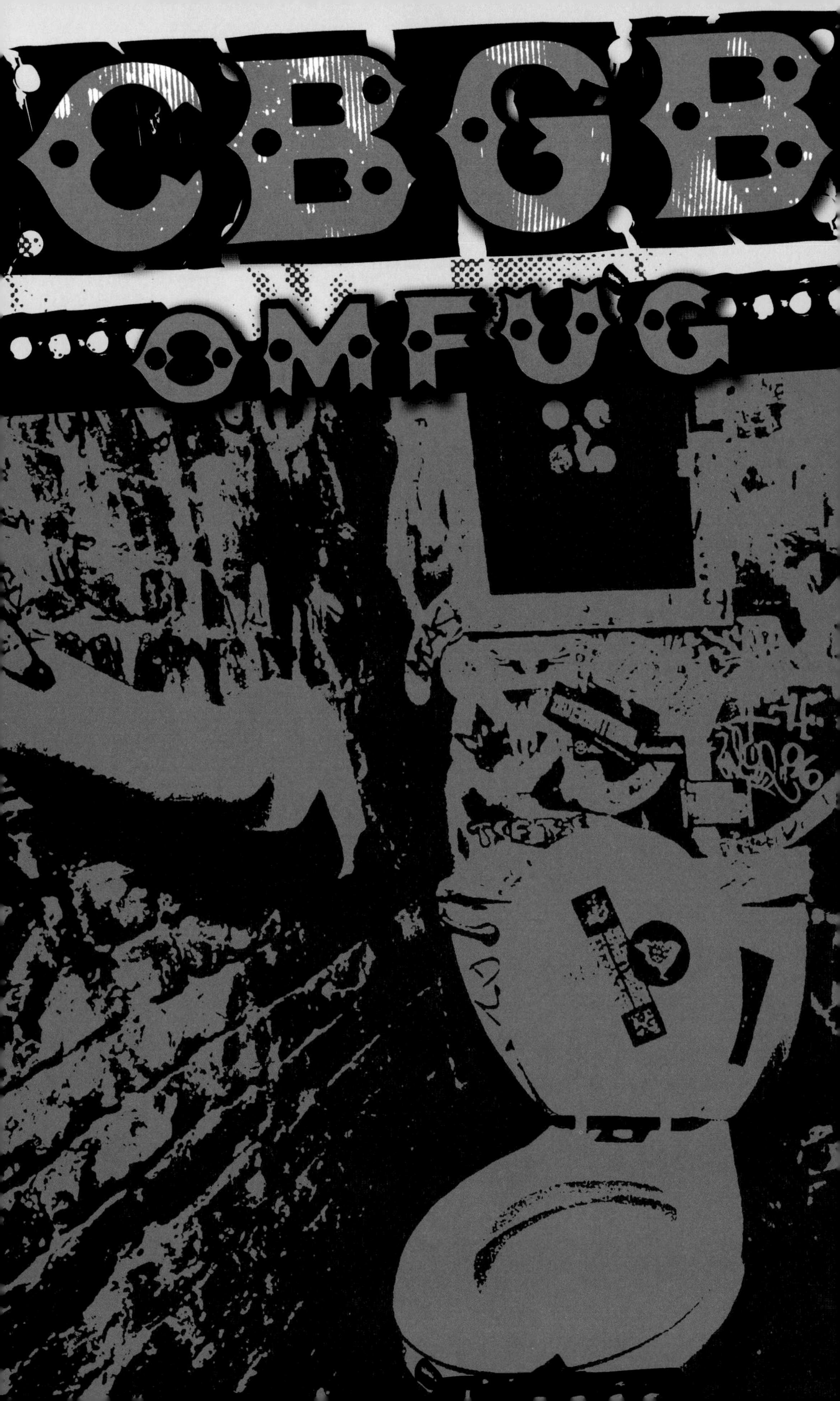
CBGB
OMFUG

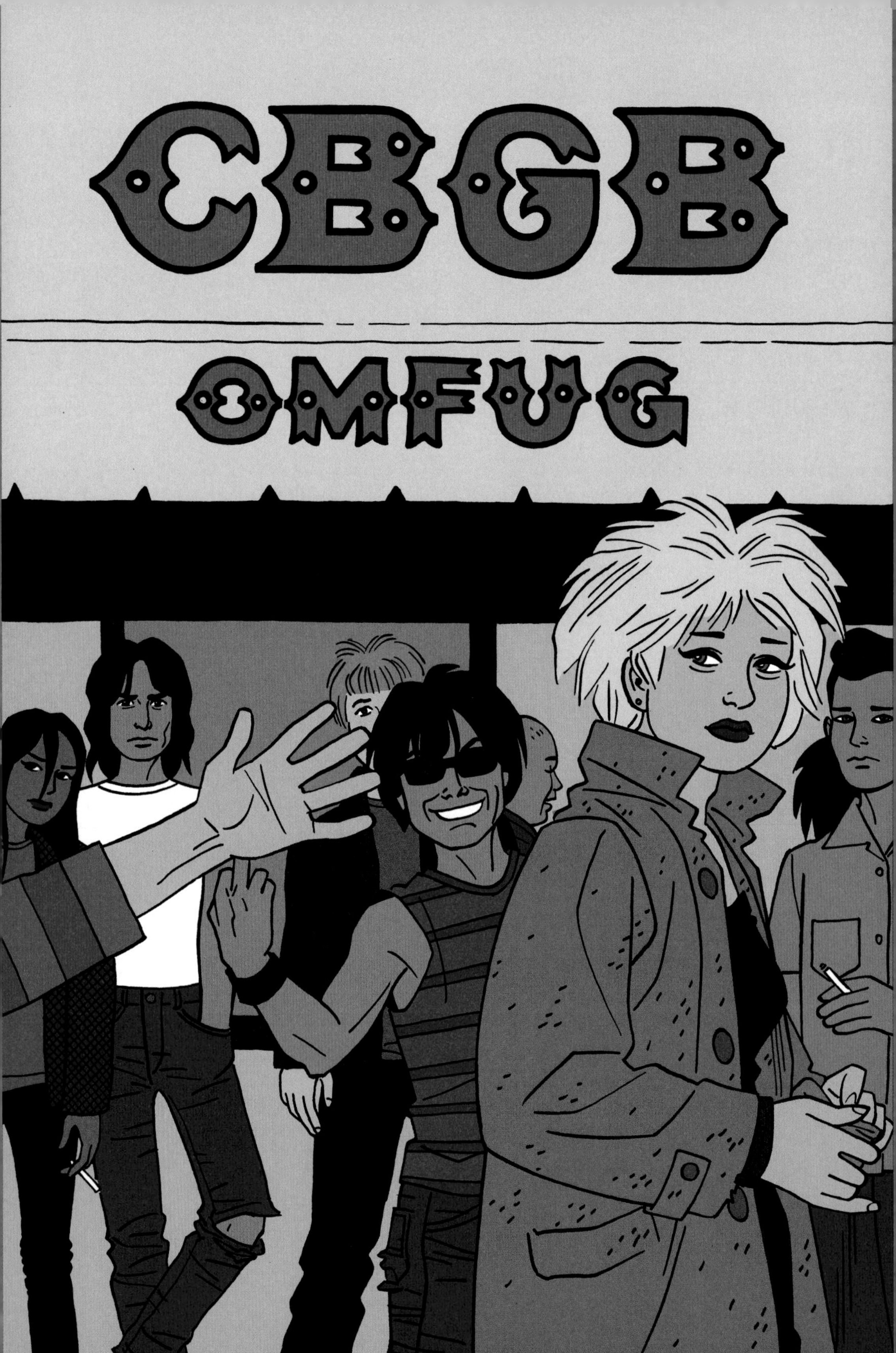
CBGB
OMFUG

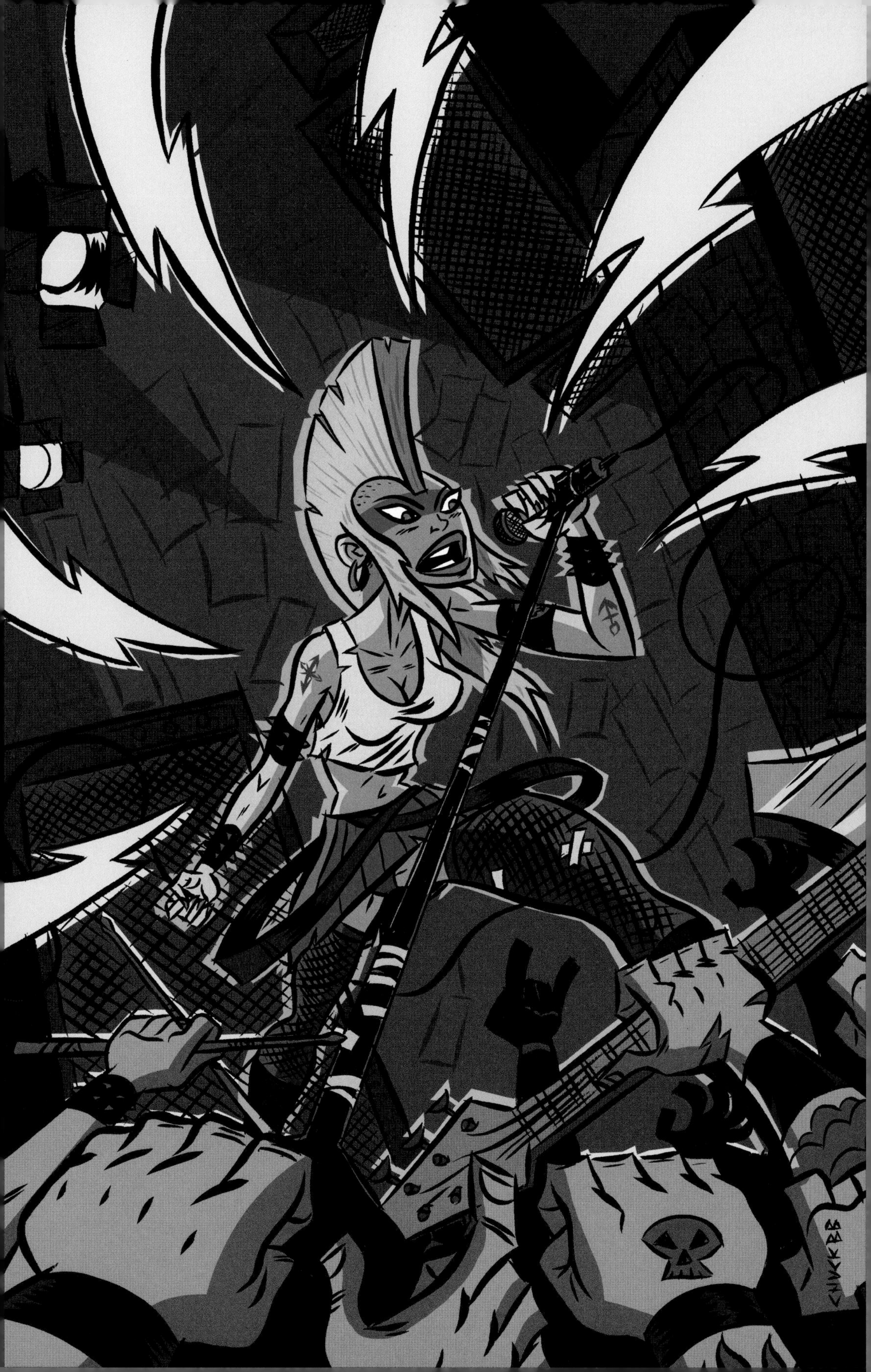

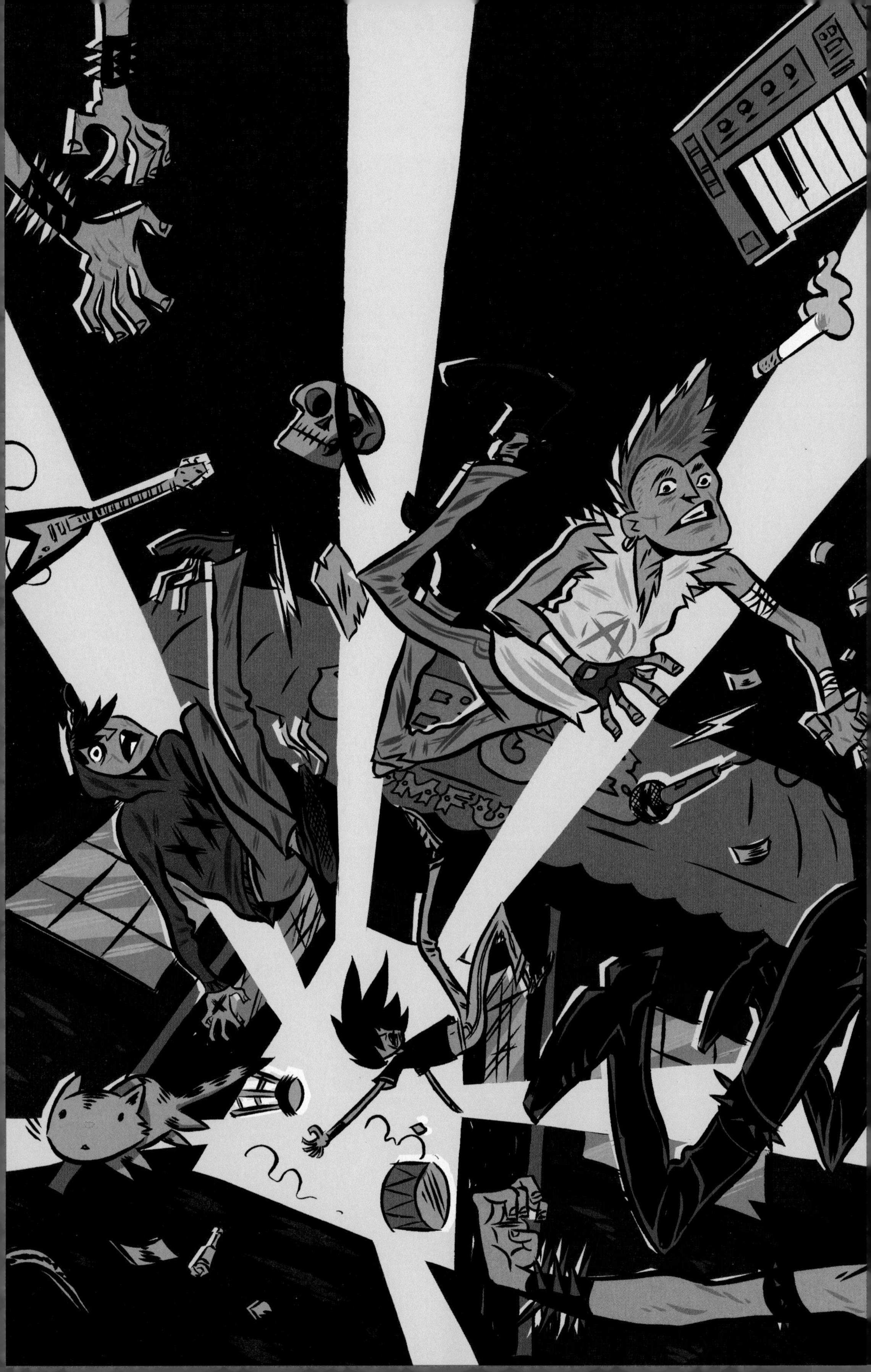

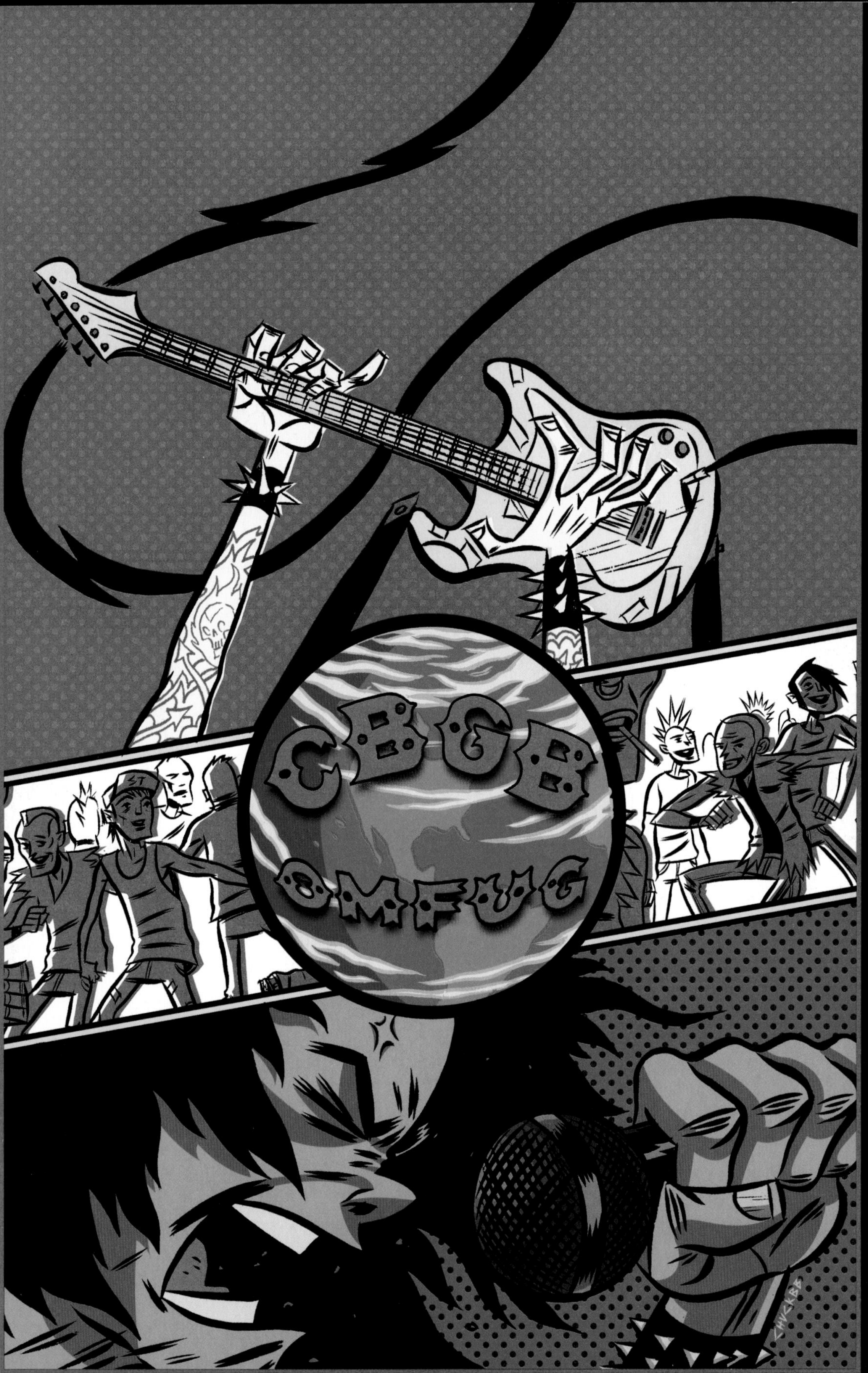
CBGB
OMFUG

CHUCK BB

PRACTICES THE LOW-BROW ART OF ILLUSTRATION AND COMICS. HE RECEIVED AN EISNER AWARD FOR HIS WORK ON THE GRAPHIC NOVEL BLACK METAL, AND IS CURRENTLY WORKING ON A SEQUEL. MOST OF HIS TIME IS SPENT AT SOME LOCATION IN AND AROUND LOS ANGELES, MOST LIKELY SLEEPING OR LISTENING TO DARKTHRONE ALBUMS ON VINYL... BECAUSE HE'S A JERK THAT WAY.

DAVE CROSLAND

IS AN AMERICAN ILLUSTRATOR WHOSE ART HAS BEEN UTILIZED IN A VARIETY OF FORMS, FROM COMICS AND APPAREL DESIGNS, TO VIDEO GAMES AND SNOWBOARD GRAPHICS. HE'S CREATED SEQUENTIAL ART FOR SEVERAL PUBLISHERS, INCLUDING BOOM! STUDIOS, ONI PRESS, IDW PUBLISHING, IMAGE COMICS, AND EC PUBLICATIONS/ DC. TO LEARN MORE ABOUT CROSLAND'S PAST WORKS, AS WELL AS HIS CURRENT & UPCOMING PROJECTS, VISIT WWW.HIREDMEAT.COM.

TOBY CYPRESS

GREW UP IN NEW JERSEY RAISING HIMSELF ON MONSTER MOVIES, PUNK MUSIC, AND SCI-FI IMAGINATIONS. GRADUATED FROM THE JOE KUBERT SCHOOL IN 1997, AND STARTED PROFESSIONALLY FREELANCING FOR MARVEL, DC, AND DARK HORSE COMICS BEFORE STARTING HIS CREATOR OWNED PUBLISHING STUDIO PUNKROCK*JAZZ PRODUCTIONS. T.CYPRESS CURRENTLY PUBLISHES RODD RACER, WHILE DEVELOPING KURSK AS AN ONLINE COMIC. HIS LATEST WORK HATESTREET IS SCHEDULED FOR RELEASE IN 2012. WWW.TOBYCYPRESS.BLOGSPOT.COM FOR MORE INFO.

JAMES DASHIELL

WAS BORN AND RAISED IN NORTH CAROLINA. CURRENTLY HE LIVES IN THE WILLAMETTE VALLEY IN OREGON WITH HIS FAMILY. HE LOVES BASEBALL, MUSIC, AND GOOD BOOKS. OTHER BOOM! COMICS TITLES HE HAS WORKED ON INCLUDE POE AND DINGO.

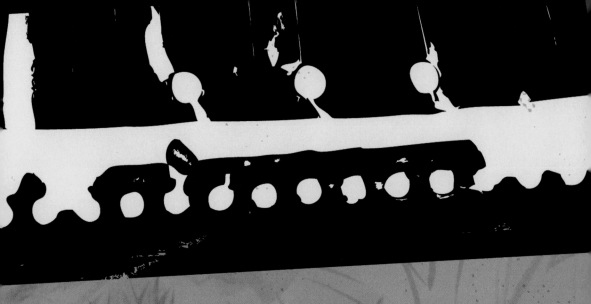

KELLY SUE DECONNICK

HAS WRITTEN COMICS FOR MARVEL (RESCUE, SIF, ENTER THE HEROIC AGE), IDW (30 DAYS OF NIGHT: EBEN AND STELLA, WITH STEVE NILES), AND IMAGE (THE EISNER AND HARVEY AWARD—WINNING ANTHOLOGY COMIC BOOK TATTOO, 24SEVEN), AS WELL AS THE ENGLISH ADAPTATIONS OF OVER 100 JAPANESE GRAPHIC NOVELS FOR BOTH VIZ AND TOKYOPOP (INCLUDING THE COMPLETE KARE FIRST LOVE, BLACK CAT, FRUIST BASKET, BLUE SPRING AND SLAM DUNK). SHE LEFT NYC IN 1992 AND NOW RESIDES IN PORTLAND, OR WITH HER HUSBAND AND TWO CHILDREN.

DAN DUNCAN

IS A FREELANCE COMIC BOOK ARTIST AND ILLUSTRATOR. HE IS A GRADUATE OF THE JOE KUBERT SCHOOL OF CARTOON AND GRAPHIC ART IN DOVER, NJ. DUE TO A ZERO TOLERANCE POLICY ON SNOW, DAN NOW LIVES AND WORKS IN CALIFORNIA, WHERE THE WARM WEATHER ALLOWS HIM TO WORK WITHOUT BEING HINDERED BY STIFF LITTLE FINGERS AND A HEAVY COAT. YOU CAN SEE MORE OF HIS WORK AT WWW.DANIELDUNCAN. NET AND HTTP://DAN-DUNCAN.DEVIANTART.COM/

MARC ELLERBY

HIS PREVIOUS ILLUSTRATION CREDITS INCLUDE LOVE THE WAY YOU LOVE FROM ONI PRESS, PHONOGRAM: THE SINGLES CLUB, AND THIS IS A SOUVENIR BOTH FROM IMAGE COMICS. HE IS THE CREATOR OF THE WEBCOMIC ELLERBISMS AND THE EAGLE AWARD NOMINATED CHLOE NOONAN SERIES. HE LIVES IN ESSEX, ENGLAND WITH HIS GIRLFRIEND ANNA.

RENATO FACCINI

WAS BORN IN RIO DE JANEIRO AND HAS A DEGREE IN DESIGN. HAS BEEN LIVING AT THE BEAUTIFUL AND COLD TOWN OF CURITIBA FOR THE PAST 3 YEARS, ILLUSTRATING FOR AGENCIES, PUBLISHERS AND BANDS IN BRAZIL, USA, UK, CHINA AND ANY OTHER PLACES HE IS NEEDED. YOU CAN SEE MORE FROM HIM AT FLICKR.COM/ ESTABELECIMENTO AND ESTABELECIMENTO.COM.BR.

ROB G

ROB G GREW UP IN COASTAL VIRGINIA WHERE HE WENT TO VIRGINIA COMMONWEALTH UNIVERSITY. AFTERWARDS HE MOVED TO NEW YORK CITY AND CO-PUBLISHED HIS FIRST COMIC BOOK TEENAGERS FROM MARS. SINCE THEN HE HAS WORKED ON MANY OTHER COMIC BOOKS AND GRAPHIC NOVELS SUCH AS DETECTIVE COMICS, THE COURIERS, AND REPO. HE ALSO HAS DONE EXTENSIVE STORYBOARD AND ILLUSTRATION WORK FOR NUMEROUS VIDEOGAMES, FILMS, MAGAZINES, AND BOOKS. HE CURRENTLY LIVES IN PORTLAND WITH HIS WIFE AND BUNNY.

KIERON GILLEN

IS BEST KNOWN FOR THE CRITICALLY ACCLAIMED IMAGE URBAN-FANTASY/MUSIC-CRITICISM COMIC PHONOGRAM. WHEN NOT LOVINGLY CARESSING VINYL HE WRITES COMICS INVOLVING ACTUAL PLOTS WHICH SELL COPIES FOR COMPANIES LIKE MARVEL, AVATAR AND BOOM. THESE INCLUDE TITLES LIKE THOR, GENERATION HOPE, THE HEAT AND LOTS MORE. ENTER HIS NAME INTO GOOGLE. IT'LL SAVE INK.

JAIME HERNANDEZ

IS ONE OF THE MOST CELEBRATED AND VITAL CARTOONISTS ALIVE. ORIGINALLY HAILING FROM OXNARD, CALIFORNIA HE CHANGED COMICS FOREVER WHEN HE STARTED LOVE & ROCKETS WITH HIS BROTHERS GILBERT AND MARIO. THE SERIES CONTINUES TO THIS DAY. HIS COMICS AND ILLUSTRATION WORK HAVE BEEN FEATURED IN NUMEROUS PUBLICATIONS, INCLUDING THE NEW YORK TIMES AND THE NEW YORKER.

SAM HUMPHRIES

LIVES IN LOS ANGELES AND IS A WRITER OF COMIC BOOKS LIKE FRAGGLE ROCK AND CBGB. HE IS ALSO A PHOTOGRAPHER OF LADIES AND HOUSEPLANTS. IN A PREVIOUS LIFE HE WAS THE ARCHITECT OF MYSPACE COMIC BOOKS. YOU CAN FIND HIM ONLINE AT SAMHUMPHRIES.COM.

KIM KRIZAN

IS THE ACADEMY AWARD®—NOMINATED SCREENWRITER OF THE FILMS BEFORE SUNRISE AND BEFORE SUNSET. HER FIRST COMIC BOOK, THE CRITICALLY—ACCLAIMED ZOMBIE TALES: 2061 WAS PUBLISHED BY BOOM! STUDIOS. KRIZAN IS AN ANAIS NIN SCHOLAR AND HER ARTICLE "HUGH'S STAND: REVELATIONS OF A LETTER FROM HUGH GUILER TO ANAIS NIN" WAS RECENTLY PUBLISHED IN THE LITERARY JOURNAL A CAFE IN SPACE. KRIZAN TEACHES CREATIVE WRITING AND SCREENWRITING AT UCLA EXTENSION.

JOHN LAYMAN

IS A POOR, SAD, BITTER OLD MAN, WHO CARES NOTHING ABOUT ANYTHING BUT HIS BUCKKNIFE COLLECTION AND KEEPING HIS REFRIGERATOR WELL—STOCKED WITH FRUIT PIES. HE WRITES A COMIC BOOK CALLED CHEW. LETTERS IT, TOO.

R ERIC LIEB

IS A WRITER/PRODUCER OF COMIC BOOKS, MOVIES, AND VIDEO GAMES, BELIEVES THAT BREVITY IS THE SOUL OF WIT, AND CAN BE FOUND ONLINE AT NOCLEVERNAME.COM

JOHNNY LOWE

IS A LETTERER WHO HAS WORKED ON COMIC BOOKS AND GRAPHIC NOVELS FOR SUCH COMPANIES AS BOOM! STUDIOS, WILDSTORM, IMAGE/SHADLOWLINE, BIG CITY COMICS, DESPERADO, LAYNE MORGAN MEDIA, BLUEWATER PRODUCTIONS, AND DEVIL'S DUE.

ANA MATRONIC

IS THE FEMALE LEAD SINGER FOR THE GENRE–BENDING GROUP SCISSOR SISTERS. THEIR SELF–TITLED DEBUT ALBUM WAS THE BEST–SELLING ALBUM IN THE UK FOR 2004. THEIR COVER OF PINK FLOYD'S "COMFORTABLY NUMB" WAS NOMINATED FOR A GRAMMY FOR BEST DANCE RECORDING. THE GROUP HAS ALSO WON THREE BRIT AWARDS AND A GLAAD MEDIA AWARD FOR OUTSTANDING MUSIC ARTIST. MATRONIC HAS ALSO BEEN FEATURED ON THE SINGLE "JETSTREAM" BY NEW WAVE LEGENDS NEW ORDER.

GIORGIO PONTRELLI

WAS BORN AND RAISED IN BARI, LIVING FOR YEARS IN ROME. IN ITALY HIS WORK HAS BEEN PUBLISHED BY THE EDITORIALE AUREA, THE BD EDITIONS, TRIDIMENSIONAL, ARCADIA AND MANY OTHER PUBLISHERS. IN THE U.S.A. HE HAS BEEN PUBLISHED BY HEAVY METAL MAGAZINE. IN FRANCE HE HAS BEEN PUBLISHED IN SOLEIL AND MODULE ETRANGE. THIS IS HIS FIRST WORK FOR BOOM! STUDIOS. SINCE 2003 HE HAS TAUGHT AT THE INTERNATIONAL SCHOOL OF COMICS IN ROME, PESCARA AND JESI.

MR.SHELDON

STUMBLED UPON THE WONDERFUL WORLD OF VHS SEX FILMS WHEN HE WAS BUT A LAD IN HIS HOMELAND OF AUSTRALIA. NOW, LIVING IN THE CITY THAT INVENTED SEX, LOS ANGELES CALIFORNIA, MR.SHELDON CHANNELS DECADES OF SEXUAL FRUSTRATION ONTO PAPER IN THE FORM OF COMICS, FOR ALL THE WORLD TO SEE. HE IS THE CREATOR OF THE ZUDA COMICS TITLE: SUPERTRON, AND ARTIST FOR THE COMIC ROCK OPERA THAT IS KILL AUDIO. HE LOVES HIS FAMILY, HIS GIRLFRIEND, HEAVY METAL MUSIC IN ALL ITS FORMS, THE REFLECTION OF HIS FACE ON THE GREASED BREASTS OF PLUS SIZE STRIPPERS, AND YOU. HE IS 25 YEARS OLD.

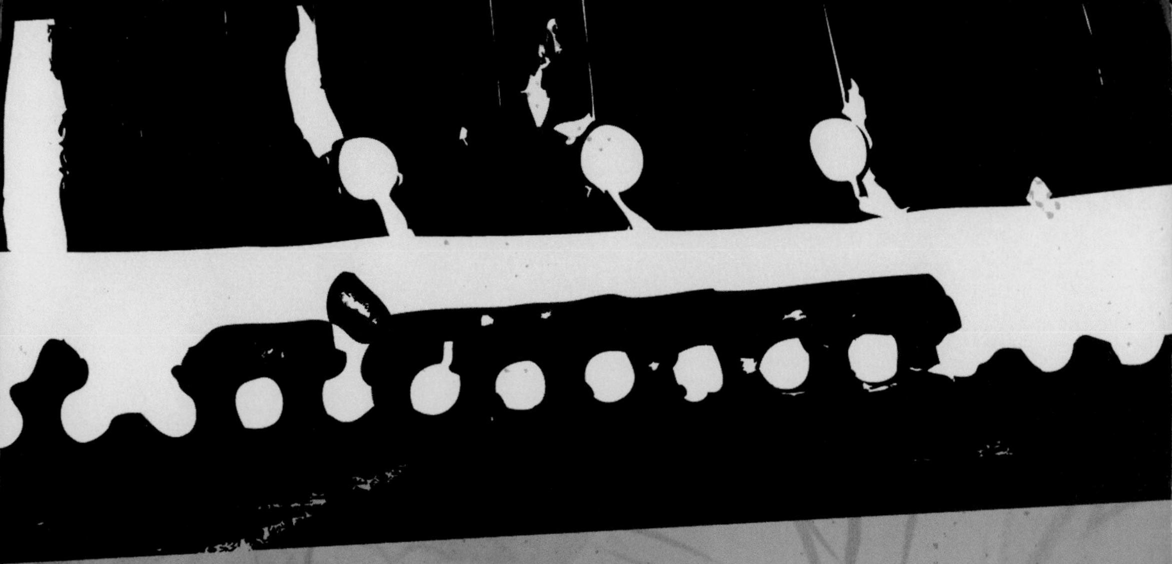

JESSE BLAZE SNIDER

IS A COMIC BOOK WRITER, VOICE-OVER ACTOR, TV/RADIO HOST, SEMI-PRO FOOTBALL PLAYER AND MOST NOTABLY A MUSICIAN. HE IS BEST KNOWN FOR HIS NEW FAMILY REALITY SHOW GROWING UP TWISTED ON A&E. SNIDER'S BOOM! STUDIOS PROJECTS INCLUDE WRITING DISNEY/PIXAR'S TOY STORY AND BOOM KIDS! TITLE, MUPPET SNOW WHITE.

LOUISE STALEY

WAS GENERAL MANAGER AT CBGB FOR 20+ YEARS, WORKING AS HILLY KRISTAL'S TRUSTED LIEUTENANT; RESPONSIBLE FOR BOOKING THE SHOWS AND ALL ARTISTS AND MANAGEMENT RELATIONS. CONSIDERED ONE OF THE LEADING AUTHORITIES ON THE CLUB, STALEY HAS AN UNCANNY SENSE FOR FINDING A JEWEL BEFORE ANYONE ELSE. SHE BOOKED HUNDREDS OF UNKNOWN BANDS THAT WENT ON TO BE SUPERSTARS, INCLUDING RADIOHEAD, SMASHING PUMPKINS, TOOL, SOUNDGARDEN, CROWDED HOUSE AND LIVING COLOUR. SHE CO-MANAGED TWO NATIONAL TOURS FOR THE WARNER BROTHERS ACT FOSSIL, AND HAS SPOKEN AT NUMEROUS MUSIC CONFERENCES AROUND THE COUNTRY. SHE OVERSEES CBGB'S DIGITAL PROPERTIES AND REVIEWED ALL THE STORIES IN THE BOOM! SERIES.

ROBERT STEVEN WILLIAMS

WRITES FICTION AND SONGS. HIS SHORT FICTION HAS APPEARED IN CARVE MAGAZINE, THE ORANGE COAST REVIEW, AS WELL AS POETS & WRITERS MAGAZINE AND BILLBOARD. ROBERT WAS A FINALIST IN THE RAYMOND CARVER SHORT STORY CONTEST. HE'S STUDIED SONGWRITING WITH ROSANNE CASH, AND JIMMIE DALE GILMORE. HE WORKED CLOSELY WITH THE LATE, ESTEEMED FICTION WRITER, BARRY HANNAH. HE'S BEEN HELPING CBGB FOR THE PAST THREE YEARS ON A VARIETY OF PROJECTS INCLUDING OVERSEEING THIS COMIC BOOK SERIES WITH BOOM! STUDIOS. FOR MORE ON ROBERT, VISIT RSWMUSIC.COM OR ROBERT STEVEN WILLIAMS ON FACEBOOK.

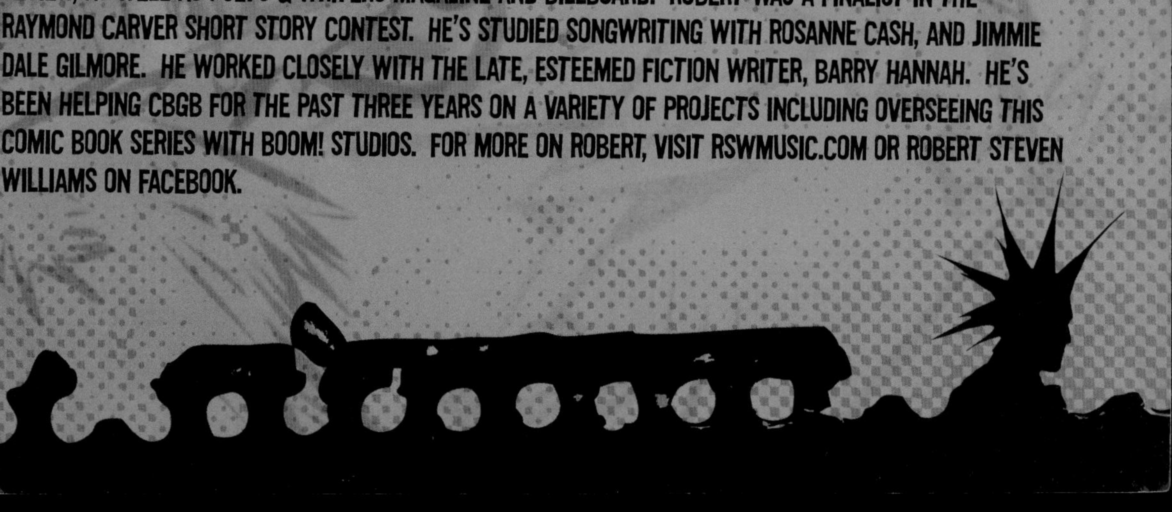